Victims of Crime

Victims of Crime

Policy and practice in criminal justice

Matthew Hall

WILLAN
PUBLISHING

Published by

Willan Publishing
Culmcott House
Mill Street, Uffculme
Cullompton, Devon
EX15 3AT, UK
Tel: +44(0)1884 840337
Fax: +44(0)1884 840251
e-mail: info@willanpublishing.co.uk
website: www.willanpublishing.co.uk

Published simultaneously in the USA and Canada by

Willan Publishing
c/o ISBS, 920 NE 58th Ave, Suite 300
Portland, Oregon 97213-3786, USA
Tel: +001(0)503 287 3093
Fax: +001(0)503 280 8832
e-mail: info@isbs.com
website: www.isbs.com

First published 2009

ISBN 978-1-84392-381-7 hardback

British Library Cataloguing-in-Publication Data

A catalogue record for this book is available from the British Library.

Project managed by Deer Park Productions, Tavistock, Devon
Typeset by GCS, Leighton Buzzard, Bedfordshire
Printed and bound by T.J. International Ltd, Padstow, Cornwall

Dedicated to the memory of Linda Mary Hall
(1952–1989)
Mum

Contents

List of abbreviations *ix*
Acknowledgements *x*

1 Victims, victimology and policy-making **1**
Researching victims 1
Victims in academia and politics 3
Raising questions 9
Methodology 12
Book structure 14

2 Victims in criminal justice: rights, services and vulnerability **16**
Victim 'rights' 16
Facilities, services and support for victims 27
Vulnerable and intimidated victims as witnesses 31
Ways forward 39

3 Victims of crime: a policy chain? **44**
Victim policies? 44
Interpreting the 'policy' 45
Victims and witnesses: shaping the 'policy' 45
Politics, pressures and influences: deconstructing the 'policy chain' 47
A policy chain? 88

4 A narrative-based model of victim-centredness in criminal trials **95**
Storytelling and narrative 95
Stories in criminal trials 100
Victims' narratives and account-making at the heart of criminal justice 102

5 Victims in criminal trials: victims at court **116**
The Witness Service 116
Prosecutors and victims 121
Wider facilities and information at court 123
Waiting at court 124
Domestic violence: 'one on its own'? 143
Victims at court 146

6 Victims in criminal trials: the trial itself **150**
Calling witnesses 150
Giving evidence 153
Reactions to evidence 164
Special measures 170
The impact of crime in criminal trials 178
Victims and witnesses after trials 186
Victims at the heart of criminal justice: principles or practice? 188

7 Victims 'at the heart' of criminal justice: a discussion **191**
What would it mean to have a victim-centred criminal justice system? 191
What factors have driven this 'policy'? 216
What has putting victims 'at the heart' of the system meant so far in practice? 218
Final points 228

References *231*
Index *249*

List of abbreviations

BCS	British Crime Survey
CICS	Criminal Injuries Compensation Scheme
CJS	Criminal Justice System
CPO	Case Progression Officer
CPS	Crown Prosecution Service
DCA	Department for Constitutional Affairs
ECHR	European Convention on Human Rights
ETMP	Effective Trial Management Programme
LCJB	Local Criminal Justice Board
OCJR	Office for Criminal Justice Reform
PSA	Public Service Agreement
SAMM	Support After Murder and Manslaughter
VIS	Victim Impact Statements
VIW	Vulnerable and Intimidated Witnesses
VPS	Victim Personal Statement
WAVES	Witnesses and Victims Experience Survey
WCU	Witness Care Unit
WSS	Witness Satisfaction Survey
YOT	Youth Offending Team

Acknowledgements

This book would not have been possible without the enduring help, support and encouragement of family, friends and colleagues too numerous to name. A large debt is owed to colleagues at the School of Law at the University of Sheffield, including Professor Sir Anthony Bottoms and Drs Gwen Robinson and Stephen Farrall. Very special thanks go to Professor Joanna Shapland for her unwavering commitment and sound guidance at every stage of this project.

My thanks also go to the many lawyers, practitioners, court staff and administrators who participated in this study both as respondents in interviews and as the focus of observation sessions. To this I must add my gratitude to all the defendants, witnesses, and victims of crime involved in the trials observed for this research, who acquiesced to my presence at this most difficult time for all involved. Special thanks must go to the Area Manager of Her Majesty's Courts Service in the anonymous area under review, who gave so freely of his time to ensure my access arrangements and was a constant source of information and advice. I am also indebted to the many policy-makers and other personnel at the Home Office, Office for Criminal Justice Reform, and Department for Constitutional Affairs, who found time in their busy schedules to speak to me on a wide range of issues.

Finally, I would like to thank my wife Claire, whose limitless patience and love made this book possible.

Chapter 1

Victims, victimology and policy-making

> My government will put victims at the heart of the criminal justice system. (Queen's Speech of 15 November 2006)

By the time Tony Blair's New Labour government was setting out its policy on victims of crime in such stark tones at the end of 2006, victims had already undergone a radical metamorphosis from the 'forgotten man of the criminal justice system' (Shapland *et al.* 1985) to the subjects of extensive official attention and legislative change. Indeed, by this point, the pledge to put victims 'at the heart' of the system, and to achieve 'victim-centred' criminal justice, was itself well established in official policy rhetoric. The pledge had already appeared in multiple policy documents, including the seminal 2002 White Paper *Justice for all* (Home Office 2002). In the years that followed, victims of crime have remained a topical and pervasive issue for politicians, policy-makers, the media and academics in the twenty-first century.

Researching victims

Initial planning for the research set out in this volume began in 2003, shortly after the summer publication of the government's 'New Deal' strategy to deliver improved services to victims and witnesses (Home Office 2003a). By this point, victimology was already a well-established (if somewhat diverse) (sub)discipline with its own journal – the *International Review of Victimology* – and associated debates and conjecture. Nevertheless, as the initial research and the review of literature and policy developments continued, clear gaps were uncovered in our present state of knowledge. In short form, the reviews exposed a marked absence of up-to-date, first-hand empirical data on the position of victims during the most symbolically powerful component of the criminal justice process, the criminal trial itself (Tyler 1990). Furthermore, the pace of change in this area indicated the need for a re-evaluation of the policy situation: especially one which took account of wider, international and societal factors beyond the United Kingdom. Few studies had combined the political and policy-making side of the victims issue with questions about that policy's practical implementation thus far in the context of local criminal justice areas and individual courts. Indeed, few commentators had questioned directly what a genuinely victim-centred criminal justice system (CJS) might look like in practice at all.

Following the above observations, the goal of this book is to examine New Labour's pledge to put victims of crime at the heart of the criminal justice system in England and Wales. The central questions to be addressed are:

1 What would it mean to have a victim-centred criminal justice system?
2 What factors have driven this 'policy'?
3 What has putting victims 'at the heart' of the system meant so far in practice?

Drawing on ethnographic techniques – including courtroom observation, qualitative interviews and surveys – the research discussed in this book was particularly concerned with the place of victims in criminal *trial*s. It will demonstrate that while much has been done to assist victims throughout the criminal justice system in a practical sense, cultural barriers and the practices of lawyers, advocates, benches and court staff have not caught up with these good intentions. It is further argued that this 'policy' is in fact driven by a multitude of goals and political pressures, not all of which are conducive to victims' needs. Broadly speaking, this has resulted in central government relinquishing responsibility for victims in favour of local implementers, without the necessary financial backing. The study concludes by proposing a model of victim-centred criminal justice, which emphasises a victim's ability to construct a 'narrative' during the trial process and thereby derive therapeutic outcomes.

Victims in academia and politics

It is conventional in most writings in this area to begin with a discussion on how victims became the focus of such widespread academic and political attention. Rock (2007) rightly points out the complexity of this exercise given the divergence of opinion among scholars on the exact foundations/founders of victimology. Kearon and Godfrey (2007) similarly warn against the academic tendency to 'force social phenomena into false chronologies' (p. 30). As such, it is perhaps more accurate to say that this chapter provides *one* overview of the development of the academic (sub)discipline of victimology. It will then move on to introduce and critique existing research on the proliferation of victims within policy-making circles, this being an even more contested issue and a key focus of this research.

Victimology and conceptions of crime victims

The advent of modern victimology came in two waves. The origins of the discipline trace back to Von Hentig's (1948) arguments against clear-cut distinctions between victims and offenders. Von Hentig suggested that individuals could be prone to victimisation, and even precipitated it through lifestyle choices. The term 'victimology'[1] is usually attributed to Frederick Wertham (1949) or sometimes to Benjamin Mendelsohn (Kirchhoff 1994). The early victimologists continued these 'precipitation' debates up to the late 1950s and early 1960s (Mendelsohn 1956; Wolfgang 1958; Amir 1971; Fattah 1992). At this point, Schneider (1991) argues that victimology was set off in two directions, as a discipline concerned with human rights, and also as a subdiscipline of criminology concerned specifically with victims of crime.

The second victimological wave originated from the United States in the late 1960s. Pointing and Maguire (1988) discuss how the 'victims movement' in the USA was driven by a host of 'strange bedfellows' concerned with different aspects of victimisation ranging from feminists[2] and mental health practitioners to survivors of Nazi concentration camps (see Young 1997).[3] Victimology was therefore very much an international development, and while US (and, later, British) victim surveys revealed new details about crime victims (Mawby and Walklate 1994), Heidensohn (1991) also notes the role played by the European women's movement. The United Nations also drew attention to victims (Joutsen 1989) and various international meetings were hosted on the topic by the Council of

Europe and HEUNI throughout the 1970s and 1980s (Mawby and Walklate 1994).

Certainly in its earlier years, victimology was far from a unified discipline. Maguire and Shapland (1997) note how victim groups in the United States adopted aggressive, political strategies emphasising victim rights, while the European schemes emphasised service provision. The 1970s saw disputes arise between those victimologists who focused on the provision of services to victims, and those interested in broader research-driven victimology (Van Dijk 1997). Conflict also arose between 'penal victimology' – focused on criminal victimisation and scientific methods – and 'general victimology' encompassing wider victimisations, including natural disasters and war (Cressey 1986; Spalek 2006). Broadly speaking, research-driven penal victimology characterised much of this early work.

As the view gradually developed that victims of crime were being neglected by the criminal justice system – and perhaps for political reasons (Elias 1986) – the study of crime victims took centre stage (Maguire 1991).[4] In a seminal contribution, Nils Christie (1977) argued that conflicts had been monopolised by the state:

> [T]he party that is represented by the state, namely the victim, is so thoroughly represented that she or he for most of the proceedings is pushed completely out of the arena, reduced to the triggerer-off of the whole thing. (p. 5)

Such views have led many recent commentators to propose alternative justice models, often based on restorative justice principles (Dignan and Cavadino 1996; Dignan 2002a, 2002b; Braithwaite and Parker 1999; Young 2000). For Dignan (2005) this is because policies and practice relating to victims of crime within the criminal justice system have led only to their 'partial enfranchisement' at best within that process.

Conceiving 'victimhood'

Generally speaking, the concept of 'victimhood' as understood by academics has gradually expanded along with the subdiscipline of victimology itself and its recent focus on those affected by crime. That said, recent years have seen a dramatic increase in the pace of this expansion, to the point that the victim is now described by Kearon and Godfrey as a 'fragmented actor' (2007: 31). Clearly there has been a marked change in the two decades since Christie (1986) famously argued that only certain stereotypically ideal victims achieve victim status in the public's eye or in the criminal justice system. Characteristics then attributed by Christie to the ideal victim include: being weak; carrying out a 'respectable project'; being free of blame; and being a stranger to a 'big and bad' offender. To be labelled as a *bona fide* victim Christie argued that one must first conform to this ideal and then 'make your case known' to the justice system. The presumption that 'real victims' necessarily become involved with the justice system has led to the victim's role often being shrouded in that of the witness giving evidence in court, which will be discussed in Chapter 3. This is problematic, given that the majority of crime probably goes unreported and most victims therefore never come into contact with the criminal justice system (Maguire 2002). As such, Jackson (2004) has argued that much of the victim policy at present is actually focused on a relatively small group of (mainly vulnerable and intimidated) *witnesses* rather than victims *per se*.

Elias (1983, 1986) and Rock (1990) draw on similar arguments to suggest that society's narrow conception of victimisation is brought about by selective definitions of crime construed for political purposes. While this may oversimplify the complex interaction of social processes which leads to an activity being labelled as deviant,[5] the point remains very significant in the context of any attempt to understand the driving forces behind victim policies. Such arguments led to the development of so-called 'radical victimology' which expanded notions of victimhood to include 'real, complex, contradictory and often politically inconvenient victims of crime' (Kearon and Godfrey 2007: 31). For example, it is now known that there is considerable overlap between victims and offenders (Hough 1986; Dignan 2005). We have also recognised 'indirect' victims, including the friends and family of 'primary' victims and the bereaved survivors of homicide (Rock 1998). Of particular relevance has been the growing appreciation for the problem of 'secondary victimisation', the notion that poor treatment within the criminal justice system may constitute a revictimisation (Pointing and Maguire 1988: 11). Such ideas have contributed to the recent emphasis on recasting victims as the *consumers* of the criminal justice process (Zauberman 2002; Tapley 2002).

Victims as state policy

As with the development of victimology itself, several attempts have been made to identify driving forces behind the renewed policy interest in victims of crime. In an early examination, Van Dijk

(1983) categorises reforms intended to 'do something' for victims into four victimogogic ideologies. The label 'victimogogic' was intended to distinguish such measures from victimology's wider goals of counting and gathering information on crime victims.[6] For Van Dijk (1983), victimogogic measures can be based firstly on a care ideology, emphasising welfare principles. Policies can also fall under a resocialisation or rehabilitation banner, with offender-based goals. The third victimogogic ideology is the retributive or criminal justice model, stressing just deserts. Finally, the radical or anti-criminal justice ideology involves resolving problems without resorting to the formal criminal justice system. Van Dijk also notes two broad dimensions to victimogogic measures, which remain valid in the recent policy context. The first is the extent to which victims' problems are incorporated as factors to consider within the criminal justice process. The second dimension is the extent to which victims' interests are goals in their own right, or whether they are intended to feed back into decision-making regarding offenders.

Examining why victims have become a significant policy issue clearly affords insight into the limits of such policies. Nevertheless, Van Dijk's construction is restricted to an examination of political ideologies. As such, he does not discuss the wider network of factors – including international influences or social issues like race and secularisation – that may lead to different policies being put into operation.[7]

Robert Elias has argued that victimogogic policies in the USA were actually a tool to facilitate state control:

> [V]ictims may function to bolster state legitimacy, to gain political mileage, and to enhance social control. (Elias 1986: 231)

The argument is that politicians use victims as political ammunition in elections, and later to insist on increasingly punitive measures. Hence, Fattah (1992) characterises victimogogic measures as 'political and judicial placebos' (p. xii).

Both Elias and Fattah therefore look more closely at the driving force(s) behind such ideologies, which takes our understanding forward. Nevertheless, the concentration on punitiveness may distract attention from a still wider range of influences, that might help us understand *why* political mileage can be gained through the appearance of supporting crime victims in the first place.[8]

In a series of publications, Paul Rock charts the development of victim policy initiatives in Britain and Canada (Rock 1986, 1990, 1993,

1998, 2004). A recurring theme throughout these studies is the lack of any unified or consistent policy. Rather, says Rock, the appearance of a unified victims strategy only develops *retrospectively*:

> [P]olicies for victims sometimes seemed to have little directly to do with the expressed needs of victims themselves and more to do with other politics. And they attain meaning only within the larger framework which those politics set. (Rock 1990: 38)

In a recent instalment, Rock (2004) examines the pressures leading to the Domestic Violence, Crime and Victims Bill.[9] A number of influencing factors are discussed, including: consumer-orientated thinking; human rights issues; international developments; vulnerable and intimidated witnesses; the development of reparation processes[10] and the Macpherson Report. In Rock's view, while making victims a party to criminal proceedings was ruled out by 2003, such influences assured that 'notions of victims' rights never disappeared' (Rock 2004: 570). To escape this impasse, Rock argues that politicians and policy-makers compromised by introducing statutory service standards for victims[11] and witnesses backed by the Parliamentary Commissioner:

> [T]hey [victims] were never to be recognized fully as formal participants in criminal proceedings, their eventual standing was to be resolved by a clever *finesse* of the problem of rights that was to be floated as the possible kernel of new legislation. (Rock 2004: xvii, emphasis in original)

Despite its extremely detailed analysis, the key drawback of Rock's methodology is his tight focus on specific institutions (such as the Home Office). As such, there is no consideration of how victim policies link to wider social trends. Also, while Rock has studied the policy background and the implementation of such measures (Rock 1993), these analyses are not combined. It is therefore difficult to draw links in Rock's work between the creation and development of policies and their actual implementation.

Adding the macro element

Victim policies can also be understood as products of broader social processes. Boutellier (2000) argues that, in our post-modern society of secularised morality, the moral legitimacy of the criminal law is no longer self-evident. For Boutellier, the only public morality to survive this secularisation is the awareness people retain for each other's suffering. This leaves us with a *negative* frame of reference for morality, where no consensus remains on what constitutes 'the good life' but there is agreement enough to acknowledge the suffering of others. This makes victims of suffering a focal point for establishing the moral legitimacy of criminal law. Hence, the criminal law becomes the 'basal negative point of reference for a pluralistic morality' (p. 65). The pain suffered by crime victims becomes a metaphor for wrongful conduct, replacing metaphors of community or collective consciousness. Boutellier calls this the 'victimalization of morality'.

In recent years victims have indeed become more prominent in criminal justice policy with a particular emphasis on those whose suffering seems to be greatest; including survivors of homicide, the victims of domestic violence and childhood victims of sexual abuse. This might, however, suggest that the policy of putting victims at the heart of the system will be limited to those victims whose suffering is readily acknowledged by society, meaning Christie's ideal victims.

Garland (2001) also explains the emergence of victim policies with reference to broader social change. As with Boutellier, Garland's argument is that victims in late-modern society (in America and the UK) have become a core benchmark for determining the success of criminal justice. For Garland, this development is grounded in the collapse of support for penal-welfarism in the 1970s, constituted by a loss of faith in the rehabilitative ideal. This heralded a 'fundamental disenchantment' with the criminal justice system and a loss of faith in its ability to control crime. Consequently, we have seen a shift in focus away from the causes of crime on to its consequences, including victimisation. Victims then become central to criminal justice policy for two reasons. Firstly, governments faced with such problems will redefine what it means to have a successful criminal justice system, by portraying crime as something the state has little control over. The government therefore focuses on the management of criminal justice and the provision of service standards which leads to victims – as the new customers of the system – being afforded increased participation in the process.

Secondly, under these conditions, victims become agents of punitive segregation. In the face of growing concern that little can be done about crime, Garland argues that governments deny their failure by turning to ever more punitive policies, such as mandatory minimum sentences and 'three strikes' legislation. Victims are used to justify such measures by governments appealing to their 'need' to be protected and have their voices heard.

Garland's view clearly corroborates the suggestion that victim policies are grounded in wider political concerns, specifically the need to give the criminal justice system a politically popular goal that is also *achievable*. Indeed, Garland's tone is one of criticism for governments who 'exploit' victims to these ends. Boutellier seems less disapproving in that the victimalisation of morality seems to transcend politics.

Attention should also be drawn to the connections between victim policy and the development of governance. This will be discussed in greater detail in Chapter 3 but, suffice to say, aspects of this policy seem to reflect the features of decentralised service provision and wider consultation strategies associated with governance. Several authors have drawn links between various aspects of criminal justice policy and the emergence of governance (Crawford 1997; Loader and Sparks 2002). Governance is also a key aspect of Garland's (2001) position given above.

Having now set the scene, the remainder of this chapter explains what this research project set out to achieve and briefly discusses the methodologies employed.

Raising questions

Using the government's pledge to put victims at the heart of the criminal justice system as a starting point, three primary research questions were formulated for this research, which will be discussed here along with the associated issues and hypotheses.

What would it mean to have a victim-centred criminal justice system?

This first research question raises a whole host of different issues, including what it would mean practically, legally, politically and philosophically to have a genuinely victim-centred system and what such a system might look like. Most commentators agree that the present system of criminal justice is not victim-centred. This book goes further, however, to argue that it is possible to convert this system into one worthy of the label without resorting to fundamental reforms. The concept of 'fundamental' versus 'non-fundamental' reform will be discussed in greater detail in Chapter 2. Essentially it is argued that the former implies altering the basic tenets or aims of the adversarial system, and that politically this is not a feasible option for policy-makers. Notwithstanding this, little attempt has been made to assess how victim-centredness can be achieved without altering the system we have now, especially as moves towards restorative justice processes must be categorised as fundamental reform. Affording victims decision-making power (in some cases) may also constitute fundamental reform but – as will be argued in Chapter 3 – consultative participation in the process and the notion of victims having rights and party status within proceedings would not, as these would not vitally alter the existing process or the existing roles of those within it.

With these points in mind, I will argue that a victim-centred trial would have three main features. The first of these is that such trials would be practically set up and organised to respond effectively to the needs of victims in terms of facilities, procedures, personnel and so on. Secondly, I will argue in Chapter 4 – and expand in Chapter 7 – that a truly victim-centred trial process would be one that understands and accommodates as far as possible victims' narrative constructions of incidents and experiences. Such a system would therefore seek to reduce the many instances in the present system where victims are prevented from constructing a full narrative account of an incident during a criminal trial, and thus miss out on the possible therapeutic benefits of doing so. It will be argued in Chapters 4 and 7 that trials are in fact already characterised by narrative and storytelling. Indeed, in England and Wales the present adversarial model has already accommodated – in the case of vulnerable or intimidated witnesses giving evidence though pre-recorded examination in chief – a much less restrictive form of evidence-giving without apparent prejudice to the interests of defendants. Finally, and linking the other two features described above, a victim-centred trial process would be one in which the underlying occupational cultures of those working within it (court staff, solicitors, barristers, judges, magistrates and so on) are genuinely receptive, understanding and proactive to victims' needs. It is further argued that these three components can be applied beyond trials to the wider criminal justice system in order to arrive at a genuinely victim-centred system.

The key to achieving these three components of victim-centredness is to afford victims rights which are justiciable from within the criminal justice system through the proactive interjection of lawyers and judicial actors. Given that we have now reached the stage where victims are said to have rights – through a Victim's Code of Practice (Home Office 2005f) – this is not so much a fundamental reform as a change in the justiciability of these existing rights.

What factors have driven this 'policy'?

The wealth of official action in this area means it is now manifestly unfeasible to argue simply that the needs of victims and witnesses are being ignored by policy-makers, as had previously been the case. Questions remain, however, as to the exact nature of this pro-victims and pro-witnesses policy that seems to have developed over recent years. As such, this project set out to identify the driving force (or forces) behind official actions on victims and witnesses.

The word 'policy' has been placed in inverted commas here because it is not to be assumed that the totality of measures and developments relating to victims (and witnesses) actually constitute a unified and consistent policy at all.[12] In fact the strategy is constituted by a whole range of different influences, what Rock has called 'other politics' (Rock 1990). This is important because policy documents only discuss a limited range of officially recognised influences. Commentators such as Elias, however, suggest that government policies (certainly those relating to victims of crime) may have a much deeper, and often less overt, political purpose (Elias 1986). Chapter 3 will demonstrate that the victims policy has indeed been driven over time by a web of political factors.

Such debates leave us with three conceivable interpretations of the victims 'policy'. Firstly, there is the straightforward possibility that all these reforms are in fact part of a consistent and unified strategy to assist victims and witnesses. The second possibility is that actions which, incidentally, assist victims and witnesses may be grounded in a quite different set of political concerns. The third possibility is that, now that victims and witnesses seem to have achieved at least rhetorical acceptance in the political system, new policies are being re-packaged as the continuation of work for these groups, but are in fact intended to achieve other aims such as, for example, increasing efficiency. Of these three possibilities, it is submitted that a combination of the second and third seems the most likely, and this contention was tested during the course of this research.

What has putting victims 'at the heart' of the system meant so far in practice?

In real life the criminal justice system faces a whole host of practical and organisational difficulties every day. As one solicitor remarked during the course of this project:

> The wheels of justice do not run smooth. They're square. And falling off. (a solicitor appearing at Courts A and B)

Add to this the influence of occupational cultures within the criminal justice system – traditionally geared around the exclusion of victims (Shapland *et al.* 1985; Jackson *et al.* 1991) – and one is faced with the real possibility that the policy and the practice of this victim-centred system are very separate things (Rock 1993).

From the outset, it was expected that this project would reveal marked development in the provision for victims and witnesses in criminal trials compared with most previous ethnographic work focused around courts (Shapland *et al.* 1985; Jackson *et al.* 1991; Rock 1993; Tapley 2002). It was hypothesised that the practical infrastructure to assist victims would be significantly developed (separate waiting rooms, facilities for video-linked evidence and so on). It was also predicted that the culture of criminal justice professionals would now be somewhat softened to the plight of victims and witnesses, although more traditional views would still be present and possibly widespread. The fieldwork also paid particular attention to the mechanisms by which victims and other witnesses were dissuaded or openly prevented from making accounts by evidential rules, working practices, courtroom environment and so on, as it was felt that the facilitation of victims' full narrative accounts within the trial process would be the least developed aspect of a victim-centred system.

Overall, what I expected to find from this part of the research was that genuinely victim-centred trials are not yet forthcoming. Nevertheless, as noted above, it was hoped to observe within existing procedures the clear potential to make them more victim-centred without resorting to truly fundamental reform.

Methodology

In order to address the above questions, data was collected throughout 2005 and the first half of 2006 at three criminal courts in the north of England. Two of these courts – Courts 'A' and 'B' – were magistrates' courts. Magistrates' courts deal with the vast majority of criminal cases in the English legal system, offences punishable with a fine up to £5,000 and/or imprisonment up to six months. The most distinctive feature of these courts is that they are presided over by lay members of the local community as judges of both fact and law. Court 'C' was a Crown Court centre dealing with more serious criminal cases. Courts A and C are situated in a large northern city, whereas Court B serves a fairly large town nearby. Access was arranged through the individual court managers and the Area Manager of Her Majesty's

Courts Service, with the support of the presiding judge at the Crown Court.

The data from all three courts falls into three categories: courtroom observations of criminal trials; qualitative interviews with practitioners and court staff; and a court user survey distributed to victims and witnesses via the Witness Service[13] at Court B. Further interviews were conducted with criminal justice administrators in the local area under review and with central policy-makers at the Home Office, Office for Criminal Justice Reform (OCJR) and Department for Constitutional Affairs (DCA).[14] These latter interviews were designed to shed light on the formation of the victim policy and the challenges of its local implementation.

Trials were selected for observation based on the apparent likelihood that they would involve civilian (non-police) witnesses and victims. This was established by examining the charge(s) and gathering information before the trial from court ushers, clerks, and lawyers. 'Trials' here means criminal proceedings originally scheduled to determine the guilt or innocence of defendants facing criminal charges, but also includes shorter proceedings where the trial must be adjourned (postponed) or the need to establish guilt or innocence is removed (which will be termed 'otherwise resolved trials' in this research).

Observations were carried out from the public gallery and recorded on paper, which is the only legal method available. Observations were semi-structured and the anonymity of all participants was strictly preserved. The notes were then subject to a grounded analysis (Glaser and Strauss 1967) to draw out themes. Interviews with criminal justice practitioners and administrators were also conducted in a semi-structured fashion whereby respondents were encouraged to dwell on areas they considered important. This helped expose the occupational priorities of the groups under review. Interviews were tape-recorded – informed consent having been gained – and transcribed. They were then the subjects of further grounded analysis, with the assistance of the NVivo software package.

Through these methods, a dataset of 23 interviews and 247 observation sessions was compiled, along with an analysis of relevant legislation and guidance documents. Overall, while it cannot be claimed that either the interviews or the observational data are statistically representative of the whole criminal justice system in England and Wales, no particularly distinguishing characteristics were identified in relation to the courts or the interviewees. As such, it is hoped that these results will be of use to scholars and practitioners in

England and beyond as an indication of how moves to put victims at the heart of the criminal justice system are being received and applied in practice. In addition, a major benefit of observational methodology is that it captures the human element that so characterises the 'fog of half-knowledge, guesses, and intimations' at the start of trials (Rock 1993: 276), where difficulties may be partly explained by the attitudes of lawyers and other actors in the process.

At this stage, it is important to emphasise two general points regarding the intended scope of this research. Firstly, notwithstanding the government's pledge to centralise the victim within the criminal justice system as a whole, this project was especially concerned with the operation of criminal trials. Even more specifically, the project sought to examine the role of victims within the substantive trial procedure prior to the sentencing stage. Secondly, this research was concerned with criminal justice rather than restorative justice. Many commentators have suggested restorative justice models as a solution to the problems faced by victims in criminal justice (see Dignan 2005). As a consequence, relatively little work has been done on the notion of achieving victim-centredness in the existing criminal justice system. Given that the vast majority of victims must still deal with the traditional criminal justice model even in the light of restorative options, we ignore this model at our peril, or certainly the peril of victims. Nevertheless, in taking this stance I by no means dismiss the significance of the restorative movement, as this will clearly continue to gather pace and become increasingly important to crime victims in the future. Many advocates of restorative justice retain in their theorising a place for more traditional forms of case disposal (see Dignan 2002a; Braithwaite 2002). As such, the following discussions adopt the view of Bottoms (2003) who argues in terms of a separation between the criminal justice and restorative justice systems.

Book structure

The rest of this book is divided into six more chapters. Following this section, Chapter 2 will provide an overview of research and commentary on some of the key issues pertinent to this research. In so doing, the chapter will also begin to tackle the question of what it might mean to put victims at the heart of criminal justice. Chapter 3 will review in detail the development of policies relating to victims and analyse these policies pursuant to the second research question, drawing on interview data from policy-makers and document analyses. Chapter 4 will discuss the concept of narrative, setting out an argument for its incorporation within criminal trials. Chapters 5 and 6 will present the empirical results from courtroom observation sessions. Chapter 7 will discuss all the results in light of the three research questions and present an overall model of victim-centred criminal justice based on all the evidence gleaned from this research.

Notes

1 The term has been described as 'a rather ugly neologism' (Newburn 1988: p. 1).
2 The role of second-wave feminism is emphasised by Kearon and Godfrey (2007).
3 Doak (2003, 2007) suggests that early victimology was quite punitive. Arguably, however, this is more a characteristic of modern victimology in the present climate of punitive populism (Brownlee 1998; Garland 2001).
4 Although the field of zemiology has continued to address victimisation through social harms beyond crime and criminology (Hillyard 2006).
5 What is sometimes called 'critical victimology' (Mawby and Walklate 1994).
6 The term fell out of fashion, although has appeared in recent literature (Davies 2007).
7 See Chapter 4.
8 Especially when confidence in the criminal justice system is lacking (Garland 2001).
9 Now the Domestic Violence Crime and Victims Act 2004. See Chapter 4.
10 Which, rightly or wrongly, Rock associates with restorative justice.
11 Now found under the Victim's Code of Practice (Home Office 2005f).
12 As has recently been suggested (Home Office 2003a).
13 The Witness Service is a voluntary organisation run by victim assistance charity Victim Support, intended to provide information and services to witnesses attending court to give evidence.
14 All data being gathered prior to the creation of the Ministry of Justice in March 2007.

Chapter 2

Victims in criminal justice: rights, services and vulnerability

Having established as far as it is possible the scope of victimology and victims of crime, the following chapter will review contemporary questions raised by victimologists concerning the place of such victims within an adversarial criminal justice system. Three important areas of debate are highlighted: victim rights; the provision of facilities, services and support to victims; and victims giving evidence in criminal trials, including vulnerable or intimidated victims. This is not an exhaustive list of matters dealt with by victimologists as a whole, but encompasses the key issues relating to the questions raised in the last chapter, and the main debates surrounding victims within criminal trials specifically.

Victim 'rights'

Underlying many of the debates in this and subsequent chapters is the notion of victims having 'rights' within the criminal justice process. It is a notion which has proved controversial. Whereas most accept the 'normal rights' of defendants (Ashworth 2000), many have refused to accept rights for victims on similar common-sense grounds (Ashworth 2000; Edwards 2004). This is not to say there is not a general consensus in the literature that victims should receive information, courteous treatment and protection from the justice system (Zedner 2002). The main debates, however, centre on the structures and procedures that must be in place to guarantee such facilities, and whether this should be done by affording victims rights. In fact, the modern debate on victim rights revolves less around the specific content of those rights and more on the mechanisms for their delivery and accountability (JUSTICE 1998).

Furthermore, this tacit acceptance of a standardised list of what Ashworth calls 'service rights'[1] distracts from the growing – but far more contentious – calls for 'some form of procedural right of participation within the system' (Doak 2003: 2). Edwards (2004) has labelled 'participation' 'a comfortably pleasing platitude' (p. 973) which is rhetorically powerful but conceptually abstract. In his discussion, Edwards describes four possible forms of victim participation in criminal justice. The most significant casts victims in the role of *decision-makers*, such that their preferences are sought and applied by the criminal justice system. Less drastic would be *consultative* participation, where the system seeks out victims' preferences and takes them into account when making decisions. Edwards sees the traditional role of victims in terms of *information provision*, where victims are obliged to provide information required by the system. Finally, under *expressive* participation, victims express whatever information they wish, but with no instrumental impact, here Edwards highlights the danger of victims wrongly believing their participation will actually affect decision-making.

Assessing rights

A common distinction drawn in these debates is that between 'service rights' and 'procedural rights'. For Ashworth (1993, 1998, 2000), victim participation should not be allowed to stray beyond service rights into areas of public interest. Ashworth is particularly concerned by victims being afforded the right to influence sentencing (and other decision-making within the process), citing the difficulties of testing victims' claims and taking account of unforeseen effects on victims (Ashworth 2000). The more limited service rights Ashworth has in mind include respectful and sympathetic treatment, support, information, court facilities and compensation from the offender or state, but exclude consultative participation (Ashworth 1998: 34).

These arguments have been influential; however, Ashworth's thought seems to be grounded in the defence perspective, incorporating the assumption that there is a zero sum game between victim and defendant rights. The difficulty with Ashworth's argument is that he does not elaborate on why victims should not have input into sentencing or other decisions. Even if affording victims some rights could prejudice the defence, Ashworth offers no mechanisms to resolve such conflicts. Sanders *et al.* (2001) classify Ashworth's argument as a normative defence of the due process approach. Sanders and Young (2000) argue that both service and procedural rights fail to cater for the interests of victims, as does the traditional 'due process versus crime control' dichotomy (p. 51). Hence Sanders (2002) suggests an alternative victims' rights approach, combined with inquisitorial-style systems in the short term, then moving towards restorative justice. Sanders therefore ignores the possibility of incorporating victim rights within the present system of adversarial criminal justice, and instead advocates the more fundamental notion of changing the nature and goals of the system. He gives little indication, however, as to why inquisitorial or restorative models would be better for victims (see Brienen and Hoegen 2000).

Sanders *et al.* (2001) disagree with Ashworth's view of service rights as a solution to victims' problems because they feel that poorly conceived service rights also marginalise victims. This is demonstrated by difficulties encountered during the piloting of One-Stop Shops[2] (Hoyle *et al.* 1999). Cape (2004) also takes up the argument that service rights have been poorly implemented, although it is not clear how this invalidates Ashworth's basic view that – in principle, properly conceived and resourced – service rights would benefit victims. As an alternative, Sanders (2002) presents an inclusive model of criminal justice which expressly rejects victim decision-making because:

> [This] would fuel the 'us' and 'them' non-relationship and therefore social exclusion ... The aim would be to listen to victims' information and their views, but decision-making would be based on clear objective criteria derived from inclusive approaches such as the 'freedom perspective'. (p. 218)

Nevertheless, problems lie in the assumed existence of 'clear objective criteria' of a higher standard than the victim's own opinion, or decision. Conversely, Erez (1991) argues that harm, for example, can *never* be measured objectively. Sanders *et al.*'s (2001) view also seems to assume a vengeful victim at a time when much of the recent evidence suggests many victims do not fall within this category (Doak and O'Mahony 2006; Shapland *et al.* 2006). The notion of listening but not acting upon victims' opinions also suggests a danger of raising and dashing their expectations, a key criticism of the One-Stop Shops (Hoyle *et al.* 1999).

A better argument against victims making decisions was provided by the JUSTICE Committee (1998), which became concerned that domestic violence victims were being *burdened* with prosecution decisions. In its report the Committee maintained that the police practice of asking these victims whether they would support a prosecution implied that the state is unwilling to fulfil its duty to police and prosecute such crime. The report therefore recommended a system of victim consultative participation on matters such as bail and the effects of giving evidence. The decision-maker should listen carefully to victims, but such consultation may or may not influence decision-making and it would be important not to raise victims' expectations. On prosecution decisions specifically, the report maintained there should be no duty on the Crown Prosecution Service (CPS) to consult *all* victims, although those making prosecution decisions should have access to information about the effects of the offence on the victim.

The 'freedom perspective' referred to above is an attempt by Sanders and Young (2000) to replace the service/procedural rights distinction with a more sophisticated tool. Unlike Ashworth, Sanders and Young propose a mechanism whereby the rights of victims and defendants are balanced by maximising *freedom* within the system. Thus, says Sanders (2002, 2004), providing *information* to victims increases their freedom without reducing the freedom of defendants. Conversely, Sanders and Young (2000) argue that if victims' opinions sway decision-making this reduces the freedom of offenders more than it increases the freedom of victims,[3] and hence constitutes an unacceptable right. Consulting victims on the discontinuance of their cases, however, is justified provided the final decision is made by the CPS based on an objective evaluation of the balance of freedoms.

Nevertheless, the apparent need to quantify freedom makes Sanders and Young's approach problematic. Furthermore, this model promotes considerable debate as to who would be charged with determining net freedom. If this role were to fall to judges, this raises the further important question of whether appeals – or long-drawn-out trials-within trials – could be run based on the argument that freedom during a criminal trial had not been maximised. Such proceedings would inevitably involve the kind of complex legal argument that once again excludes victims from the process.

Victim rights in sentencing

Erez (2000, 1999, 1994) has concentrated attention on victims' participation rights specifically within the sentencing procedure, and how these may be afforded through victim impact statements (VIS).

VIS statements developed in the USA for victims to communicate information to the court about the effects of crime. These were adopted in Britain in October 2001 as 'victim personal statements', although the British system excludes judicial consideration of comments made by the victim on sentencing (Lord Chancellor's Department 2001).

Ashworth (2000) argues that the involvement of victims in sentencing has been used as a means of legitimising a punitive stance against offenders (see also Elias 1986). For Ashworth, it is unjust for unpredictable or unusual impacts upon victims to affect sentence. Ashworth also warns against falsely raising victims' expectations of their role, while agreeing with Victim Support (1995) that victims should not be burdened with decision-making responsibilities in this area.

Despite such views, in a system grounded on proportionality, it may be the very cases where the impact of crime is unusual where the victim's input into sentencing becomes useful. Ashworth's second concern echoes that of the JUSTICE Committee (1998) regarding the burdening of victims with decisions. Nevertheless, consultative participation coupled with proper explanation need not burden victims unduly, and as a due process argument Ashworth offers no evidence to the contrary. The difficulty concerning victims wrongly led to believe they will be making decisions[4] can also be resolved through enhanced information provision.

Erez (1999, 2004) also challenges Ashworth's warnings. She begins by conceding that VIS statements currently have little impact on sentencing (Morgan and Sanders 1999). For her, the blame for this lies with resistant cultures of practitioners, especially the widely held view that only 'normal' levels of impact should affect sentences (Erez 1999). On this point, Sanders *et al.* (2001) see VPS statements as fundamentally flawed because they rarely contain unexpected ('abnormal') information. Conversely, Erez maintains that exposure to victim impact statements will furnish practitioners with a more realistic appreciation for the normal impact of crime (Erez and Rogers 1999; Erez 1999). As such, Erez (1999, 2000) argues that VPS statements will only influence the *proportionality* of a sentence, and may also achieve restorative ends for victims (Erez *et al.* 1997).

Erez's (1999) contention regarding proportionality is based on studies from America and Australia (Erez and Rogers 1999) which purport to demonstrate that VIS statements are generally not used as a vehicle for communicating vindictive opinions to the court, if only because they are edited by the police and other parties. As such, she suggests a VIS can influence sentences in either direction, and that their overall affect on sentencing is partly hidden in the statistical analyses:

> [S]ome changes in [sentencing] outcomes do occur, but they are hidden as in the aggregate they offset each other. Without victim input, sentences might well have been too high or too low. (Erez 1999: 548)

Sanders *et al.* (2001) heavily dispute the notion that VIS statements can reduce sentence severity (see also Giliberti 1991). Although the authors are unable to disprove Erez's argument empirically, they note that such findings have not been replicated (by Davis and Smith 1994; Morgan and Sanders 1999).[5] Furthermore, Erez appears to base her conclusions on the word of practitioners. That said, Erez's view on the lack of victim vengefulness is supported by evaluations of restorative justice in both Northern Ireland (Doak and O'Mahony 2006) and Britain (Shapland *et al.* 2006). These indicate that victims tend not to advocate disproportionately punitive punishments. It also appears that the public become less punitive when they are better informed about the justice system (Mattinson and Mirrlees-Black 2000). Of course, Sanders *et al.*'s argument is not that victims are generally vindictive and punitive, 'simply that non-punitive victims rarely make a VIS' (2004: 104).

A zero sum game?

Despite reaching very different conclusions, Erez and Sanders and Young agree that a trade-off between the rights of victims and defendants (that is, a zero sum game) is not inevitable. For Erez, procedural rights afforded to victims through victim impact statements do not unjustly affect defendants, but rather improve sentence accuracy in terms of just deserts, while Sanders and Young avoid a conflict of rights by maximising the freedom of all sides. Although both solutions are subject to critique, the underlying rejection of a zero sum game hints that it is possible to move beyond these rather restrictive due process arguments in this discussion of what victim-centred criminal justice might entail.

Indeed, Garland (2001) sees this zero sum game as the product of a punitive ethos espoused by governments in an effort to deny the failure of the justice system to reduce crime. The position is summarised by Hickman (2004):

> [F]airness to victims is not a zero sum game. It can be achieved without detracting from the rights of the defendant. The fact that this government wishes us to think otherwise is a profoundly political matter. (p. 52)

Jackson (1990, 2004) has remarked on the dominance of 'balance' rhetoric within criminal justice discourse, in this case the balance between victim and offender rights. Nevertheless, the above discussion seems to suggest that the zero sum game is a product of its time rather than an objective reality.

Enforceability?

True rights must have some mechanism for their enforcement (Jackson 2003). This was a key observation made by Fenwick (1995) of the Victim's Charter issued by the Conservative Government (Home Office 1990). Fenwick branded the Charter as 'seriously misleading' (p. 844) owing to its lack of enforcement provisions. The issue of *enforcing* victim rights will be dealt with in some detail in Chapter 7. Suffice to say, however, that unenforceable rights would seem manifestly unsatisfactory in the context of the government's pledge to put victims at the heart of criminal justice.

Enforceability is at the heart of the modern debate on the *form* of victim rights, as opposed to their *content* (JUSTICE 1998). Chapter 3 will demonstrate that – thus far – the government has relied on complaints mechanisms outside the criminal justice process as a means of enforcing such rights as it purports to afford to victims in the criminal process. If this process is to become genuinely victim-centred, however, this brand of 'externally enforceable' rights also seems inadequate. If enforcement comes only from external complaints procedures then one might argue that the services afforded to victims remain expectations (JUSTICE 1998; Shapland 2000) with victim rights limited to the right to complain *outside* the criminal justice process. Such 'externally enforceable' rights therefore exile victims to the periphery of the system. As such, Jackson's (2003) critique can be expanded by suggesting that rights will be taken far more seriously if enforcement comes from within the criminal justice process itself (internally enforceable rights). This position has received considerably less attention in the existing literature[6] and will be developed during the course of this volume.

Finding victim rights: early developments

Government policy in the UK has fluctuated from the language of rights in the first Victim's Charter (Home Office 1990) to 'service standards' in the second Charter of 1995, and reverted back to rights in the 2002 White Paper *Justice for All* (Home Office 2002). The use of such terminology in the first Charter replicated the language in the preamble to the UN's 1985 *Declaration of Basic Principles of Justice for Victims of Crime and Abuse of Power* – which the Charter was intended to implement – and which spoke of 'measures in order to secure the universal and effective recognition of, and respect for, the rights of victims of crime and abuse of power' (p. 1).

Generally, both the Declaration and the Council of Europe's *Recommendation on the position of the victim in the framework of criminal law and procedure*[7] of the same year were concerned with service rights. A few participatory rights were indicated, including the weighing up of victims' injuries and losses by the court when determining compensation. At Part A, Paragraph 6b, the Declaration refers to allowing victims' views and opinions to be 'presented and considered at appropriate stages of the proceedings where their personal interests are affected, without prejudice to the accused'. This is significant, as it suggests victims' preferences will be taken into account. Neither document sets out any form of redress if standards are not met.

The second (1996) version of the Victim's Charter does not mention rights, only service standards related to information, support and protection (Home Office 1996). The JUSTICE report (1998) also dropped this language to recommend reforms based on victims' 'legitimate expectations'. We may persist with labelling these as service rights, although there is an absence within the Charter of enforcement mechanisms other than the complaints procedures of individual agencies. By now victims' role as (voluntary) information providers was clearer, and indeed the second Charter did foresee victims' *stated* opinions influencing decision-making:

> If you are worried about being attacked or harassed as a result of the court case you should tell the police. They will tell you what can be done and tell the CPS so that they can let the court know at the time bail is being considered. (p. 10)

The 'worry' mentioned here would be based on a victim's *beliefs* about their overall situation. Although there is no emphasis on the system to seek out such beliefs, this does suggest *consultative* participation, as the implication is that bail decisions may be influenced.[8] The Charter also states that victims' concerns are to be considered before releasing offenders on bail or licence. The enforcement potential of any of these rights remains suspect, however, and still originates from complaints procedures outside the criminal justice process itself. Of course, victims must also be made aware of their rights, and on this point the 2002/03 British Crime Survey (BCS) indicated that only 13 per cent of victims had heard of the Charter (Ringham and Salisbury 2004).

Later developments: moving towards documented, internally enforceable rights?

We may now be moving closer to a stage where victim rights are clarified and documented within international instruments, statute and case law that also provide enforcement mechanisms from within the criminal justice process.

Case law developments may indicate that victims have rights under the European Convention on Human Rights (ECHR), which would be enforceable from within the criminal justice process in England and Wales through the Human Rights Act 1998. For example, there are now a number of rulings to the effect that keeping witnesses anonymous (say, because they are intimidated) does not breach a defendant's Article 6 right to a fair trial, provided the evidence can be challenged (*Baegen* v. *Netherlands*,[9] *Doorson* v. *Netherlands*[10]). This became a point of some media interest when, in June 2008, the House of Lords' judgment in *R* v. *Davis (Iain)*[11] ruled that witness anonymity was in most cases incompatible with the common law and therefore beyond the court's jurisdiction. The government responded by pledging to swiftly change the law to reverse the ruling and 'protect witnesses' (BBC 2008) and the Criminal Evidence (Witness Anonymity) Act was rushed through the House of Commons in July 2008, which essentially abolished the common law in this area and reinstated a judge's discretion to make witness anonymity orders.

The case of *Sn* v. *Sweden*[12] confirms that Article 6 does not grant the defence an unlimited right to secure the appearance of witnesses in court (Ellison 2003). This might indicate subtle moves towards allowing witnesses to decide for themselves as to whether they give evidence. The case also maintains that witnesses can give evidence through recorded interviews without breaching Article 6. Doak (2003) suggests that victims might also find favour under Articles 3 and 8 if they are treated in a degrading manner by the criminal justice system or the state fails to protect their rights to privacy when giving evidence.

The European Court has resisted interpretations of the Convention which afford victims more explicit influence over decision-making in sentencing (*McCourt* v. *UK*[13]) although in *T and V* v. *UK*[14] the parents of a young murder victim were allowed to make representations to the Court (Rock 2004). In the domestic case of *R* v. *Secretary of State for the Home Department and another*, ex parte *Bulger*[15] the Divisional Court held that the family of a murder victim did not have standing to seek judicial review of any tariff set in relation to the murder.

Under domestic case law, judges should certainly seek out the impact of offending on victims (*Attorney General Reference No.2 of 1995* (*R* v. *S*)[16]) (Shapland 2002). This might suggest that victims have a right to provide such information.[17] Furthermore, *R* v. *Perks*[18] indicates that a sentence can be moderated if it aggravates the victim's distress or the victim's forgiveness indicates that his or her psychological or mental suffering must be very much less than would normally be the case. Thus, in certain circumstances, the victim's choice to forgive a defendant becomes relevant to sentencing (Edwards 2002).

We now also have the EU Council's 2001 Framework Decision on victims' standing in criminal proceedings. The Decision is steeped in the language of rights, including the right to compensation and damages, the right to provide and receive information, the right to be treated with respect for the victim's dignity, the right to be protected at various stages of the procedure and the right to have allowances made for the disadvantages of living in another member state from the one in which a crime is committed. Article 2 of the Decision requires member states to ensure victims have 'a real and appropriate role in criminal proceedings', suggesting participatory rights, albeit not involving victims in decision-making roles. States are obliged to ensure these standards are met, suggesting these rights may be enforceable, and therefore a step closer to a more robust form of rights.

The Domestic Violence, Crime and Victims Act 2004 sought to implement the Framework Decision through a statutory Code of Practice (Home Office 2005f). The Code's basis in statute is significant, although its provisions are not law and its enforceability remains with the complaints procedures of individual criminal justice agencies. If dissatisfied with the outcome of such procedures, members of the public can report the matter to their Member of Parliament who can refer it to the Parliamentary Commissioner for Administration for investigation. So far this procedure has brought questionable results, with only 30 cases brought to the Parliamentary Commissioner as of June 2008. Furthermore, most of these cases were dismissed on the grounds that the victims involved had not exhausted all other complaints mechanisms (Casey 2008). In addition, a new Victims and Witnesses Commissioner is to be charged with monitoring the operation of the Code, although it has not been said that discontented victims can complain directly to him/her and – as of June 2008 – no appointment has been made to this post (*ibid*). It is envisaged that victims can take their complaints to the statutory Victims' Advisory Panel, but neither the Panel nor the Victims and Witnesses Commissioner will have powers of investigation or redress,[19] although the Commissioner is being touted as a champion of victims' rights (Home Office 2006c).

As such, the test of any rights under the Code may again lie in their enforceability, and on this we find ourselves in the same position as the Victim's Charters. If these provisions are rights, it seems they are still only enforceable outside the criminal justice process. Indeed, the judiciary are not included as parties with any obligations under the Code. The substantive text of the Code refers only to the right to make a victim personal statement and the right to a review of a decision from the Criminal Injuries Compensation Authority. The latter seems to be another service right, the former sounds more participatory. As under the Victim's Charter, parties within the CJS are obliged under the Code to take account of a victim personal statement when making decisions, although Edwards (2004) notes the difficulty in clarifying exactly what form of participation is being afforded here.

Victims are to be *consulted* under the Code regarding their opinions, mainly in relation to the release of serious offenders. To this end, the probation service is required to *seek out* and pass on the representations made by victims (of mentally disordered offenders and road traffic offenders who intended to cause physical injury or damage to property) to those responsible for the prisoner's/patient's release. Parole Boards must take account of victims' representations in conditions placed on offenders' licence and supervision. The police must record any views a victim expresses on applying for 'special measures' to help them give evidence in court,[20] although there is no mention of a CPS obligation to consider such views. While the Code for Crown Prosecutors (CPS 2004) maintains that victims' views are relevant when deciding on the public interest test or the acceptance of pleas, it is surprising that this was not also spelt out in the statutory Code.

Overall, while the Code is grounded in statute, enforcement mechanisms remain largely as if this were not the case. Furthermore, the Code is still mainly concerned with service rights. The same is true of the Witnesses' Charter (Home Office 2005g) and the draft CPS Children's Charter aimed at child victims and witnesses (CPS 2005a). Both abstain from the term 'rights' and are modelled around legitimate expectations, enforced through complaints procedures external to the criminal justice process.[21] As such, Casey (2008) has recently argued that this system still fails to adequately meet the needs of victims and, in particular, is failing to address the *overall* response a victim receives from the criminal justice system.

A more significant role for the views of victims has been hinted at in a consultation paper on the introduction of victims' advocates to represent homicide survivors in court. Again the consultation emphasises 'the importance of seeking the view of victims in prosecution decisions' (Home Office 2005b: 12). The consultation also envisages the victims' advocate expressing victims' views to the prosecutor at the pre-trial stage so they can be taken into account. This seems to imply something closer to party status, because victims are not only consulted, but have mechanisms in place to ensure the outcomes of such consultation are presented to the court for its consideration. Examples of issues on which victims may want to express views are given as: bail (and conditions); withdrawal or downgrading of charge; discontinuance of criminal proceedings; applications for reporting restrictions and trial management matters. This still excludes sentencing, but expands upon any similar lists seen previously in official publications and may therefore indicate an increased acceptance of the right to more *consultative* participation for victims.

Facilities, services and support for victims

The considerable debates above notwithstanding, arguably the grievances of victims in the criminal justice system have less to do with the controversial issues of participation or rights and more to do with a lack of basic services. This section will deconstruct the notion of service rights to identify precisely what victims need from the system.

Early studies

One of the first examinations of victims in the criminal justice system was Maguire and Bennett's (1982) study on burglary victims. Their findings indicate that the majority of victims were more concerned with the public relations or service provision of the police than their investigative role, albeit possibly because they could only judge police effectiveness by the former. Similar sentiments were echoed in Shapland *et al.*'s (1985) *Victims in the Criminal Justice System*, which demonstrated that victim satisfaction with the police dropped as cases progressed through a criminal justice process which failed to live up to their expectations. This finding was later confirmed by Jackson *et al.* (1991) in Belfast's magistrates' courts and the Crown Court. Key to Shapland *et al.*'s argument was the understanding that a victim-orientated system need not look significantly different from the existing one. Victims were not wishing to run the system, but rather expressed a desire for better information, consultation over decisions to drop or vary charges and to be treated respectfully. The authors noted that the changes required to achieve this were more *attitudinal* than *structural*. This indicates that addressing the occupational cultures of criminal justice practitioners is crucial.

Further light was shed on these issues by Rock's (1990) analysis of the social world of a typical English Crown Court. This study was based on one court and focused attention on witnesses as opposed to victims *per se*. As such, there is little discussion on how different parts of the criminal justice system come together and co-operate to assist victims. Nevertheless, Rock's conclusion confirmed that witnesses were kept at the margins of the court's social community and received little support. Such findings again indicate that providing support and services to victims within criminal justice is largely a *cultural* challenge.

Later studies

The report of the JUSTICE Committee (1998) made recommendations concerning victims at all stages of the criminal process, based on evidence submitted by all its agencies and other organisations. One cultural 'blind spot' identified in their report was the need to pass information about victims and witnesses between agencies. Generally, courts accepted the benefits of keeping prosecution and defence witnesses apart as they waited at court, but were less savvy when it came to more basic human responses to these issues, such as preventing intimidation through security and watchfulness.

Overall, the JUSTICE Committee advocated a criminal justice system based on service standards, backed by national Codes of Practice with a statutory Victims Commissioner as the ultimate point of complaint. The Committee was clearly in favour of extending greatly the services, support and facilities being offered to victims of crime by the courts. Consultative participation was also part of the JUSTICE scheme – at least in relation to probation decisions post-sentence – and the voluntary provision of information to judges regarding sentence.

Lord Auld also discussed victims in his report on the Workings of Criminal Courts (Auld 2001). Auld framed his analysis not just in relation to victims, but all members of the public. This pre-empts an important debate – taken up in the next chapter – concerning the wider implications of public-orientated reforms being used to address an over-professionalised criminal justice system (Christie 1977), and whether policy-making in this area is actually concerned with the public in general rather than victims specifically. Auld's (2001) report noted that the scheduling task of matching High Court judges to cases for which their individual areas of expertise would be most valuable distorted the system in a number of ways 'that are unjust and upsetting' to victims and others (p. 239). Auld also concedes that some witnesses at court are forced to wait for extended periods and are then bewildered at the course a case might take: for example when prosecutors accept a plea to a lesser offence. Auld argues that such concerns pose a serious risk of alienating the public, and especially victims, from the criminal justice process.

As a solution, Auld advocates more robust management and preparation of cases so that trials run to a more predictable plan. His report also called for clear understandings to be established at the beginning of a case as to who is responsible for keeping the victim informed on progress. Nevertheless, Auld dismisses the notion of *consulting* victims over decisions, arguing that such consultation would place great pressure on them, leaving them open to intimidation and raising false expectations. Auld also believes that victims lack the necessary objectivity and knowledge or experience to be consulted in this way and that 'at the pre-trial and trial stages of the process it has yet to be established that the alleged victim is in truth a victim' (p. 500).

While putting undue pressure on victims is clearly a legitimate concern, it is doubtful that merely *consulting* victims would cause undue upset, especially in light of Shapland *et al.*'s (1985) findings that some victims want to be consulted over prosecution decisions. Intimidation is also a legitimate concern, but one which is dependent on individual (probably more unusual) cases. The belief in objective factors on which to base decisions has already been critiqued, whereas it is difficult to see what 'knowledge or experience' a victim needs to form an opinion as to whether they would like a case to proceed. Finally, the return to notions of the alleged victim is surely a step backwards, as it carries connotations that such individuals should be denied services and support unless they are officially endorsed as truth-tellers who have suffered.

Auld's dismissal of victims' procedural involvement is based on concerns and assumptions about their vindictiveness and vengefulness (critiqued above) and is basically another due process argument. As such, Auld is advocating service rights and hinting at the existence of the zero sum game. The report dismisses 'more radical suggestions' like giving victims party status. Like Brienen and Hoegen (2000), Auld argues that the continental *partie civile* or auxiliary prosecutor models afford few practical advantages to victims.

Victimisation and witness surveys

In recent years, victims' experiences of support mechanisms have been included in victimisation surveys. For example, the 2002/2003 British Crime Survey shows that only one fifth of victims who reported an incident to the police and wanted more information actually received it. The BCS also indicates that victim satisfaction with the police is linked to the outcome of their investigation, specifically whether an offender is charged and/or victims' stolen property recovered (Allen *et al.* 2005).

The Witness Satisfaction Surveys (WSS) (Whitehead 2001; Angle *et al.* 2003) and the Vulnerable and Intimidated Witness (VIW) Surveys (Hamlyn *et al.* 2004a, 2004b)[22] both confirm that witness satisfaction with the criminal justice system is related to perceptions of courteous treatment, especially by the police. At court, 80 per cent of prosecution witnesses and 72 per cent of defence witnesses remembered receiving some information about the process beforehand in the 2000 WSS, mainly through leaflets. Receiving information about court visits had a significant impact on witnesses' overall satisfaction. Information for all witnesses was lacking in relation to how long the whole visit to court would take and on what to bring to court.

Between the 2000 and 2002 WSS, the number of witnesses having contact with the Witness Service went from 51 per cent in the first survey to 81 per cent in the second. This can be explained by the establishment during the intervening period of a Witness Service at all magistrates' courts. The surveys also showed that 10 per cent of witnesses had a pre-court familiarisation visit before the day of the trial in both 2000 and 2002 (12 per cent of victims in 2000). On the day itself, the 2002 survey shows that a further 57 per cent of witnesses had the opportunity to look around the court before proceedings. Child witnesses and victims were more likely to have a pre-trial familiarisation visit compared to other witnesses.

Overall, in the 2000 sweep, 17 per cent of witnesses had to wait more than four hours to give evidence (9 per cent of victims) although most waited only up to one hour (31 per cent). Forty-three per cent of victims had to wait up to one hour and 28 per cent waited up to two hours in 2000. The 2002 survey suggested that waiting times had increased slightly. In 2000, 73 per cent of prosecution and defence witnesses were put in separate waiting rooms, which rose to 83 per cent in 2002. Again, waiting times were linked with witness satisfaction.

Vulnerable and intimidated victims as witnesses

While the role of victims in sentencing and the various services and support facilities available to victims at different stages of the process have been the subject of a great deal of academic and policy attention, the rights of victims relating to the evidential process itself are seldom debated. As such, this section will identify specific victim needs during the evidential process to be addressed in a victim-centred system.

Identifying the problem

Giving evidence is often a difficult and mystifying experience. Indeed, the JUSTICE Committee (1998) concluded that the level of intimidation and upset experienced by some witnesses while giving evidence was against the interests of justice. Hence, witnesses may find themselves being asked confusing, unpleasant questions in a legalistic style they find baffling (Hamlyn *et al.* 2004a, 2004b). They are then often required to present their answers in a wholly unnatural and restricted manner (see Danet 1980; Shapland *et al.* 1985; Rock 1993; Luchjenbroers 1996; Ellison 2002).[23]

Many of these practices reflect conventions steeped in the traditions of advocacy. Carlen (1976) notes how judicial proceedings in the magistrates' courts are facilitated by 'the systematic manipulation of temporal, spatial and linguistic conventions' by professionals (p. 128). The assumption that victims may be interrupted while giving evidence but lawyers should not be, the notion that victims should face the bench and the idea that there is a 'correct speed' at which to give evidence are therefore all deeply engrained cultural working practices. Crucially, however, such unofficial understandings are not fundamental to adversarial evidence, certainly not in terms of written rules of procedure, conduct, or laws. Indeed, the JUSTICE Committee (1998) thought it strange that criminal justice practitioners considered it necessary to see the witnesses live in the witness box at all and were in favour of screening off adult and child victims or of evidence being given via video-link.

Rape victims were among the first witnesses to be recognised as facing particular challenges while giving evidence (Holmstrom and Burgess 1978). Temkin (1987, 1999) has argued that giving evidence can be the most traumatic element of being a victim aside from the actual offence and that reaching the trial stage might itself be difficult for these victims because of the poor response by police.[24]

Victims of domestic abuse may also be especially vulnerable or intimidated while giving evidence. Cretney and Davis (1997) give the example of Linda Roberts, who attended magistrates' court committal proceedings only to be left alone in a waiting room, fearful that the defendant would find her. At the subsequent trial, Roberts found herself unable to go through with her evidence. Like Temkin, Cretney and Davis criticise the attitude taken by the police (and prosecutors and sentencers) towards such victims. Their argument is that police are unable to look beyond the relationship that exists (or existed) between complainant and accused and work on the assumption that the complainant victim will withdraw support. The authors argue that this blaming of victims becomes a self-fulfilling prophecy, born of a negative and uninterested police attitude. Temkin (1987) and Cretney and Davis (1997) therefore both emphasise the role of *occupational cultures* as a key prerequisite to victims' discomfort in giving evidence. Indeed, many of the problems faced by victims and witnesses described above are not grounded in the adversarial model *per se*, but on the attitudes of those within it, especially the advocates who elicit evidence.

In 1998 the *Speaking Up for Justice* report responded to growing calls for something to be done to assist especially vulnerable and intimidated witnesses giving evidence. Based on distinctions drawn by Healey (1995) a 'combined' approach was advocated to identify such witnesses. Witnesses could thus be vulnerable by reason of personal characteristics (disability, mental and physical disorders) but also for wider circumstantial reasons (being related to or involved with the defendant). From a review of relevant research, *Speaking Up for Justice* revealed that the intimidation of *victim* witnesses (whether or not they are also vulnerable witnesses) is more widespread than the intimidation of *non-victim* witnesses. Women were more at risk from intimidation than men and intimidation is more likely when the witness knows the offender, who in most cases perpetrates the intimidation. Both points were confirmed in the British Crime Survey of that year (Tarling *et al.* 2000). Intimidation was especially prevalent in cases of rape, domestic violence, racial harassment and crimes against sexual minorities. The 1998 BCS showed that three quarters of reported incidents of intimidation were verbal and only 8 per cent were – in the victim's view – intended to prevent him/her giving evidence. Overall, 8 per cent of victims had suffered some form of intimidation, 15 per cent when the victim knew the offender (Mattinson and Mirrlees-Black 2000).

The 2002 Witness Satisfaction Survey (Angle *et al.* 2003) indicated that 26 per cent of witnesses feel intimidated by an individual and 21 per cent by giving evidence. Intimidation by individuals was especially prominent among victims (27 per cent), women (26 per cent) and child witnesses (30 per cent). Overall, 42 per cent of all witnesses and 51 per cent of victims were intimidated by either the process or an individual. Fifty-six per cent of witnesses were intimidated by defendants and 35 per cent by official sources, including lawyers, police, court staff, judges and magistrates.

Finding solutions

Intimidatory cross-examination also concerns Ellison (1998, 2001, 2002). For Ellison, the difficulties faced by rape and other victims during cross-examination are grounded in the inadequate regulation of the process and the combative features of the adversarial system. Traditional mechanisms of restricting inappropriate cross-examination through the discretionary intervention of the judge are insufficient, because this may conflict with a judge's duty to ensure fair proceedings. Similarly, argues Ellison, the adversarial nature of criminal justice in England and Wales means advocates approach their task with a combative mindset.

Ellison is especially critical of reform introduced in the Youth Justice and Criminal Evidence Act 1999, especially the advent of so-called 'special measures'. Special measures are facilities such as video-links and screens designed to assist vulnerable and intimidated victims and other witnesses give evidence in court in a more relaxed, less oppressive manner. The measures are frequently cited in official documentation as evidence of the government's significant commitment to putting victims at the heart of the justice system (Home Office 2006a). Certainly special measures constitute one of the most visible and obvious amendments to the criminal process over recent years.

Despite such rhetoric, however, Ellison (2001, 2002) views special measures as a less significant development. Certainly these reforms were far more modest than the system of pre-recorded cross-examination for children envisioned by the Pigot report 10 years earlier (Advisory Group on Video Evidence 1989; Hoyano and Keenan 2007). For Ellison, the 1999 Act embodies an 'accommodation approach' through which the tenets of the existing adversarial system of justice are preserved and more radical reform is resisted. Ellison is not alone in these kinds of arguments. I have argued elsewhere that most special measures do not significantly increase a witness's verbal contribution to the evidential process (Hall 2007). The last chapter also noted Rock's (2004) impression that the Domestic Violence, Crime and Victims Act of 2004 was a compromise designed to avoid accepting victims as parties in criminal trials. According to Ellison, measures which deviate least from the traditional adversarial model are also least effective in alleviating stress and securing the best possible evidence. In the same vein, Victim Support (2002b) calls for more comparisons with inquisitorial criminal justice to temper the excesses of cross-examination.

Ellison's view clearly implies that the best means of assisting vulnerable and intimidated victims during evidence is to alter the character of the adversarial process. Arguably, however, these problems are more dependent on the attitude of lawyers asking questions than on the specific adversarial nature of the system. What is needed is not a fundamental alteration of the system, but rather its civilisation. This implies treating victims with courtesy – as people rather than sources of evidence – and installing professional aversions to interrupting victims giving their evidence or resorting to aggressive questioning styles. Such rules of civility are common in other professions that promote conjecture, including academia.

We will note in a moment the findings of witness surveys that seem to indicate special measures are having a beneficial impact on witnesses giving evidence under the existing adversarial justice model. In addition, Brienen and Hoegen (2000) argue that, although the process of cross-examination has remained largely unchanged, the 'rough edges' have been taken off by recent reforms. This is not to say that such measures have matured to a point where the problems faced by victims giving evidence are nullified. Birch (2000) notes how 'poorly served' witnesses with learning difficulties will be by the 1999 reforms and labels the Act 'a somewhat hurried piece of work, enacted to fulfil election promises' (p. 223). Crucially, however, Birch's underlying view is not that refined special measures would be incapable of assisting victims in an adversarial system, but that their impact will be minimal while practitioners remain sceptical of the measures.

Pre-recorded examination in chief

Possibly the most significant of the special measures is the capacity for vulnerable child witnesses to give evidence via pre-recorded examination in chief in s. 27 of the 1999 Act. Under this provision, witnesses are interviewed in advance by a police officer in the less intimidating surroundings of specially designed police interviewing suites. These interviews are recorded on videotape or DVD and then played in court during the trial. The theory is that this will largely replace a witness's examination in chief in court and therefore reduce the time he or she spends answering questions during the trial itself, making the whole experience less distressing.

In examining the operation of such interviews, Davies and Westcott (1999) confirmed the vulnerability of very young witnesses and the need to present questions in a way they can understand. Children required support throughout the process, which included adequately preparing them for the interview and giving them proper closure. The language used and the conduct of the interviewer were essential not only in terms of supporting the child but also to avoid children simply going along with implications or suggestive questioning.[25] Overall, the author advocates a flexible approach to interviewing child witnesses, allowing scope for open-ended questions and the child's 'free narrative' responses. Davies and Westcott (1999) and Welbourne (2002) agree that a focus on evidentially building a case and preparing young witnesses for court were insufficient to meet the needs of vulnerable children.

Such findings led to the publication of new guidelines for police officers conducting these interviews (Home Office 2001a). These emphasised the importance of preparing witnesses for the interview and for the interviewer to have regard to the interviewee's specific circumstances, including their race and level of cognitive understanding/disability. The guidelines also set out the benefits of establishing rapport with interviewees in order to reassure them and assess their level of understanding. The document emphasises the interview's progression from rapport to a free narrative (during which the witness should not be interrupted) to more specific questioning. The operation of pre-recorded examination in chief in English courts hints that the adversarial model is capable of incorporating a wider form of evidence, which may be beneficial to victims. The existence of such evidence already in the system implies that its application can be successfully expanded to more victims and witnesses, just as video-links, screens and so on were extended to adult witnesses as special measures in 1999.

Witness surveys

Witness surveys have provided some indication as to the impact of special measures and other reforms intended to assist vulnerable and intimidated witnesses. Results from the 2002 Witness Satisfaction Survey (Angle *et al.* 2003) revealed a number of improvements in witness satisfaction (Whitehead 2001). Seventy-eight per cent of witnesses were satisfied with their experience of the criminal justice system and 71 per cent of victim witnesses were satisfied overall. Eighty-six per cent of victim witnesses reported being satisfied with the conduct of the prosecution lawyer in their case and 92 per cent were satisfied with the conduct of the judge. Nearly all (96 per cent of) witnesses thought they were treated courteously by the lawyer on their side. Witnesses who were treated courteously by lawyers on both sides and were given the opportunity to say everything they wished were much more likely to be satisfied overall compared to other witnesses. Overall, the strongest predictor of witness dissatisfaction with the system was the feeling they had been taken for granted (Angle *et al.* 2003).

Such findings indicate that witnesses can still be satisfied with the criminal justice system after being subject to the adversarial model of evidence. Regarding evidence, it seems that victims and other witnesses want a simple extension of the courteous and civilised treatment they require from the rest of the system. This supports the assertion that the manner in which lawyers conduct themselves during evidence is key, not the process itself.

The Vulnerable and Intimidated Witness Surveys were generally supportive of special measures (Hamlyn *et al.* 2004b). Overall satisfaction amongst VIWs rose between the first and second phases of the survey by 5 per cent, although the 69 per cent of VIWs reporting satisfaction was lower than the 78 per cent of *all* witnesses reporting satisfaction in the WSS. Witnesses rated special measures facilities highly, with a third reporting they would have been unable or unwilling to give evidence without them. Witnesses who used special measures were less likely to feel anxiety than those who did not.[26] Nevertheless, the report commented that 'there is still some way to go before the needs of VIWs are met' (Hamlyn *et al.* 2004b: xv).

The NSPCC has also commissioned research on video-links, which involved speaking with 50 young witnesses who had given evidence (Plotnikoff and Woolfson 2005). The authors suggest that 'the essentially compulsory use of TV links for young witnesses in cases of sex or violence' (p. 11) restricts the options available to children. This may go against Article 12 of the 1990 UN Convention on the Rights of the Child, which requires decision-makers to involve children in the decision-making process on matters relevant to their lives. The report suggests that – given a genuine choice – some children might choose to forgo the TV link in favour of being screened off from the defendant and gallery in the courtroom.

The suggestion that special measures are being forced upon victims is a troubling one (Hall 2007). In the application of special measures provisions under the Youth Justice and Criminal Evidence Act 1999 – and following the *No Witness, No Justice* scheme (Home Office 2004g) – vulnerable and intimidated witnesses are supposed to be identified as such at an early stage by police officers. To this end, police officers taking a witness statement on the standard MG11 form should also submit an MG2 initial witness assessment. This latter form records details of the witness's vulnerability or intimidation and any special measure necessary to improve the quality of evidence (Home Office 2004h).

It is nevertheless difficult to adduce from the police guidelines how exactly the assessment of vulnerability is to be made. The MG2 does contain a section where officers must 'give the views of the witness as to why the [special] measures sought are required'. This implies consultative participation on the issue of special measures, although there is no indication as to how a witness who *does not* want to give evidence this way (even when they are so entitled) would make this view known. The Home Office guidance document for witnesses – *Witness in Court* (Home Office 2003g) – indicates that the court will 'take account' of witnesses's views when making decisions on special measures (p. 21). That said, the police guidelines are also clear that children under 17 in cases of sexual offences or violence, neglect or abduction will be considered 'in need of special protection' and 'benefit from strong presumptions' that their evidence will be given by pre-recorded examination in chief and video-link 'unless the court considers the measures will not maximise the quality of evidence'. The MG2 form itself is even more prescriptive in this regard:

> If either a) [sexual offences] or b) [offences involving violence, cruelty or abduction] apply, then the child witness is 'in need of special protection' and the admission of a visually recorded interview, if available, is mandatory and any other evidence must be given by a live link. (Home Office 2004h: 39)

This is an interpretation of s. 21 of the Youth Justice and Criminal Evidence Act 1999, which sets out the special protection to be afforded to witnesses under 17 years of age. Here, s. 21(3) confirms that the 'primary rule' is that any pre-recorded evidence in chief is admissible, and that all other evidence should be given via live video-link. Nevertheless, a court can depart from this principle if it believes such facilities will not maximise the quality of a witness's evidence (s. 21(4)(c)). Crucially, s. 19(3)(a) of the Act requires courts to take account of any views expressed by the witness when making this determination. This subsection also applies to all other witnesses, including those who do not fall under s. 21, but are still automatically eligible for special measures because they are under 17 years of age (s. 16(1)(a)) or a complainant in respect of a sexual offence (s. 17(4)). Thus, in most cases, it seems unlikely that young witnesses will be compelled to give evidence via special measures against their will. This includes most young witnesses falling under s. 21, as in most cases this surely would not maximise the quality of the evidence. In a similar example, while adult complaints of sexual offences are automatically entitled to special measures under s. 7(4), the Act clearly states that such victims can give up this automatic right under this subsection.

Of course, this is all dependent on victims and witnesses being clearly informed that they are not obliged to give evidence through special measures. In Chapter 6, however, it will be shown that witnesses are not always presented with the alternatives.[27] Hence, this does raise the concern that at least some children may be afforded little choice over whether they give evidence through special measures.[28] Essentially the difficulty seems to be that the Act, and the resulting guidance documents (Home Office 2004h), do not account for witnesses who are automatically eligible for special measures but do not wish to give their evidence in this way.[29] Arguably, compelling witnesses to give evidence through special measures without any consultative participation is contrary to the spirit – if not the letter – of the 1999 Act.

Ways forward

This chapter has introduced the most pertinent debates in modern victimology concerning victims of crime within the criminal justice system, with particular reference to the court process. It is clear that there is significant conjecture at both the academic and policy levels on many of these key issues, especially regarding the nature of victims' rights and victims' participation in the process. As these debates go on, studies continue to show that the needs of victims are not being met (Applegate 2006). Before moving on to discuss the policy process in greater detail in the next chapter, it is worth pausing at this point to reflect on the broad implications of the above discussions for the government's pledge to deliver victim-centred criminal justice.

Fundamental reform?

A key question for reformers implementing policies to put victims at the heart of the criminal justice system is the extent to which such reforms constitute a fundamental alteration of the existing criminal justice process. The issue then becomes whether reforms of this nature are a necessary and justified means of achieving this objective. The introduction of special measures under the Youth Justice and Criminal Evidence Act 1999 illustrates the complexities surrounding such questions, for while superficially these reforms appear very significant, Ellison (2001) among others believes they merely preserve the tenets of the existing adversarial model. Such arguments imply that there are definite limits of reform beyond which governments and policy-makers are unwilling to go to achieve a victim-centred justice system. The question effectively becomes not just whether victims are being put at the heart of criminal justice, but whether this is achievable through what Rock called 'finesse' (2004: 571) and accommodation rather than more fundamental reform of the existing system.

For Ellison, a more fundamental programme of reform would clearly involve a move away from adversarial criminal justice. In this construction, fundamental reform would mean altering the nature of the system and the roles and goals of those within it. Moving towards an inquisitorial system, for example, would require fundamental change in the practices of all involved. Moves towards restorative justice would also be fundamental, as they necessitate changes in the goals of the process from conviction to restitution, and many changes in the process itself.[30] It would also be a fundamental change to alter the basic system of evidence which, in Ellison's view, special measures have failed to do. Non-fundamental reform, on the other hand, would simply adapt the manner in which the existing system operates and how its participants perform existing roles.

To expand this debate, we can draw upon the key question of whether victims should become decision-makers in the criminal justice process. Employing the distinction between changing the system and adapting its operation, some decision-making on the part of victims might constitute fundamental reform. If victims were permitted to decide whether or not to pursue a prosecution, for example, this would constitute an essential shift in the role of the Crown Prosecution Service, and therefore a fundamental change. The same would be true if victims selected sentences, as this would usurp the role of judges and magistrates.

Nevertheless, official resistance to fundamental reform does not preclude the victim from any participation within the process, and certainly not from having opinions canvassed and weighed up by prosecutors and judges, such that they may have a real impact. So, while victims selecting sentences can be ruled out, a non-fundamental change would allow them to present information on the impact of crime – or *opinions* as to sentence – and have that information considered by judges. The notion that decision-makers within the system base their decisions on all available information is already a basic principle within the criminal justice process. Hence, promoting mechanisms to ensure that information from all sources, including the victims, is available to such decision-makers represents non-fundamental reforms. Ultimately the same decisions are being made by the same actors, and thus the system itself does not change.

While victims making decisions on sentence and prosecution must be seen as fundamental reforms, non-fundamental reform would afford them the discretion to choose whether they give evidence in the first place. In England and Wales the system is already based on the voluntary provision of evidence. Indeed, as there is no legal duty to report crime, evidence will always be partial. Hence it would be a non-fundamental reform to minimise the exceptions to this rule (courts' discretion to summon witnesses). This is particularly relevant in domestic violence cases, where victims are often unwilling to give evidence (see Cretney and Davis 1997). It might be argued that this gives victim witnesses the power to end a prosecution in cases where there is no other evidence (a fundamental reform). Nevertheless, the absence of good evidence is an issue already dealt with routinely by police and CPS, hence the emphasis remains on the existing system to gather as much evidence as possible and to provide an environment in which the victim is happy to give evidence.

Providing such an environment is also a non-fundamental reform. For example, professional standards can be changed such that prosecutors are expected to keep victims informed and treat them courteously, without impacting on the process. Similarly, fostering a change in attitudes among practitioners to minimise inconvenience to victims – even if this inconveniences professionals and courts – does not remodel the system itself. In the same vein, one could preserve the basic adversarial nature of evidence, but adapt practices to minimise hostility and to allow victims to speak more freely.[31]

Earlier in this chapter, the controversial notion of victim rights was discussed. In principle, however, securing the application of non-fundamental victim reforms by giving victims rights would not in itself constitute a fundamental change in the system. This is especially true if rights are enforced through existing features of the process. For example, fostering the expectation that judges will step in if victims are interrupted unnecessarily during their evidence is simply a formalisation of an existing (if discretionary) judicial function. This of course means that the *enforcement* of rights and the remedies available to victims when they are breached is key.

Another key debate is whether giving victims the status of parties in criminal proceedings would constitute fundamental reform. Interestingly, while most commentators in this area make reference to this issue, there has been little specific discussion of what constitutes party status. The most likely understanding seems to be that a party has representation in the trial procedure through which their views and (perhaps) opinions are presented to the court for the bench to take into account. This suggests that making victims a party to the case need not take us much further than the consultation and consideration of the victims' position already accepted as non-fundamental reform above. The key addition here is that the presentation of this position to the court is guaranteed through the advent of representation. As such, this again does not change the fundamental process of decision-making or the respective roles of existing parties (defendant and state) and is therefore a non-fundamental reform.

What the above discussion illustrates is that a great deal more can be done for victims within the present adversarial criminal justice system than is often implied in the literature. The remainder of this book will therefore pursue the notion that victim-centred criminal justice need not be particularly different from the system we have now (Shapland *et al.* 1985). In other words, it will question the assumption espoused by Ellison and others that victim-centredness can only be achieved through fundamental reforms. Of course, non-fundamental reforms may well be easier to apply in the face of deeply engrained occupational practices. Such reform may also suggest changes that are not resource-intensive, such as treating victims with courtesy.[32] As such, putting victims at the heart of criminal justice would seem a far more achievable proposition if it could be accomplished without fundamentally altering the criminal justice system.

Notes

1 See below.
2 This scheme was intended to make police the 'one-stop shop' for victims wanting information about the progress of cases they were involved with. The pilots were deemed a failure when it became clear that police did not have all the relevant information and could not adequately explain the decisions made by the Crown Prosecution Service. See Chapter 3.
3 It is not clear whether the authors believe this is because such sentencing would be excessively punitive or because it would lead to inconsistency within the system.
4 There is little evidence to suggest victims want such decision-making power (JUSTICE 1998; Auld 2001; Tapley 2002).
5 Sanders *et al.* do not attribute this to differences between the UK, American and Australian systems.
6 Although see Doak (2007).
7 Recommendation 85(11).
8 Albeit, it is telling that this is not expressly stated.
9 Application No. 16696/90, 26 October 1995.
10 [1996] 23 EHRR 330. Although in June 2008 the House of Lords' judgment in *R* v. *Davis (Iain), The Times*, June 19, seems to restrict the use of anonymous evidence in British courts. The government has responded by pledging to swiftly change the law to reverse the ruling and 'protect witnesses' (BBC 2008).
11 *The Times*, 19 June 2008.
12 Application No. 34209/96, 2 July 2002.
13 [1993] 13 EHRR 379.
14 [2000] Crim. LR 287.

15 [2001] All ER 449.
16 [1995] Crim. LR 835.
17 The Victim's Code of Practice refers to a victim's right to make a victim personal statement.
18 [2000] Crim. LR 606.
19 The Parliamentary Commissioner for Administration could *recommend* agencies provide redress following an investigation.
20 See p. 33.
21 Although 'legitimate expectations' were originally conceived as legal obligations enforceable through ombudsmen or judicial actors (JUSTICE 1998).
22 Although note that both surveys concentrate on witnesses, some of whom will be victims, rather than victims as a distinct group. Discussion of the VIW surveys will be taken up below. It remains to be seen how the new Witnesses and Victims Experience Survey (WAVES) will add to the picture provided by these surveys.
23 See Chapter 4.
24 Lees (2002) makes a similar point.
25 Bull and Corran (2002) suggest that the *manner* in which an interviewer speaks to a child may be as influential as the words used.
26 Early concerns from practitioners and the judiciary regarding the impact of special measures on jurors was addressed by Davies (1999) who found that while juries did prefer 'live' evidence this did not affect their decision-making.
27 See p. 171.
28 There appears to be no case law to assist us with our interpretations of s. 21 on this point.
29 The disadvantages to witnesses of giving evidence via video-link in particular are discussed in Chapter 6.
30 While the government has of course invested heavily in investigating the merits of restorative justice programmes (Shapland *et al.* 2004), these have grown up in parallel to the adversarial system, and are arguably diversionary processes (Dignan 1992; Young and Goold 1999).
31 See Chapter 4.
32 Although some victim-centred reform may require significant resources, such as the advent of special measures.

Chapter 3

Victims of crime: a policy chain?

Victim policies?

This chapter sets out to identify the driving forces behind the progression of official actions on crime victims and asks whether such actions can be classified as a unified strategy.[1] This is important because relevant policy documents tend to discuss a limited range of influences. Commentators such as Elias, however, have suggested that victim policies may have less overt, political, purposes (Elias 1986). Rock (1990, 1998, 2004) has covered many of the earlier developments in this area in great detail. As such, this chapter will focus attention on developments from the advent of the New Labour government in 1997, especially the period from 2004 onwards.

The key argument set out below is that victim policies have been derived from a wide variety of different political pressures and areas of activity, not all of them conducive to victims' needs. As such, it may be a mistake to think of victims as a single policy. Such pressures/areas include: the nature of policy-making; the mechanisms by which national strategies are implemented locally; developed understandings of victimhood; greater distinctions drawn between victims and witnesses; the work of victim assistance groups; wider reform agendas (financial concerns, efficiency, a target culture, the multi-agency approach); so-called populist punitiveness; international influences; the development of rights discourse and macro influences.[2] Such characteristics of reform are far from unique to the area of victim policies, reflecting broader political trends, especially in relation to governance (Crawford 1997; Jordan *et al.* 2005).

Interpreting the 'policy'

Three possible interpretations of government action on victims will be considered in this chapter. Firstly, there is the possibility that all such actions are part of a consistent, unified strategy to assist victims and witnesses. The second possibility is that actions that, incidentally, assist victims and witnesses may be grounded in a different set of political concerns. This is certainly what Rock found when studying the politics of victims relating to the development of Victim Support in the mid 1980s and early 1990s, when ideas concerning reparation 'proved to be the Trojan horse which carried victim support schemes to political prominence' (Rock 1990: 345). A third possibility is that – victims and witnesses having achieved at least rhetorical acceptance in policy-making (Rock 2004) – new policies are being packaged as the continuation of work for these groups but are in fact intended to achieve other aims such as increasing efficiency in the justice system or, in the words of Elias:

> [V]ictims may function to bolster state legitimacy, to gain political mileage, and to enhance social control. (1986: 231)

All three interpretations can no doubt be applied to some aspects of the government's work on victims. The central question, however, is whether this work is all part of the same thing, or instead reflects many different politics.

Victims and witnesses: shaping the 'policy'

In July 2003 the Home Office published a national strategy to deliver improved services for victims of crime and witnesses called to give evidence in court (Home Office 2003a). Titled *A new deal for victims and witnesses*, the report pulled together the various strands of government action in this area – compensation; information provision; support for vulnerable and intimidated witnesses; funding for the Witness Service and so on – and presented them as a unified strategy.[3] This was achieved within the broader context of a multi-agency approach and standards articulated through the government's Public Service Agreement (PSA) targets. So, the *new deal* not only sets out future measures, it also provides a clear example of a strategic approach to victims and witnesses policy, which has also been employed in other areas of policy-making like health (Greener 2004) and education (Selwyn and Fitz 2001).

Nevertheless, the *deal* is also a misleading document in so much as – in common with most other policy documents relating to victims and witnesses – it implies a clarity and consistency of purpose (internally and in relation to all past measures) which does not reflect the complexities and practicalities of actual policy-making. This chapter will demonstrate that the occasional publication of review documents like the *new deal* is merely the latest product of an ongoing process of policy-making characterised by complex interactions between government departments, the parliamentary and political process and ideological movements domestically and abroad. As such, this is an example of what is usually termed 'governance', defined by Crawford as:

> [A] pattern of shifting relations which involve: the fusion of, and changing relations between, the state, the market, and civil society; a move from 'social' to 'community'; greater individual and group responsibility for the management of local risk and security; and the emergence of new forms of management of public services and structures for policy formation and implementation. (1997: 6)

Much of the development in policy-making and implementation over recent years seems to reflect such ideas, in this and other areas of reform. For example, in the context of education policy, Bache (2003) notes:

> The term 'governance' implies an increasingly complex set of state–society relationships in which networks rather than hierarchies dominate policy-making. (p. 301)

The concept of 'policy networks' and wider 'policy communities' (Jordan *et al.* 2005) reinforces the argument that victims policy is likely to derive from multiple sources rather than a simple decision on the part of hierarchical policy-makers to address this issue. Consequently, the snapshot provided by examining the progression of policy documents from the *new deal* right up to the most recent CJS strategic plan for 2008–11 (Criminal Justice System 2007) only provides static impressions of a dynamic process.

For a more intricate understanding of official policy regarding victims and witnesses, such documents must be examined in the context of wider and preceding developments. This was clearly illustrated by Rock (1990), who suggests that while the larger framework set by politics suggests a unified strategy, those politics may not individually be aimed at assisting victims themselves.

A policy chain?

The impression derived from documents like the *new deal* and more recent publications is that past and present actions related to victims and witnesses are indeed part of some consistent strategy to improve their lot. Policy-makers inevitably link a government's recent actions to a succession of previous actions, each new document generally referring to the last in a manner reminiscent of citing legal precedent. In this way official policy documents tend to be linked together in a chronological chain of policy-making.

The 2003 *new deal* is a particularly good illustration of this strategy, devoting three pages to recounting the government's record on victims and witnesses. Indeed the title *new deal* echoes the 2002 chapter *A better deal for victims and witnesses* from the White Paper *Justice For All,* a title also used for a chapter in the government's criminal justice review of the year before (Home Office 2001b, 2002). Similarly, the 2003 Inter-Agency Working Group on Witnesses' report *No Witness, No Justice* and its accompanying Ministerial Response both open with a reference to Labour's pledge to put victims and witnesses at the heart of the criminal justice system, also found in *Justice for All.* The chapter *A better deal for victims and witnesses* itself began by recounting the government's earlier work in assisting Victim Support and the expansion of the Witness Service (Rock 1990). That this should be the case is not at all surprising because, as Rock (1986, 1990) observed in England and Canada, policy-making often requires the latest innovations to be packaged as a *continuation* of work that has already been done and has therefore already met with political acceptance.

Politics, pressures and influences: deconstructing the 'policy chain'

In light of the above observations this research project set out to conduct a thematic analysis of victims policy documents, reforms, and the views of relevant policy-makers. The data was analysed not chronologically, but by areas of political activity and pressure. The aim was to deconstruct and debunk the myth of the policy chain in relation to victims (and other policy areas) while exposing the complex interaction of influences that really drive such reforms.[4]

At the same time, such analysis also reveals the limitations of the existing reform agenda.

The nature of policy-making

As noted above, the policy-making process is inevitably portrayed as sequential and ordered, with all present actions being linked to previous developments. One good example relates to the concept of victim right, introduced in Chapter 2. Here there was a perceptible development of policy from the first Victim's Charter of 1990[5] to a more refined second Victim's Charter (based on service standards) to the Victim's Code of Practice: a compromise of non-fundamental reform and externally enforceable rights (Home Office 2005f). The wheels of progress were greased throughout by a succession of reports (Auld 2001), consultations (Home Office 2005g, 2005h) and pilots (Hoyle *et al.* 1999).

In another example, the recent history[6] of the development of special measures to assist vulnerable and intimidated witnesses can be traced back to the initial government funding of the Crown Court Witness Service announced in 1991.[7] Limited provision for pre-recorded examination in chief (for children) then arrived in the Criminal Justice Act 1991 and then – via the *Speaking Up for Justice* report (Interdepartmental Working Group on the Treatment of Vulnerable or Intimidated Witnesses in the Criminal Justice System 1998) – came the rollout of special measures under the Youth Justice and Criminal Evidence Act 1999. We have recently seen the extension of pre-recorded examination in chief to adult vulnerable witnesses, and now to adult victims of sexual assault giving evidence in the Crown Court (Criminal Justice System 2007). At the time of writing (summer 2008) the government has announced that it will be proposing extensions in special measures provisions for vulnerable and intimidated witnesses, especially in cases involving guns and other offensive weapons (Office of the Leader of the House of Commons 2008). The government has also reacted very speedily following the judgment in *R* v. *Davis (Iain)*[8] from the House of Lords in June 2008, in which it was ruled that witness anonymity was in most cases incompatible with the common law and therefore beyond the court's jurisdiction. The government responded by rushing the Criminal Evidence (Witness Anonymity) Bill through the House of Commons in July 2008: which essentially abolished the common law in this area and reinstated a judge's discretion to make witness anonymity orders.

Such policies then do not appear from nowhere, or at least are not portrayed as such by policy-makers. The need to ground reforms on well-established principles also means such measures (once initiated) must be consolidated, assessed and refined. Having introduced practical reforms over the last few years in the Youth Justice and Criminal Evidence Act 1999, the Criminal Justice Act 2003 and the Domestic Violence, Crime and Victims Act 2004, from 2004 onwards there is a sense that policy-makers are trying to win over criminal justice practitioners and administrators to produce occupational cultures and practices more conducive to tackling victims' needs.

One example of this consolidation process has been the general shift towards collecting information from victims and witnesses themselves through the Witness Satisfaction Surveys, the Vulnerable and Intimidated Witness Survey and the new Witness and Victim Experience Survey (WAVES). This tendency to consolidate reforms with empirical evidence reflects wider trends towards rational or evidence-based policy-making (Lawrence 2006), the emphasis now being on 'what works' (McGrath 2000; Sanderson 2003; Shaxson 2005). Consolidation may also reflect what Rein and Rabinovitz (1978) termed the 'principle of circularity', whereby policy formation feeds into implementations, which feeds into policy evaluation and contributes to the formation of new or developed policies (Nakamura and Smallwood 1980).

This all implies that policy-making at any given time will be restricted by the limits of what is presently acceptable in political terms. So, for example, in the 2001 review of the Victim's Charter the creation of a minister for victims was dismissed on the grounds that victims would be better served as a shared responsibility between justice agencies (Home Office 2001d: para. 29). What we see here is the distribution of the victim issue along a horizontal axis of policy-making – linking different departments, agencies and interest groups – rather than along a vertical axis of hierarchical power relationships in a single agency or policy-making organ, this being another feature of governance (Matheson 2000).

Interviews conducted for this research confirmed this impression of victims as a shared priority:

> Even though we have got this Unit here in OCJR, there's still a huge amount of work happening across other departments, and even across other places in OCJR. So in the DCA there's the victims and witnesses branch, within the Home Office there's people doing work on domestic violence, doing work

> on vulnerable and intimidated witnesses. (representative of the OCJR)

That said, it was suggested with specific reference to the *new deal* that generalising priorities and responsibilities in this way could have negative implications:

> That was a really useful document, but looking at it now we felt it had perhaps too many priorities and it wasn't always clear who was going to be responsible for delivering on them, and so over the past year we have felt that we really needed quite a tight focus, particularly on the PSA [confidence] target. (representative of the OCJR)

Nevertheless, at this stage, a victims minister was too radical to contemplate, and would remain so until the appointment of Fiona Mactaggart to this position in 2005. Interestingly, however, the above quotation does emphasise the *delivery* of guaranteed standards (see Home Office 2005d), something which was lacking in the largely unenforceable first Victim's Charter (Fenwick 1995). This would imply putting victims at the heart of criminal justice now involves guaranteeing and enforcing minimum standards (perhaps rights) as discussed in the last chapter. On this point, Nakamura and Smallwood (1980) have noted the growing importance of the *implementation* stage of policy-making and Bache (2003) argues that policies are not really 'made' until they are implemented.

Arguably the restrictive views adopted in the Auld Report of 2001[9] set the tone for the development of victim policy over the next few years, this being essentially Ellison's (2001) accommodation approach discussed in the last chapter. This impression was confirmed by policy-makers:

> I think that the thrust of policy has been working with the system that we have got, how we can best improve it, and I think you can really clearly see all the reforms fitting around that. (representative of the OCJR)

A similar view was echoed by local administrators in the area under review:

> It seems to me that any significant further changes will involve a decision being taken about whether the court process in

> England and Wales is about the adversarial system ... or the more continental idea of the inquisitorial system ... As I understand it, from a philosophical and principle point of view the decision is that we will remain with the adversarial system and I think – given that – future changes are likely to be around the edges. (the Justices' Chief Executive of the local Magistrates' Court Committee)

Such views support the position taken in the last chapter that the possibility of victim-centredness within the *present* criminal justice system must be further explored. To this end the lack of internally enforceable rights in the Victim's Code of Practice and the exclusion of the judiciary from any obligations under the Code have already been noted. That said, while the government's reluctance to place obligations on judges is understandable – and consistent with the principle of reduced compulsion that characterises governance (Bache 2003) – it is questionable whether the exclusion of judicial actors from the remit of the Code and the Victims and Witnesses Commissioner will provide the best results for victims.

The limits of the present reform agenda are further revealed through the Witness Satisfaction Survey (Angle *et al.* 2003) where, on the issue of intimidation, the court felt that increasing the information available was probably the only option because:

> Given the formality of the judicial process, particularly in the Crown Court, it would be difficult and perhaps not desirable, to make the process unintimidating. (p. 57)

Overall, it seems clear that, to these policy-makers, putting victims at the heart of the system does not mean fundamentally reshaping the system around them, but is rather an attempt to adapt the existing model to their needs. It was this kind of approach which lead to Rock's (2004) 'finesse' in which the language of more far-reaching reform is employed ('rights for victims') but not the operational reality. The argument here is that while non-fundamental reform may be sufficient to achieve victim-centredness, one can go a lot further towards granting victims genuine rights and participation within the system than has presently been achieved without fundamentally changing it.

Another fundamental aspect of policy-making procedure is the need to adapt policies to suit contemporary situations and – in particular – levels of support. So, for example, in 2004 a government suggestion that 'industry' foot the bill for compensating victims was hastily withdrawn in the face of opposition from employers citing the likely rise in cost of employer liability insurance (Home Office 2004a). Consequently, the reforms that eventually appeared in the Domestic Violence, Crime and Victims Act 2004 were more modest, introducing a surcharge placed on some convictions and laying down provisions for the future reclaiming of money paid by the state compensation scheme from the offender.[10] Subsequent consultation suggestions to the effect that narrowing down state compensation to those seriously injured will reduce administrative costs illustrate how governments and policy-makers adapt their strategies when proposed reforms elicit unfavourable responses (Home Office 2005d).

Interactive policy-making

As well as necessarily following on from previous reforms, measures, or rhetoric, a more recent development in the nature of policy-making seems to involve consulting directly with those who are or will be affected by reforms. This was particularly apparent after 1999, when the need to assess the application of reforms under the Youth Justice and Criminal Evidence Act of that year necessitated a challenge to the long tradition in policy-making in this area of failing to consult any victims (Williams 2005).

Up until this point, victims themselves had surfaced on the policy scene in a most *ad hoc* manner, far removed from the modern focus on evidence-based policies discussed above. Hence, the 1964 introduction of the Criminal Injuries Compensation Scheme (CICS) was largely based on a presumption that victims wanted it, and might turn to vigilantism without it (Rock 1990).[11] Such examples are far from unique to victim policies. Ellis (2005) for example recounts how 'youth' became a policy concern for the Conservatives in the 1960s based on a mistaken belief that this group threatened Conservative values.

Nevertheless, the need to assess the impact of the 1999 Act prompted the government to engage with victims and witnesses more directly. Consequently, the introduction of the Witness Satisfaction Survey and the Vulnerable and Intimidated Witness Survey was designed to chart how witnesses had reacted to the introduction of special measures, the extension of the Witness Service, and the progress towards relevant targets (Kitchen and Elliott 2001; Whitehead 2001).[12] One interviewee from the DCA confirmed that reviewing previous research was no longer enough, and that one had to talk to the victims themselves, hence the creation of institutions like the Victims' Advisory Panel in

2002 (representative of the DCA 2005). That said, the victim members of the Panel are mainly indirect victims of homicide, and therefore do not represent the vast majority of crime victims. In addition, Casey (2008) criticises the fact that the Panel has only been chaired thus far by ministers and government officials, while none of its proposals have been explicitly accepted by the government. Nevertheless, the attempt to bring victims into the policy-making process reflects wider government strategies in which – pursuant to New Labour's 'Third Way' (Giddens 1994; Leggett 2000; Crawford 2001) – attempts have been made to establish wider 'policy communities' in many areas of reform.

This is so-called 'interactive' policy-making (Mayer *et al*. 2005) by which stakeholders such as local communities (Pearce and Mawson 2003; Irvin and Stansbury 2004), the elderly (Priestley 2002) and children (Tisdall and Davis 2004) are given a voice in policy-making. Broadly speaking, the principle is that all those who will be affected by a policy decision should have some involvement in its formation (Cabinet Office 1999; Williams 1999). This has been especially apparent in relation to victims of domestic violence, albeit arguably the relevant forums have not been overly successful (Hague 2005).

Another representative of the DCA gave his opinion on gathering first-hand views from local courts:

> I've always worked in Whitehall ... never worked on the front line – been in a court dealing with cases, so very much an ivory towers man – but very keen to actually go out there and actually listen to what happens. So I've been along and visited 15 to 20 courts and asked them 'What are the problems you face on the front line? (representative of the DCA, courts innovation branch)

Policy-makers therefore seem increasingly willing to gather front-line information, a philosophy very much supported by local interviewees:

> It's quite concerning for the people on the ground – the operational people – to really read into a lot of this [national policy] documentation. That whilst the ideas are good, firstly they come from a background of some ignorance in terms of what actually happens anyway, and secondly come from a very idealistic stance where there's no concerns/issues around the practical implications. (the District Legal Director at Court A)

It is interesting to note that the manner in which such first-hand data were gathered could influence the overall character of such policies. For example, in the area of police reform, policy-makers were concerned with the satisfaction of users of police services as a whole, but their performance measures afforded victims particular attention:

> The wider issue about *all* contact with the police is important … but, interestingly, the performance measures we have at the moment [local surveys based on the standardised Policing Performance Assessment Framework] are heavily weighted towards the satisfaction of the victims, because the user satisfaction surveys we have in place at the moment only get feedback from victims. (representative of the Police Reform Unit)

The PPAF is the primary method of assessing the progress of such reform in local areas relating to the police. For the rest of the criminal justice system, a new Witness and Victim Experience (WAVES) survey is now utilised (representative of the OCJR). Nevertheless, an independent report by Casey (2008) criticises the government for failing to publish the results of the WAVES survey publicly: presently only the Local Criminal Justice Boards (LCJBs) have access to this data. As such, it is not clear whether WAVES is weighted in favour of obtaining the views of witnesses, victims or the public in general.

Buying reform?

The content and pattern of delivery of many of the victim reforms may lead some to the conclusion that these have been used to 'buy' public support for other, less popular measures. For example, it is probably relevant that the Halliday Report on sentencing was due to be published a few months after the 2001 review of the criminal justice system, *Criminal Justice: The Way Ahead* (Home Office 2001b). Halliday would criticise traditional prison sentences of less than 12 months and suggest a greater role for community supervision (Halliday 2001). The Labour government were by now very mindful of appearing soft on crime (Cavadino and Dignan 2002). As such, one can see the increasing concessions to victims and witnesses made in *The Way Ahead* as a way of securing the political capital to take a more constructive view of offenders and their sentencing which was, of course, a practical necessity given the ongoing penal crisis but one which the public was not terribly inclined to accept (see Rock 1986; Walklate 2007).

This tendency for governments to buy support for less popular measures is not exclusive to the UK. In Canada, Rock (1986) concludes that to gain support for the abolition of the death penalty the Federal Government included it as part of a wider Peace and Security Package, which was assembled in a rather *ad hoc* manner and included victimisation surveys (Rock 1986). Later in this chapter, it will be demonstrated how victim policies are often combined with more punitive measures, which may represent a similar effect. The notion of placating the public by combining victim reform with more controversial measures returns us to the important question as to whether this policy is really concerned with victims at all, or instead with wider notions of the 'general public' or the 'normal, law-abiding citizen' (cjsonline 2006c; Home Office 2006b).

Overall, it seems likely that the government's current view of what 'at the heart of the system' means will depend on contemporary political influences and pressures. Indeed, the evidence suggests that the policy-makers themselves sometimes have no clear answer to this question, which is illustrated by the implementation of the victim personal statement scheme.[13] It is clear that on the introduction of this scheme there was confusion among criminal justice agencies as to whether it was intended to act as a tool of expression for the victim, or to assist the system by providing more information on which to base decisions (Hoyle *et al.* 1999; Morgan and Sanders 1999). Edwards (2004) argues that the participatory goals of victim personal statements have never been clarified, and could be expressive, consultative or informative. This confusion surrounding the purposes of the VPS prompts us to fall back to questioning the existence of any consistent policy at all. The reality may be that 'at the heart of the system' sometimes means providing information, sometimes means consultation, sometimes means both and sometimes means neither, depending on the circumstances at the time. As such, it is only when the different policies and developments are taken together – and arranged into a policy chain – that the impression of consistent purpose is created.

Influencing the local context

It is not only the public that must be won over to new reforms, but also the local actors charged with implementing them. As noted by one OCJR policy-maker:

> We can't do anything if the Local Criminal Justice Boards don't buy into it. (representative of the OCJR)

Created in April 2003, the 42 Local Criminal Justice Boards (LCJBs) were intended to manage the justice system more effectively through local co-ordinators (Home Office 2003a). Boards are made up of high-level (administrative) representatives from different criminal justice agencies in the local area. Central policy-makers interviewed for this research stressed the need for effective communication between the centre and local service providers to get policy implemented. For example, one interviewee from the OCJR suggested that the main problem with the Youth Justice and Criminal Evidence Act 1999 was that parts of it were unspecific and open to wide interpretation. In addition, the view has been noted that documents like the *new deal* bombard local agencies with a large number of priorities. The OCJR's response to this was to produce a delivery plan (OCJR 2005) containing seven key objectives alluded to in the quotation below. Nevertheless, even these priorities required clarification for local implementers:

> I felt that those seven priorities are very very high level and they're very broad, and certainly if I was somebody who worked in a Local Criminal Justice Board area I wouldn't necessarily know what I was supposed to do with that. (representative of the OCJR)

So, for example, one policy-maker from the OCJR explained disappointing take-up rates for victim personal statements in terms of local agencies not really understanding their purpose. Priority four is that victims' views will be sought and used in the criminal justice process and, as such, the relevant tool kit spelt out how a VPS should be collected and used in an effort to boost their implementation.

Implementing criminal justice policies like these clearly brings numerous challenges. This is especially the case when dealing with non-statutory local bodies – as the LCJBs used to be before April 2004 – who do not have their own finances[14] and 'in a sense don't exist', because such bodies are not expressly subject to the authority of central policy-making Units (representative of the OCJR). Of course, this also implies a lack of accountability (see Crawford 1997), and enforceability of victim rights. One way around such problems has been for the OCJR to provide a delivery fund of £150,000 from which small grants have been awarded to the local agencies making up the

LCJBs. Of course, this is a very small sum indeed compared to the £25 million afforded to Victim Support (2006), itself a tiny proportion of the budget for the entire criminal justice system. This system also ensures that the OCJR retains control of the local implementation of relevant measures.

The most common way of applying central policies in local contexts has been for the centre to set national minimum standards and then allow each local area to implement these in their own way – through the LCJBs – following individual impact assessments:

> The messages they [the centre] are giving out is that of a national framework with a strategy, but with local discretion and decision-making. (the Regional Director of Legal Services (Justices' Clerk))

For the police, such strategies went beyond victims and witnesses to encompass citizen-focused policing in general. Again, this hints at a wider scope for such policies, aimed at the public in general rather than just victims. These standards were, however, formulated with reference to the Victim's Code of Practice to ensure consistency across the spectrum. The Police Reform Unit also organised practitioner networking events to disseminate best practice (representative of the Police Reform Unit).

Members of the LCJB in the area under review were clear that they did enjoy a degree of autonomy from the centre but – contrary to the above sentiments expressed in Whitehall – they were more inclined to consider themselves accountable to the OCJR and the National Criminal Justice Board. The local view was thus that national standards essentially compelled the Board to take action:

> For example ... conditional cautioning, they were desperate to get pilots for conditional cautioning ... there was a feeling in [local] CPS and police that we couldn't take any more at this time and we wanted to defer it and we did defer it for a few months, but then they came back to us – sweet talked us – and they particularly wanted an area to pilot it and we have agreed to it. (the Regional Director of Legal Services (Justices' Clerk))

As such, it was not usually a case of the Board or its constitutive agencies fervently agreeing to each new requirement – which would be more in keeping with notions of governance (Bache 2003) and interactive policy-making (Mayer *et al.* 2005) – although the Board had been successful in deflecting some requirements for limited periods.

Take, as an example, the national implementation of the *No Witness, No Justice* scheme, designed to promote witness attendance at court (Home Office 2004g). At the pilot stage, the police in the local area under review were given a wide remit to run tailored initiatives. Nevertheless, when the national minimum standards were delivered, local actors found themselves with less discretion:

> We've had to fit the national model, I'd say 50 per cent of everything we've done at the pilot had to change. (a witness care unit manager)

As one police chief noted:

> These so-called pilots, we got the feeling that whatever the outcome they would be implemented. (a police chief inspector)

Hence, it is clear that although the policy of allowing local implementation of national strategies does afford LCJBs some measure of discretion, the reality is that while the strategies and standards themselves are applied in a broad, untailored manner, local agencies have little alternative but to follow the centre's lead. That said, it was clear that local difficulties like those described above have fed back to central policy-makers to some extent, reflecting Rein and Rabinovitz's (1978) principle of circularity (see above):

> Finally I think they are beginning to realise as a corporate voice now [that] if 42 [police] forces are coming back and only two can actually hit the minimum standard then there is something that they ought to be listening to. (a witness care unit manager)

In terms of the influence of the Board itself, it is clear that its members are top management figures from each agency, and as such the Board has a lot of influence on those agencies:

> The whole point of it [the Board] is it's got the chief officers on it, these are people with purse strings, these are people with clout. (the Regional Director of Legal Services (Justices' Clerk))

Disagreements within the LCJB were apparently rare, but when they occurred members would:

> Use our skills of negotiation and persuasion to try and come to a consensus. (*ibid*)

Another interviewee described the LCJB as 'a very polite setting' without much robust contention or debate (Youth Offending Team Manager 2005). Indeed, some argued that the lack of a genuine power of compulsion was a disadvantage for the LCJB and 'doesn't allow it to be as proactive as it could be' (the director of a private prison).

A representative of the Department for Constitutional Affairs (2005) said that the DCA could apply certain 'levers' to influence the courts. Here, the chain of influence stretched from the DCA, which could make recommendations to the Courts Service Board, which were then passed on through the regional and area directors to the individual court managers and, finally, to operational staff on the ground. This helps to illustrate the complex delivery operation and the so-called 'vertical axis' of policy-making (Matheson 2000). The DCA also relied on word of mouth between neighbouring areas to spread the merits of specialist courts. In the area under review, there was regular communication between local agencies and neighbouring areas, especially to swap ideas regarding the local implementation of national standards:

> It's funny, we received something through from my equivalent in [a neighbouring area] the other day saying to us, how are *you* going to do it? (a police chief inspector)

In its most recent CJS Strategic Plan (Criminal Justice System 2007) the government has formalised this notion of swapping ideas between locals through the establishment of 10 LCJB 'beacon' areas to act as examples and distributors of best practice. The beacon approach is also intended to give individual areas more freedom over the 'definition and implementation' (p. 17) of nationally imposed targets and schemes.

Hartley and Benington (2006) have stressed the importance of inter-organisational sharing of information in a wide range of policy areas. In this context, it was also clear that local agencies are able to take concerns to the LCJB if they feel national standards overlook important issues. For example, the local Youth Offending Team (YOT) manager expressed frustration at the exclusion of young people from the new WAVES survey:

> This is something I've raised with the Local Criminal Justice Board ... and the Board have accepted that and I've actually self-delegated the task of going away to come up with something we can do locally to try to redress that to get the views of young people who are victims in the criminal justice system. (a Youth Offending Team Manager)

The same interviewee noted that there was little point taking operational-level issues to the Board because the Board was comprised of the highest-level representatives of the agencies and it was more productive to go straight to lower-level representatives.[15] The YOT manager was also keen to emphasise how gaining a place on the LCJB for the YOT had been an important breakthrough for the recognition of the service. This is in contrast to Victim Support and other voluntary organisations, which have no place on the Board. Hence, it is questionable whether Local Criminal Justice Boards do achieve genuine change for the benefit of victims when they are made up of administrators rather than victims or other customers of the criminal justice system.

The Local Criminal Justice Boards seem to be clear examples of the 'new forms of management of public services and structures for policy formation and implementation' referred to by Crawford (1997: 1). Nevertheless, administrators may be said to have an interest in promoting efficiency and reducing costs rather than innovating to provide services to victims. This is not to say individual Boards may not become particularly enthusiastic about victims,[16] but as a whole this system relies on the enthusiasm of individuals rather than the combined or inherent goals of the body itself.

Local funding

As in most areas of policy and administration, funding was an issue of some concern among local service providers and agencies. Very little central funding had been made available for many of the victim and witness initiatives necessary to achieve national standards. For example, the probation service in the area under review had been required to take money from the local pot to fund its victim contact duties under Multi-Agency Public Protection Arrangements (MAPPA). As such, the YOT manager referred to above had to personally negotiate funding for his initiative to plug gaps in the WAVES survey from local resources. The same was true of the Youth Offending Team more generally, which contracted out some of its victim contact work to the charity REMEDI. Again the YOT had received no central funding for these measures, nor was it to receive any money to help meet the standards under the new statutory Code. The local private prison also had a MAPPA role to play in contacting victims of very serious offences before the release of offenders that prompted no extra funding from the centre.

Funding was also a prominent concern in the organisation of the joint CPS/Police witness care unit (WCU):

> Years ago there was a declaration that [the] CPS were going to be the guardians of witnesses in the future,[17] and really they've never really had the resources to do that, they've always relied on the police to have witness liaison clerical staff … in fact it's still 95 per cent police. (a police chief inspector)

This was despite the fact that the CPS had received central funding for *No Witness, No Justice* initiatives (Chief Crown Prosecutor). Nevertheless, it was clearly emphasised that the WCU was competing with completely separate initiatives for scarce resources:

> What tends to happen is the Chief will look at the overall budgets and say, 'Well, I want some of that for automatic number plate recognition for counter-terrorism measures.' So I can't quite manage my own budget … perhaps naivety compelled me to declare what we'd got! (a police chief inspector)

That said, one court administrator accepted that many of the initiatives necessary to help victims and witnesses did not cost a great deal of money:

> There were plenty of excuses over resources, it hasn't cost us that much to set this up at all. (the Clerk to the Justices at Court B)

Some respondents – especially local administrators – believed that more funding should also be available to help voluntary agencies provide a more professional service:

> I would put the money not necessarily into statutory organisations, but into voluntary organisations so that the follow-up and the additional work is there, and particularly into services like counselling and mental health help. (representative of the probation service)

Applying to the Home Office for increased funding has certainly been a permanent occupation for Victim Support. Indeed, the Chair of Victim Support's National Board of Trustees has called for a substantial increase of government funding to £60 million (Victim Support 2003). Nevertheless, the government has often drawn on its grants to Victim Support[18] to illustrate its work in supporting victims (Home Office 2001a, 2003a). The charity is sometimes portrayed as a quasi-government department on the basis that it has established itself within the inner circle of CJS organisations (Rock 1998; Home Office 2003a). If this were indeed the case, however, one might argue that the degree to which Victim Support has found itself permanently obliged to press the government for increased funds from the Home Office – and their subsequent need to establish a reserves policy in the event of funding being withdrawn (Victim Support 2006) – suggests an absence of any long-term or fixed strategy.

Local responsibility?

It seems clear that the government's strategy on providing support to victims is one of local agencies taking responsibility for delivering services – usually with existing funds – which meet national targets, distributed through the Local Criminal Justice Boards. The advantage to this is that local bodies have the discretion to tailor activities to fit their own needs. Nevertheless, a less flattering interpretation sees the government portioning out responsibility for victims to local actors. Parallels may be drawn with the government's tendency to depoliticise issues, keeping at arm's length the political character of decision-making, as discussed by Burnham (2001) in the economic sphere.

Under this construction, the government's maintenance of victims as a shared priority becomes more understandable. Support must be offered for the most part through existing local funding rather than through the centre. Indeed, as far as funding is concerned, victims could not be further from the heart of the system, even if one includes the state funding provided to Victim Support and the cost of the Criminal Injuries Compensation Scheme. As discussed above, it is also questionable whether Local Criminal Justice Boards are the best agencies to coordinate the delivery of such local support, as they are not inherently interested in victims *per se*, but rather in meeting targets handed down from the centre. Setting these targets does not however fulfil the government's obligation to provide the victim-centred model of criminal justice we have been promised, especially as it is the local agencies who are held accountable (certainly in their view) if such policies do not meet required standards.

Growing understandings of victimhood

As the policy chain has developed, so have official understandings of victimhood and what it means to be a victim of crime.[19] For example, in its list of 'victims with particular needs', the *new deal* referred to several groups that were traditionally sidelined: including bereaved families,[20] victims of human trafficking and victims of domestic violence. The *deal* also included victims of anti-social behaviour within the ambit of victimhood, which technically extends the definition beyond victims of crime.[21] Indeed, when it was pointed out how witnesses in anti-social behaviour hearings could not have access to special measures under the Youth Justice and Criminal Evidence Act 1999 (the relevant provisions being restricted to *criminal* proceedings) the DCA worked to get the law changed.[22] The *deal* also recognised the vast majority of victims who never come into contact with the CJS, emphasising the role of government services outside the justice system, especially housing and healthcare services.[23]

The extension of victimhood continued in the Sexual Offences Act 2003, which reformed the definition of sexual victimisation to reflect more accurately the harm and suffering of victims experiencing sexual acts not previously falling within the category of rape.[24] By the time the Domestic Violence, Crime and Victims Bill was published in December 2003, the accompanying explanatory notes suggested that the Bill's definitions of victimhood were:

> [W]ide enough to include victims of offences of which no offence was reported to the police or no suspect was charged or convicted ... and witnesses who are not actually called to give evidence. (Her Majesty's Stationery Office 2003: 3)

This perhaps indicates a departure from the often-criticised convention of referring to 'alleged' victims in accordance with the defendant's presumed innocence (Rock 1993).[25] The reforms under the Sexual Offences Act 2003 also seem to indicate a move towards defining victims by their suffering rather than through more exclusionary legal definitions. Indeed, the government's 2005 consultation document on creating a tougher framework for road traffic offences (Home Office 2005a; Home Office 2005e) argues that such a framework should accurately reflect the 'devastating consequences' suffered by the victims of such crime. Consequently, several policy-makers and practitioners interviewed for this study said they would try to put themselves 'in the shoes of the victim' (representative of the DCA).

With the piloting of victims' advocates to represent the indirect victims (survivors) of homicide in court now under way, the government has effectively afforded party status to this small percentage of indirect victims, who just a few years ago might have been largely ignored by the justice system (Home Office 2005b; Home Office 2005c). Such development in official definitions of victimhood and provision for such victims is intricately connected with other factors influencing the policy chain, especially the victim assistance groups, which have been particularly influential in developing appreciation for the needs of victims outside the criminal justice system (Victim Support 2002a). It will be seen below that the recognition of victims of domestic violence and human trafficking has also been greatly influenced by international pressures.

The general image is therefore one of a reform agenda which seeks out and introduces services to meet the needs of traditionally hidden victims of crime (see Casey 2008). There is, however, a key proviso, which is that most of these new victims would also fall within the classification of ideal victims. So, while victims are being defined more by their suffering, it is a stereotypical notion of suffering by which they are being judged.[26] Thus, while special measures may now be available to victims of anti-social behaviour, in practice they still appear to be mainly afforded on a case-by-case basis to ideal victims deemed worthy of them (Hall 2007). There has been relatively little attempt to address head on the reality that many victims are also previous offenders. There have been even fewer developments towards recognising victims for whom the public often feels little sympathy, especially corporate victims of economic crime (Williams 2005).

Distinguishing victims and witnesses

The general focus on ideal victims has also tended to merge victims and witnesses into a single category. This is in line with Christie's (1986) notion that ideal victims necessarily become involved with the criminal justice system. As such, Jackson (2004) has argued that much of the victim policy has actually been focused on a relatively small number of vulnerable and intimidated *witnesses*. It was not really until the 2000 publication of the Occasional Paper *Victim and Witness Intimidation: Findings from the British Crime Survey* (Tarling *et al.* 2000) that victims and witnesses started to be treated as separate groups with distinct needs. This paper was among the first reports collating information from (British Crime Survey) victims who were not necessarily witnesses. Increased recognition of victims as a separate group also came in the 2001 review of the criminal justice system – *Criminal Justice: The Way Ahead* – where reference is made to the problems faced by victims outside the criminal justice system (Home Office 2001b). Interestingly, however, in the list of various past schemes and policies we have come to expect in such reports, only the Criminal Injuries Compensation Scheme is identified as a measure *purely* for the benefit of victims without also linking them to witnesses.

It is telling that the 2001 policy document falls back on state compensation to illustrate the work done to support victims. This suggests that CICS (created in 1964) was at this stage still seen by policy-makers as the government's most significant response to the problems faced by victims as a distinct group, and that many of the more recent developments were still very much concerned with victims as witnesses. This is ironic given that CICS excludes a large proportion of victims (Miers 1991). Indeed, the *de facto* requirement that successful compensation applicants have co-operated with the criminal justice system effectively means CICS is again aimed at victims who are willing to become witnesses.

Nevertheless, the beginnings of support for victims outside the CJS suggests that the needs of non-witness victims were starting to be recognised. Certainly after 2001, policy documents seem to distinguish victims from witnesses more specifically and the victim personal statement scheme – launched nationally in October 2001 – is overtly focused at victims in their own right. Nevertheless, it is significant that victims will only be offered the chance to make a VPS after having already submitted a witness statement. This point may seem inconsequential, but one might conceive of situations where a case is prosecuted on the strength of other witnesses' evidence and the victims themselves wish to communicate the lack of impact to the court.

Nevertheless, by the end of 2005, the publication of a draft Witnesses' Charter seems to cement this newfound policy distinction between the needs of victims and witnesses, and even those witnesses who are not called to give evidence. This Charter sets out the 'standards of care for witnesses in the criminal justice system' whether or not they are also victims. We might add here the Prosecutors' Pledge (CPS 2005b) which – like the statutory Code – is specifically focused on victims who may be witnesses rather than witnesses who may be victims.

This issue of distinguishing victims from witnesses in policy-making helps bring together a number of the other politics identified by Rock (2004) and the present research. Chapter 2 discussed Garland's (2001) macro-level argument that governments have reacted to falling confidence in the ability of the system to control crime by redefining its success criteria in terms of the efficient management of cases and the provision of minimum standards of service to victims. This effectively prompts a philosophy of victims as consumers of the criminal justice system, which Tapley (2002) and Rock (2004) have discussed and which is also seen in other policy areas, including the National Health Service (Greener 2004). This new focus on the *process* as experienced by *victims* rather than the specific *outcomes* achieved through the participation of *witnesses* necessitates the conceptual separation of these two groups. This means gathering their separate thoughts and opinions, which we see towards the end of the policy chain with the advent of Witness Surveys (Angle *et al.* 2003).

Victim Support and other victim groups

Previous sections have already touched on the increasing importance of victim support groups and charities in the formation of relevant policies. The largest of these organisations – Victim Support – has continued to defend its apolitical, voluntary status which was instrumental in its original recognition by the government (Rock 1990).[27] That said, the organisation has arguably developed a more political character of late. This has been demonstrated through its work on the 2001 EU Council Framework Decision,[28] the publication of a 'manifesto' (Victim Support 2001) and its inclusion on the list of 'Criminal Justice System Agencies and Partners' (Home Office 2001b). The organisation also has obligations under the Victim's Code of Practice, effectively establishing it as a statutory agency (Rock 2004: 561). More recently, Victim Support has been involved in the organisation of conferences in conjunction with the Office for Criminal Justice Reforms to further the consultation exercise on proposed changes to the Criminal Injuries Compensation Scheme (Home Office 2006c).

Indeed, throughout the policy chain a certain degree of choreography has developed between the issues raised by Victim Support and the actions of policy-makers. Many (although not all) of the issues raised in Victim Support's (2001) manifesto were later found in *Criminal Justice: The Way Ahead* and/or the 2001 review of the Victim's Charter (Home Office 2001b; Home Office 2001d). Similarly, when Victim Support published its *No Justice Beyond Criminal Justice* report on the plight of victims outside criminal justice (Victim Support 2002a) this was swiftly followed by similar views being expressed in the *new deal* (Home Office 2003a). Victim Support was also actively involved in drafting the 2001 European Framework Decision, which the Victim's Code of Practice is intended to implement (Victim Support 2002b).

It therefore seems likely that Victim Support is now being consulted on almost all upcoming actions and reports relating to victims and witnesses.[29] It might therefore be tempting to think of Victim Support as the driving force pushing government reforms on victims and witnesses. Fundamentally, however, we can question the extent to which Victim Support has been afforded the political ability to truly sway policy-making. Despite adopting a more professionalised character, the charity holds back from commissioning research or holding independent conferences to sway opinion, its role is more consultative. In addition, at the local level, Victim Support and other voluntary organisations are not represented – certainly in the area under review – on the Local Criminal Justice Board, albeit that the Regional Director of Legal Services suggested this might be a possibility for the future.

Contributions have also increasingly been made by the smaller, more specialist, victim assistance organisations, especially in relation to the widening of official definitions of victimhood discussed above. The views of the homicide survivors' group Support After Murder and Manslaughter (SAMM) in particular appear to have carried some weight following the consultation on victims' advocates for homicide survivors (Home Office 2005b). Indeed, in announcing the pilot for this scheme, the government was apparently following the views of SAMM and other such organisations rather than those of the judiciary and lawyers, who mainly opposed the pilots (Home Office 2005c). With the (statutory) establishment of the Victims' Advisory Panel we are told that victims will get the opportunity to feed directly into policy-making. The panel comprises victims of hate crime, burglary and anti-social behaviour, although it has been noted earlier that most of the members are indirect victims of serious violent crime, and thus atypical victims.

In sum, the policy-making process in this area has frequently involved governments reacting to calls for action from a variety of different victim assistance groups. With this comes the implication that the policy has been driven and developed on a much more *ad hoc* basis than it first appears. Rock (1998) has already described how policy-makers began taking greater account of indirect victims during the late Conservative era following pressure from organisations like

Parents of Murdered Children (POMC) and SAMM. More recently, proposals to amend the Criminal Injuries Compensation Scheme have been spurred on by the dissatisfaction of victims and relatives of victims who were injured or killed in the London bombings of July 2005 (Home Office 2005d: 17) and comparisons drawn with the US compensation systems after the New York terrorist attacks of 11 September 2001 (BBC 2006; Walklate 2007). This interpretation is consistent with Harland's (1978) impression that state compensation programmes are often grounded in the contemporary emotional and political climate, created in the wake of tragic and dramatic events or victim rallies.

The inclusion of wider organisations, beyond government agencies, in the policy-making process again brings us back to the growth of governance. While some discussions of governance predict a loss of control over policy-making for governments (Pearce and Mawson 2003), in fact governments can retain significant influence over the composition of the policy network (Richardson 2000). The position of Victim Support appears to reflect this reality, for while the charity has been accepted as what Maloney *et al.* (1994) call a 'core insider' to the policy-making network (Tisdall and Davis 2004), it has failed to establish any platform to criticise government actions. This is not to say that Victim Support has not come to play an important role in the development of victim policy. In particular, we may attribute to this and other victim assistance organisations the continued proliferation of rights language in relation to victims – especially given its contribution to the 2001 European Framework Decision (Victim Support 2002b) – and, more recently, the acceptance of the concept of victims being afforded a voice (and, with it, victims as parties) has been given new impetus through the victims' advocates pilots proliferated by SAMM. Nevertheless, the key point is that Victim Support is unlikely to be the only factor influencing government policy on victims and witnesses and is perhaps not even the most significant. Victim Support could therefore be excluded from the policy network just as easily (and probably more easily) as it was accepted.

Criminal justice and other non-victim reform

It was noted above that one possible explanation for victim reforms is that they are intended to achieve other ends that have little to do with victims themselves. As noted by one interviewee:

> [T]here's so many ways you can cut things – always so much work that overlaps – in any policy job that I've ever had. (representative of the OCJR)

This section will gather together some of the most prominent ends achieved in or connected with victim reform. These are wide-ranging, encompassing financial concerns, system efficiency, a target culture, the multi-agency approach and other goals for the system.

Financial concerns

From the outset, financial concerns have clearly had a part to play at many stages of the policy chain. One obvious example is the persistent attempts to reform the Criminal Injuries Compensation Scheme to stem the tide of ever-growing costs. As Harland (1978) notes:

> The reality of state-funded victim compensation seems to be that it is an extremely limited service available to only a minute proportion of those who suffer loss or injury as a result of crime. Too often, however, this reality is cloaked in a political show of concern for victims, while the underlying fears of costs continue to emerge in the form of programme restrictions. (p. 213)

Hence, it is not unreasonable to question whether periodic government rumblings to cease payments for non-serious injury (Home Office 2005d) have more to do with the financial cost of the scheme than with benefiting victims directly. The most recent proposal of this kind (*ibid.*) claims the new system will reflect the practical and emotional support victims say they need in the BCS, although the survey has never actually asked victims whether they would prefer such practical support to small amounts of compensation. Also, as the Victim's Charter had already guaranteed victims such services anyway, the government's justification here seems dubious.

We might also mention the government's continued development of the system of court-based compensation orders, most recently in the Powers of Criminal Courts (Sentencing) Act 2000. Such orders appear to represent an especially important symbolic recognition of victims' suffering (see Miers 1980). To this end, courts have been required to state reasons for *not* making such orders since 1988 (Miers 1991). The suggestions made in both the 2004 (Home Office 2004a) and 2005 (Home Office 2005d) compensation consultations to place more emphasis on reclaiming money from offenders would therefore seem a positive move. Of course, this would also lift the strain on the state system, as a victim is not compensated twice.

Nevertheless, in court, the limitations placed on compensation orders seem to be more culturally grounded, with judges and magistrates unwilling to impose the orders as a single penalty or to combine them with custodial sentences (Home Office 2004a). Difficulties also persist with prosecutors lacking enough information to judge how much compensation to ask for. This can lead to very small (insulting) amounts being requested, or no request being made at all, in which cases magistrates in turn are reluctant to make awards at their own discretion (Newburn 1988; Moxon *et al.* 1992). Of course, solutions here seem to lie once again with the effective communication of the impact of crime to the courts.

Also in relation to financial concerns, we have seen moves to reduce inefficiencies leading to postponements or otherwise resolved trials at court through instruments like the *No Witness, No Justice* report (Inter-agency working group on witnesses 2003) and the Criminal Case Management Framework (Home Office 2004d).[30] Such inefficiencies represent a considerable drain on resources for the criminal justice system. Of course – unlike the various schemes implemented through the LCJBs – this is *central* funding going to 'waste'. This issue of efficiency is discussed in some detail below.

One solicitor interviewed for this research adamantly blamed cost-cutting priorities for the recent focus on trial adjournments:

> No adjournments, no adjournments, that's the philosophy, and the reason why is cost, they don't want trials, they're too costly. (a defence solicitor appearing at Court B)

On this point, Valler and Betteley (2001) note that similar integrations of the economic and social policy sphere have occurred in many areas of reform.

Increasing efficiency

Throughout the policy chain, the victim question is often linked with increasing the efficiency of the criminal justice system. Indeed, there have been continued efforts throughout this period to streamline the management of criminal cases. Central to this was the introduction in 2003 of the Criminal Case Management Framework. At courts, the Framework encompasses the Effective Trial Management Programme (ETMP), which is designed to promote efficient use of court time and the speedy disposal of cases.

Issues relating to victims directly are largely absent from the Framework, which is clearly evidenced by the exclusion of youth cases – which often involve particularly vulnerable, young victims – from the ambit of the companion guidelines (Home Office 2004d). It is also telling that the prescribed aim for courts is to reduce the number of trial *postponements* rather than the number of trials that are resolved in some other way on the day they have been scheduled to run as full trials.[31] The latter category often still involve victims and witnesses attending court unnecessarily. As one local administrator put it:

> We're not monitoring cracked [otherwise resolved] trials [but] they're as much an evil in terms of the process as ineffective [adjourned] trials! ... The LCJB aren't even concerned about cracked trials any more because we've not been asked to monitor them! (the District Legal Director at Court A)

Of course, this relates back to a point made earlier concerning the local implementation of victim reform through the LCJBs. Again, it can be argued that as the Boards are comprised of criminal justice administrators rather than members with specific interests in victims *per se*, it is unsurprising that these policies become more about efficiency on implementation, even if they are not already weighted in that direction.

This drive for efficiency is also evidenced by the fact that many of the proposals for victim reforms appear in the context of wider reports aimed at streamlining the criminal justice process. This was certainly the case with the Glidewell Report of 1998 and the Auld Report of 2001. The same is also true of policy documents like *Criminal Justice: The Way Ahead* (Home Office 2001b) in which the chapter *a better deal for victims and witnesses* must be seen in its wider context, namely a review of the criminal justice system in general. Victims and witnesses were given seven out of 139 pages despite a pledge to 'put the needs of witnesses and victims more at the centre of the criminal justice system' (p. 8).

The argument that reformers are more concerned with system efficiency than victim care gained weight in October 2003, with a government proposal to resurrect witness orders. Such orders would compel all witnesses to attend for Crown Court and summary trials (Home Office 2003d). These proposals illustrate that – while improving victim and witness satisfaction and making them feel more at ease with their role in the justice system is the headline policy – these aims are still connected with the less personal goal of getting witnesses (not *victims*) to come to court. Indeed, the 2003 consultation paper itself identified a conflict of policy:

> Ensuring that witnesses attend court ... is directly relevant to the delivery of the Government's Public Service Agreement (PSA) targets on bringing more offences to justice and increasing confidence in the criminal justice system. However, it is possible that introducing a greater element of compulsion [through witness orders] might have a negative effect on the confidence in PSA (particularly the witness satisfaction element of this target). (Home Office 2003d: 3)

These proposals now appear to have been dropped. Nevertheless, the episode clearly indicates that policy-makers were, in this instance, willing to trade witness satisfaction for increased efficiency. This indicates a very different set of priorities than those implied by the pledge to put victims and witnesses at the heart of the criminal justice system or the apparent moves from an institutional-based to a citizen-based criminal justice system (Tapley 2002; Goodey 2005). It reminds us that the government is still very concerned with inefficiency and the associated low public confidence in the justice system, and that such concerns can have a large influence on measures incidentally benefiting victims and witnesses. Hence, victims and witnesses were a key issue in the criminal justice system Framework Document of July 2003 on improving public satisfaction and confidence in the criminal justice system, which is a central Public Service Agreement target (Home Office 2003c).

The proposition that efficiency goals may be behind a number of victim reforms means a conflict arises for policy-makers between providing information to victims on the one hand, and ensuring witnesses will turn up to give evidence on the other. Some elements of government policies therefore bear the hallmark of an advertising campaign. Information sources like the *Victim of Crime* booklet (Home Office 2003f) and online virtual walkthroughs for victims and witnesses (cjsonline 2006e) highlight the positive aspects of the product – the information and support available to witnesses and victims, the ability for victims to be heard through victim personal statements and special measures to counter vulnerability and intimidation – while downplaying the less appealing aspects such as intimidatory cross-examination, waiting times and the confusing, restrictive evidential process. In July 2008 policy-makers reacted swiftly to preserve this positive image of the criminal justice system, by rushing the Criminal

Evidence (Witness Anonymity) Bill through parliament. This followed the House of Lords' judgment in *R* v. *Davis (Iain)*[32] which seriously restricted the admissibility of anonymous witness evidence. In this case, much was made by policy-makers and the media of the fact that, if denied such protection, many witnesses might not come forward. The financial cost of derailing the specific murder trial at the heart of the appeal (said to be £6 million) was also emphasised (BBC 2008).

Nevertheless, giving victims and potential witnesses a less than frank image of what becoming involved in the criminal justice process entails can only impair their preparation for the experience, and ultimately increase dissatisfaction with the system. As such, there are certainly negative implications to the recasting of victims as consumers of criminal justice, which interviews confirmed has been a clear goal of policy-makers since at least December 2004 (representative of the DCA). One might therefore argue that if victims and witnesses are indeed being brought more to the heart of *a* criminal justice system, it is not the *same* 'unedited' system as that inhabited by criminal justice professionals.

Of course, it may be quite wrong to think of efficiency as a separate endeavour to supporting victims. Many interviewees were clear that providing the right kind of services for victims and witnesses would increase confidence in the justice system, boost witness attendance and therefore minimise adjournments or otherwise resolved trials. The point is rather that if this is indeed what the government is doing (or sometimes does) then to understand the larger framework of policies related to victims and witnesses we must also understand the government's intentions for the CJS and the factors driving that policy, especially given the conflicting nature of various criminal justice goals, as demonstrated by Elias:

> Like prosecutors and police officers before them, judges seem trapped by conflicting penal goals, none of which seems to argue for a very strong victim role … If judges consider victims, then they must sacrifice either uniformity or offender needs or social goals. (Elias 1986: 156)

Other goals for criminal justice

Elias's observation raises the question as to whether the current social goals of the CJS are conducive to the needs of victims. In other words, victim policy can sometimes be grounded in wider strategies to achieve certain outcomes from the criminal justice process. For example, one stated aim of the *new deal* was to provide victims and witnesses with alternative options to the court: these include restorative justice and other problem-solving remedies like anti-social behaviour processes and Community Justice Centres. At least to some extent then, the aim appears to have been to divert cases away from an overstretched criminal justice system, again boosting system efficiency (see Dignan 1992).

In the Executive Summary of the *Justice for All* White Paper, the aims of the reforms were set out as follows:

> [T]o rebalance the criminal justice system in favour of the victim and the community so as to reduce crime and bring more offenders to justice. (Home Office 2002: para. 0.3)

In this construction, reforms in favour of victims are grounded in a higher set of priorities to reduce crime and prosecute more offenders, both of which are consistently popular as political aims. It also appears that the aims of the reforms go beyond victims, to encompass once again the wider community. This is complicated by Crawford's (1997) observation that notions of 'community' are elastic and 'overflowing with meaning' (p. 300). Furthermore, if the subject of the reform agenda is now 'the community' rather than victims in their own right, this may reflect some ideal notion of the 'normal law-abiding citizen', who appears in many of the most recent policy documents:

> This Government is committed to rebalancing the criminal justice system in favour of victims of crime and the law-abiding majority. (cjsonline 2006d)

> The purpose of the Plan is to deliver a fair and effective criminal justice system that puts the victim of crime and law-abiding citizens first. (Criminal Justice System 2007: 3)

This wider emphasis on the public in victim policy rhetoric[33] was reflected in the criminal justice review document of 2006: *Rebalancing the criminal justice system in favour of the law-abiding majority: Cutting crime, reducing reoffending and protecting the public* (Home Office 2006c). Here then it is the law-abiding majority being placed at the heart of criminal justice rather than the victims themselves.[34]

Crawford (1997) and Boutellier (2000) demonstrate how 'community' in the late-modern context is a difficult concept. The 'law-abiding majority' may itself be a myth given the prevalence of unreported crime (Nelken 2002). More importantly, however, reforms intended to please this public audience will not necessarily be tailored to benefit the crime victims themselves, many of whom would not form part of this law-abiding majority (Dignan 2005). Indeed, Jackson (2003) notes the 'dubious symmetry between the interests of the victims and the community' (p. 317). In short, we might speculate along with Elias that victims are being used as political vote-catchers. As the majority of voters are probably not victims of crime (or at least would not see themselves as such) what matters to governments is to give this wider public the impression that victims are being helped rather than actually following through with providing (and financing) such help themselves.

The *new deal* places the government's work on victims and witnesses within the context of two of its Public Service Agreement targets. The first involves bringing more offenders to justice and the second calls for increased public confidence in the criminal justice system. These targets feature in many of the policy documents, and interviews with policy-makers reinforced their importance:

> We're very much focused around the PSA targets. (representative of the OCJR)

Policy-makers were particularly concerned with the confidence target and clearly appreciated that helping victims and witnesses would bring benefits to the system through increased confidence passed on by word of mouth to future potential witnesses (representative of the DCA). One policy-maker from the OCJR noted:

> I think the statistics show that whilst three quarters of people feel that [the criminal justice system is] fair and it's good for the defendants, only a third think it's the same for victims and witnesses. I think it's those sorts of statistics that have been driving things. (representative of the OCJR)

Here, this respondent is referring to British Crime Survey data indicating that while 80 per cent of adults are very or fairly confident that the criminal justice respects the rights of defendants, only 36 per cent believe it meets the needs of victims (Walker *et al.* 2006).

The emphasis on public perceptions of criminal justice had filtered down to local actors in the area under review:

> I think it's as things have become more customer oriented, there's been such an outcry in the press and even murmurings in the general public that, noticeably, what we had was not of this day and age. (a court clerk at Court C)

A number of other respondents raised the issue of media coverage and suggested this was the true driving force behind the government's policies. Indeed, one interviewee felt sure that the government encouraged reporting of certain crimes in order to justify repressive measures:

> [Politicians] are making our communities feel victimised, the extent of lawlessness, of feral wild-beyond-control children prowling our streets ... isn't the horrific problem – necessarily – it is portrayed as. (a youth offending team manager)

A target culture

The proliferation of PSA targets has occasionally led to the government facing criticism for establishing a target culture of extreme managerialism (Newburn 2003). Similar observations have been made across other areas of policy-making including education (Gorard *et al.* 2002), health (Greener 2004) and the economy (Dorey 2004). One court representative described this development in largely positive tones:

> [There has been] much more of a performance focus in the last five to seven years ... that was something that was unheard of in the public sector until the early 1990s, in courts till the mid 1990s. (the Clerk to the Justices at Court B)

Other interviewees expressed frustration at such developments, but grudgingly accepted that 'figures mean everything these days' (a court clerk at Court C). These respondents were often sceptical that performance figures could accurately convey the complexities of real-life court operation. As one district judge (and self-confessed hater of statistics) put it:

> It's a human process, you can't dehumanise it. (a district judge sitting at Court B)

Nevertheless, targets can often be useful in the context of a policy chain as a way of measuring success or justifying current measures.

In addition, setting targets – even targets that are broad brush and difficult to apply in individual areas – can compel agencies to take action:

> There needed to be a head of steam about it to get these things moving; unless there was that big push [on national minimum standards concerning witness care] then I don't think [police] forces and CPS areas would have got on with it at the rate they have. (a police chief inspector)

Conversely, the lack of targets can cause measures to stagnate. This was exemplified by the initial low take-up rates of victim personal statements:

> Because there was no target to achieve a particular take-up of victim statements it was felt that the police weren't really pushing them. (representative of Research Development Statistics and OCJR)

We have already noted the lack of interest in the number of otherwise resolved trials based on the absence of specific targets. On a more positive note, however, one Case Progression Officer[35] at Court C noted that targets made it easier to acquire central and local funding. As such, targets can drive the early implementation of new policies before they become culturally accepted practices at the local level.

Of course, national targets are not necessarily difficult to achieve, as noted by one Youth Offending Team Manager in relation to victim contact work:

> [W]e meet our national standard – I know that – but our national standard is pretty easy to meet to be honest. (a youth offending team manager)

The ease by which this particular respondent felt his agency could meet national targets may indicate that the centre is trying to delegate responsibility for victims, as opposed to reacting if targets cannot be met. Of course, this is assuming different targets are viewed as compatible, and are a realistic measure of performance in the local context. On the latter point, one Justices' Chief Executive described a perceived conflict between the targets of reducing witness waiting times and ensuring the court's time is not wasted:

> There are many performance measures and standards that are to some extent inconsistent. For example, the courts that perform best in having low witness waiting times … are the courts with very poor effective trial rates. So, the witnesses are coming to court … and they aren't waiting very long, but they are very frustrated because they didn't need to be there at all … The victim has got the biggest (the longest, the most detailed) story to tell so it's almost always the case that they're in the witness box an hour in anything like a meaningful trial. Therefore every other witness falls outside the criteria, which is the percentage of witnesses that wait for an hour or less. It's an unrealistic measure unfortunately because the only way to perform well is for your trials to crack. (the Clerk to the Justices at Court B)

Targets themselves are of course also the products of complex political interactions. By using the PSA targets as the context, policy-makers cement the (probably false) impression that this is indeed one all-encompassing strategy driven over time by unified and consistent goals.

The multi-agency approach

Moves to assist victims have also been tied up with the development of the government's multi-agency approach to public sector services, including health and education (Milbourne *et al.* 2003). Indeed the Home Office's (2003e) *Tackling Witness Intimidation – An Outline Strategy* reveals as much about the multi-agency approach as it does about intimidated witnesses. Some policy-makers interviewed for this research agreed that a joined-up approach to criminal justice, in which different agencies readily communicate, is far more logical from the victim's perspective:

> Even though people use the term 'criminal justice *system*', I'm not sure that for a long time it has been … and of course victims and witnesses are the people who do go through that system end to end. (representative of the OCJR)

That said, at the local level interviewees emphasised that communication between agencies was nothing new to them:

> I think if I'm honest it's rather naïve of the policy-makers to suggest that they've come up with this good idea and no one

> spoke to each other previously, because that just simply isn't the case. (the District Legal Director at Court A)

In many cases the continuation of such unofficial multi-agency ambitions relied on the *ad hoc* arrangements of committed individuals:

> I already had lots of contacts … it was then reliant on individual enthusiasm, to some extent, and you'd have certain bits folding because that individual would leave. (representative of the probation service)

Not all local multi-agency endeavours were functioning as efficiently as local actors would wish. For example, this probation service representative clearly believed the police were not forwarding information necessary for their victim contact work:

> You still have some people who are like 'This is *our* work, we know how to do things properly' … In terms of the victim contact work we now get names and addresses of victims without a problem, they're not always that accurate because people aren't always that good with the files. But we don't get the additional bits of information, we don't for example get ethnicity – which the police do monitor – which we could do with because when you're going out to see a victim who is still very distraught you don't in the middle of that suddenly whip out a form and say 'Can you actually tell me how you'd like to call yourself?' We don't always get information in terms of vulnerability or disability or issues that would make us more sensitive in how we approach people, for example that someone has learning difficulties, that somebody has a regular social worker. (*ibid.*)

Such concerns reflect Crawford and Enterkin's (2001) view that, practically, victim contact work in the probation service presents 'significant challenges' (p. 722). There were also administrative tensions apparent between the police and CPS in their joint witness care unit:

> It's never been proven as a concept that we must all adhere to because it works. I think it's a noble concept of having joint PC/CPS clerical and I think it would be even better if we had

> joint administrative systems ... We're still two separate bodies joined for certain functions. (a police chief inspector)

One particular example given was that of the Victim Information Bureau run by the CPS, which was still separate from the witness care unit, meaning that if the WCU needed to contact victims they would need to go through this separate body.

New Labour has championed the strategic or multi-agency approach in many areas (Milbourne *et al.* 2003). This again raises questions regarding the political influences guiding this approach and how they interact with the issues of criminal justice, witnesses and victims. Even with the creation of a victims minister in 2005, and the amalgamation of the Ministry of Justice in 2007 to coordinate CJS reform, the government does not appear to have abandoned its philosophy of victims as a shared priority between agencies and departments. It seems the minister is largely being used as a spokesperson on victim policy rather than the driving force behind renewed reform, which again implies responsibility for such reforms still rests away from the centre.

Punitiveness and expanding state control

The last chapter noted the argument of Ashworth (2000) that the involvement of victims in sentencing has been used as a means of legitimising a punitive stance against offenders. In addition, Elias (1983, 1986) has repeatedly argued that reforms put forward ostensibly in the name of crime victims have been used as a means of extending state control. Many criminologists have commented on the growth of populist punitiveness in late modernity (see Downes and Morgan 2002). The question therefore becomes whether this development is linked with the growth of victim reforms.

Certainly, the policy chain reveals many examples of victim reform being packaged in policy documents and statutes with reforms of an arguably more punitive nature. As such, there is often a sense that the government is attempting to balance the conservatism (with a small 'c') of one policy direction with the liberalness of the other. For example, at the time of its implementation, some commentators (Haines 2000) argued that the system of Youth Offending Panels and referral orders under the Youth Justice and Criminal Evidence Act 1999 (the Act that introduced special measures) would exclude defendants from the process, and was therefore punitive.[36]

We can draw on several more examples. The 2001 criminal justice review (Home Office 2001b) accepted broader notions of victims but packaged such concessions alongside provisions to tackle organised and international crime and a pledge to create 2,660 more prison places. Later, in the *Justice for All* White Paper (Home Office 2002), reforms relating to victims and witnesses were introduced alongside measures relating to the admission of hearsay, the partial abolition of double jeopardy and the possibility of trial without jury.[37] *Justice for All* also introduced proposals later enacted in the Courts Act 2003 which extended state power through the introduction of a court security service with powers of arrest and detention (see Jackson 2003, 2004).

The Sexual Offences Act 2003 also contained punitive provisions. In the accompanying guidance document the Home Office (2004f) said the Act would 'put victims first'. Nevertheless, elsewhere in the Act a conditional discharge is now considered a conviction for the purposes of the sex offenders' register, meaning people can be put on the register without being convicted of any sexual offence. In the same way, from a defendant's perspective the Criminal Justice Act 2003 brought radical reforms like the abolishment of the double jeopardy rule in serious cases where new and compelling evidence is available[38] and the wider admissibility of hearsay and evidence of bad character. The former is clearly of benefit to victims and witnesses, removing in some circumstances a complex component of giving evidence. Nevertheless, from the defence position such provisions may be viewed as prejudicing the fairness of proceedings. Furthermore, under s. 101(1)(g), a defendant's bad character can be adduced following his or her attack on another person's character, while no comparable provision is present for non-defendants. The *new deal* (Home Office 2003a) cites this as a provision that can 'limit the scope for gratuitous attacks on witnesses' character' (p. 19) but this will only be so if defendants are given clear guidance from advocates. The observation sessions conducted for this research suggest that witnesses (including victims) are just as capable of attacking defendants' characters from the witness box as vice versa,[39] but under the 2003 Act this would not necessarily lead to their own bad characters being adduced. The argument again is that victims may provide the liberal smokescreen that dilutes the impact of repressive measures.

Another revealing example was the proposed reintroduction in October 2003 of witness orders, which was discussed above. This again reflects Elias's (1986) assertion that victim reforms may be intended to increase state power. In this case, state power is extended by eroding the principle currently applied in England and Wales that the criminal justice system is based on the *voluntary* attendance of witnesses. In the Domestic Violence, Crime and Victims Act of the following year, benefits to victims (especially the statutory Code) were once again balanced by punitive provisions. Of particular note are the new jail sentences of up to five years for breaching non-molestation orders and also the court's new power to impose restraining orders even when defendants are *acquitted*. More recently, there have been further indications of a dual purpose behind victim reform. The Home Office has given its pledge to 'toughen up every aspect of the criminal justice system to take on the criminal and support the victim' (Home Office 2004c: p. 6). Indeed, throughout this 2004 strategy document the promise to support victims is almost always preceded by a pledge to catch, punish and stop more offenders from committing crime.

In July 2006, the publication of another CJS review document (Home Office 2006c) reaffirmed that:

> [T]he needs of victims must be at the heart of what the criminal justice system does. (p. 6)

Nevertheless, the choice to run 'increased prison places' as the headline in the press release accompanying this review is indicative of underlying punitiveness within the wider proposals, which include: an end to automatic one-third reductions in sentences for early guilty pleas; parental compensation orders; increased use of anti-social behaviour legislation; tougher penalties for carrying knives and 'tougher new action on alcohol'. The strategy also seems greatly concerned with speeding up the criminal justice system, a point returned to in the subsequent document *Delivering Simple, Speedy, Summary Justice* (Home Office 2006a). Once again, victim measures are here being combined with more punitive and economic reforms.

In sum, when one looks at reforms to the criminal justice system as a whole one clearly sees the more liberalised position taken towards victims contrasting with an increasingly punitive stance towards defendants. Brownlee (1998) notes a significant contradiction between recent trends towards populist punitiveness on the one hand, and moves to increase efficiency in criminal justice on the other. While the latter implies diverting offenders from the main criminal justice system, the former demands expensive punishments.

This combination of the liberal and conservative down the policy chain may be interpreted in two ways. The first is the straightforward zero sum game argument discussed in Chapter 2. This would suggest that the genuine goal of these policies is to rebalance the system in favour of victims. If this is correct, however, then measures introduced thus far suggest that policy-makers are also working on an assumption that benefits to victims can indeed be achieved by cutting back on defendants' rights, in exactly the way Ashworth (2000) deplores. The report of Casey (2008) clearly reflects the view that the balance of protection afforded by the criminal justice system is unfairly weighted towards the defendant. As such, the report frequently repeats the BCS finding that only 33 per cent of the public are confident that the system meets the needs of victims, while 79 per cent feel it respects the rights of those accused of a crime. The evidence discussed in this section clearly suggests that in each policy document and statute, the government is giving with one hand (to victims) while it takes with another (from defendants). The second interpretation is that victims are not really the focus of this policy at all, but are only the means by which the punitive polices are justified, and the state's power extended.

In terms of their implications, neither interpretation is particularly attractive. If this really is a policy about victims, then the discussion in the last chapter has shown that this goes far beyond a simple zero sum game. In other words, victims will never be put at the heart of criminal justice purely through restricting the due process rights of defendants. On the other hand, if punitiveness and control is in fact the ultimate goal of these policies, then such reforms seem unlikely to benefit victims in any genuine way in the long term. Achieving genuinely victim-centred criminal justice therefore requires solutions that avoid both sets of problems. This will be the ultimate goal of Chapter 7 in this volume.

International influences

On one level, the international influence on victim policy in England and Wales can be understood purely in terms of the increasing number of international instruments and documents appearing in the policy chain related to victims and witnesses. As such, it is evident that *specific* international pressures – from the EU, Council of Europe and UN among others – are another factor complicating the larger framework of interconnected politics. On another level, this can be understood as reflecting a broad international growth in our understandings of victimhood and victims' needs, reflecting even wider macro developments. The latter possibility will be returned to below.

The most prominent (specific) development of the recent period has been the EU Council's 2001 Framework Decision on the standing of victims in criminal proceedings. This document arguably spurred the revival of rights language associated with victims in the UK because, unlike the various recommendations made by the Council of Europe, a decision from the Council of the European Union is binding on all those to whom it is addressed and, therefore, highly significant politically in the domestic context. As such, this is an example of what is generally referred to as 'multi-level governance' with national and international levels (Smith 2004).

Victim Support points out that while the UK and Ireland have two of the best records on victims in Europe, both countries still have things to learn before they are fully implementing the Decision (Victim Support 2002b). Member states had until 22 March 2002 to introduce laws giving effect to most of the provisions and until March 2006 to implement Article 5 (Communication Safeguards), Article 6 (Specific Assistance to Victims)[40] and Article 10 (Penal mediation in the course of criminal proceedings).[41] Consequently, the Framework Decision delayed the introduction of what was then the Victims and Witness Bill – and afterwards became the Domestic Violence, Crime and Victims Act – and prompted the introduction of the statutory Code of Practice.

The proliferation of rights language in the 2001 Framework Decision is an example of a general growth in human rights discourse internationally, especially in Europe following the introduction of the European Convention on Human Rights enshrined into British law by the Human Rights Act 2000. In Chapter 2 it was demonstrated that such rights as may be present for victims under the Convention are still the topic of considerable debate. Nonetheless the Convention has arguably provided rights for victims domestically in England and Wales indirectly through the very culture of rights it instilled.

International developments have led to whole new dimensions of a given issue being incorporated within the domestic framework. Hence, the *new deal* indicates that earlier versions of the Domestic Violence, Crime and Victims Act did not place such emphasis on victims of domestic violence. Domestic violence was (and remains) very high on the international agenda and has recently prompted several recommendations from the Council of Europe on the protection of women against violence.[42]

A similar effect is discernible regarding victims of human trafficking, which has become a major international concern (Konrad 2006). The year 2002 saw the publication of the EU proposal for a

Council Directive on short-term residence permit issues in relation to victims of action to facilitate illegal immigration or trafficking in human beings. The following year, the Home Office funded the pilot Poppy projects to provide shelter and basic services to such victims. The chain of causation actually becomes cyclical, as following this the UK made human trafficking a priority during its tenure as president of the G8 and the EU, driving forward the adoption of an EU action plan on this issue in December 2005 (Ferrero-Waldner 2006) and then consulting on a domestic action plan in early 2006 (Home Office and Scottish Executive 2006).

More recently, the Crown Prosecution Service's proposed Children's Charter (CPS 2005a) refers to the UK's 1991 adoption of the United Nations Convention on the Rights of the Child,[43] specifically the obligation to 'consider the best interests and views of a child' and to afford them 'the right to legal help and fair treatment in a justice system that respects their rights' (Articles 3 and 12).

It was noted expressly by at least one interviewee that international influences were responsible for the piloting of new measures in England and Wales:

> Internationally, the idea of domestic violence courts has grown out of the drug courts model – in terms of drug courts were developed in the late 1980s/early 1990s in the US. (representative of the DCA)

Clearly the international and domestic contexts are not easy to separate in any policy context (Smith 2004). For present purposes, what is interesting is how the international victim movement broadens our narrower conceptions of victimisation and often prompts swift government action. The international sphere also provides policy-makers, academics and others with useful comparators. For example, following the publication of the 2001 EU Framework Decision, Victim Support (2002b) called for more comparisons with inquisitorial criminal justice systems to temper the excesses of intimidatory cross-examination. This has also been suggested by Ellison (2001).

Rights language

To develop a point made in the last section, the language of rights has clearly expanded internationally in recent years. Since the Human Rights Act of 2000 a human rights culture has emerged in England and Wales, leaving policy-makers more willing to depart from the purely service standards approach when it comes to victims of crime (Rock 2004). This is reflected in the more recent policy documents, which often speak in terms of creating victim rights for the first time (Home Office 2005h: 5). Since then, the policy discourse on rights for victims of crime has accelerated, such that Doak (2003, 2005) now identifies a widespread call for some form of procedural right of participation (for victims) within the system.

The Home Office's (2004c) strategy document went so far as to indicate that a robust and effective criminal justice system 'acts on behalf of the victim and supports victims and witnesses through the justice process' (p. 69). In the context of other reforms discussed above, it seems unlikely that this means the system or its prosecutors now represent victims rather than the state. Nevertheless, the use of what would have been quite radical language 20 years ago still indicates a change in policy (or, at least, rhetoric) over time. The government's CJS strategy document *Cutting Crime, Delivering Justice* (Home Office 2004e) also seemed to cast victims as *quasi* parties in the case, pitting the victim directly against the defendant:

> Criminal justice will be organised to support the victim and thwart the offender. (p.26) [44]

Of course, this again instils notions of the zero sum game. Nevertheless, policy-makers are clearly now willing to speak in terms of giving some victims their own representation in court. This is important because those with representation usually also have rights to be represented, and are usually called 'parties'. Recent years have also seen increased discussions on giving victims a 'voice' (CPS 2005b; cjsonline 2006d; Criminal Justice System 2007). This was clearly an important issue to one policy-maker interviewed for this research:

> I want the Victims' Advisory Panel to play a very important role … it's made up of victims themselves whereas most of the other boards and panels we've got, they're actually policy boards … this Panel is actually victims themselves getting a direct voice to ministers … it's actually quite incredible. (representative of the OCJR) [45]

The question throughout is whether the radical nature of these and other reforms is confined to the rhetoric used to describe them: whether calling these 'rights' reflects a development of language – precipitated by international developments like the 2001 Framework

Decision – rather than policy. This of course brings us back to the definition of rights. When questioning policy-makers on the exact nature of rights under the statutory Code this rhetoric can slip:

> It depends on what you mean by rights. We think there are certain minimum standards that anyone ought to be able to expect and we set those out very very clearly and we do expect agencies to comply to them. So I suppose it's more about minimum service standards. (representative of the OCJR)

Examining the reforms to date – and adopting the view that rights should be enforceable from within the criminal justice process – the rhetoric interpretation seems to carry greater weight.

Macro influences

The more macro-level influences on victim reform as suggested by Boutellier (2000) and Garland (2001) have been described in Chapter 2. At this stage, however, a number of features of the policy chain can be identified which seem to back up their conclusions.

Rhetorically at least, victims do seem to be taking a more prominent position in criminal justice policy. Both commentators argue that this is because the system has become defined by its treatment of victims and the addressing of their suffering. Under this construction, it is not surprising that the criminal justice system, policy-makers, and other outside agencies have sought to identify a wider range of victims, hence the expansion of our conception of victimhood. This has involved not only identifying different *categories* of victim (survivors of homicide, victims of domestic violence) but also different types of suffering (intimidation, secondary victimisation, anti-social behaviour). Thus, having excluded the victim for so long, one might argue that in this new era of moral pluralism and loss of faith in penal-welfarism, the system ironically now needs more victims in order to legitimise itself.

Hence, we have noted previously the wider definitions of victimhood found in the Sexual Offences Act 2003, which were based on the argument that other forms of sexual victimisation were just as distressing to victims as the legal definition of rape. This may reflect the wider point that victims have indeed become more prominent in criminal justice policy with particular reference to those whose suffering is accepted to be the greatest. So, while the present limitations of the victim personal statement scheme must be acknowledged (especially as it excludes the consideration of victims' opinions), this development reflects a new ethos of addressing the suffering of crime victims. Similar arguments can be made regarding special measures, the Witness Service, and the provision of information generally. Thus, we may be moving closer to defining victims by the suffering they endure.[46] Of course, this has negative implications if it leads to policies focusing only on Christie's (1986) ideal victim.

Garland (2001) also argues that governments deny the failure of the criminal justice system to solve the problem of crime by turning to ever more punitive policies, thus appealing to victims' need to be protected and to have their voices heard. As such, notions of a zero sum game develop between the needs of victims and offenders, which sustain and intensify the punitive ethos. As already discussed in this chapter, there are clear examples throughout the policy chain of victim reform being combined with more punitive measures.

Another clear indictment of the macro perspective is the fact that these developments are international in nature, especially with regard to human rights. Again this hints that victim measures are ultimately the result of broad social trends, and perhaps even inevitable in the broadest sociological context.

A policy chain?

Given the above discussion, it is submitted that victims of crime have become prominent in policy-making because actions that, incidentally, assist victims and witnesses have frequently been grounded in a quite different set of political concerns, and because – now that victims and witnesses have achieved rhetorical acceptance in the political system – new policies are being packaged as the continuation of work for these groups but which are in fact intended to achieve other aims.

It therefore seems logical to return to the original contention that, in reality, all the developments related to victims and witnesses are not actually part of the same thing. No single actor (like Victim Support) or even a small group of actors are responsible for driving this policy. In truth, this is probably not a single policy about victims and witnesses at all but one comprised of, as Rock (1990) suggests, numerous other politics. Indeed, the focus of these other politics may stretch far beyond victims of crime to encompass the public in general.

It is by now clear that calling this a 'policy chain' implies a degree of linearity and consistency which is simply not present. Rock (2004) has described these policies as more of a 'web' of developments. For Rock, there are eight main influencing focal points to this web: the structure of the Home Office;[47] the nature of policy-making; the growth of the victim as a consumer of criminal justice; the development of human rights; compensation developments; developments in reparation provision; the identification of vulnerable and intimidated witnesses; and race issues (specifically, the Stephen Lawrence enquiry).[48]

The present analysis supports these views, although I would seek to emphasise different aspects of this web. For example, it seems clear that this is a group of policies based on multi-levelled governance[49] and international developments. Many of the influences in this policy community (Bache 2003) can also be placed in the context of the wider social changes described by Boutellier (2000) and Garland (2001). Furthermore – while Rock (1998) has talked about the growth in recognition of homicide survivors as indirect victims – I would seek to emphasise the growth in our conceptions of victimhood and suffering more generally, and would cite the identification and support offered to vulnerable and intimidated witnesses as reflecting these wider developments.

Indeed, perhaps here lies an explanation for the often confusing merging of victims and witnesses into a single group. Recognising the problems witnesses face when coming to court or giving evidence brings them within the ambit of victimhood, meaning witnesses are the new victims. Finding new victims is important because, as the macro theorists have argued, criminal justice is now legitimised by the treatment of victims. This feeds into the acceptance of victims as consumers of the criminal justice system.

The overarching point is that the victim policy chain is a retrospective construction, achieved by concentrating on specific elements of much wider strategies, processes, and influences over time. Academics have had their role to play here, as their tendency is to compartmentalise such developments, placing them in order and treating them as a unified whole. It has also been demonstrated that the policy-making process itself requires new initiatives to be billed as the continuation of old ones. Hence, policy documents like the *new deal* are designed to suggest a unified and consistent strategy to assist victims and witnesses when in fact there is none.

Van Dijk (1983) argues that much of the victim movement is action-orientated, meaning that doing something for victims is often more important than constructing long-term policies based on victims' expressed needs. Thus, as priorities change, so too does the funding for new projects, like the expansion of the Witness Service. The fact that the greater part of the funding for localised victim care must come from local resources distances the centre from responsibility for such measures. This situation also implies that the continuation of funding for victim care in the long term relies on victims retaining their present status as a key political issue.

A victim policy?

These are important observations because, if accurate, they suggest that recent benefits brought to victims and witnesses are more properly understood as the *by-products* of other agenda(s). As such, the reality exposed in this and the last chapter is that many of these policy developments are open to critique, or at least have not served victims directly as well as they might.

For example, the argument has been made that victims still lack genuine internally enforceable rights. Recent developments like the Victim's Code of Practice have not taken the issue much further from the Victim's Charter introduced by the Conservatives in 1990, and the rights victims have been afforded are mainly restricted to service rights. This is partly because – as this chapter confirms – the government has subscribed to a strategy of preserving the existing justice system rather than adapting it with fundamental reform to suit the needs of victims, who have certainly never been asked directly whether they require more fundamental changes. I have suggested that non-fundamental reform as defined in Chapter 2 is a legitimate mechanism for achieving victim-centredness. Nevertheless, the government's view is far more restrictive than this, excluding victims' participation (especially consultation) within the system essentially on the grounds of a zero sum game. So, we have seen the confused introduction of victim personal statements, replete with a practice direction to ensure the views of victims on sentence are not considered (Lord Chancellor's Department 2001; Hoyle *et al.* 1999; Morgan and Sanders 1999). We have also seen the introduction of special measures, which do assist victims (giving evidence in the guise of witnesses) but fail to address the arguably more fundamental problem of questioning techniques and the occupational practices of lawyers and judges.[50]

There are also numerous indications that the government has no clear or consistent plan for implementing reform. Hence the awkward introduction in short succession of two completely separate means of reducing administrative costs in state compensation, which

I have argued may reflect financial concerns more than anything else (Home Office 2004a; 2005d). In addition, this chapter has noted the unstructured, unplanned manner in which Victim Support must permanently compete for extra funding as its role expands.

The issue of funding is key to this debate, because the lack of central money to finance the support offered to victims by local agencies strongly suggests that the government is unwilling to take responsibility for them. Instead, local agencies must find resources from existing allocations. Again this means that the continuation of support for victims is dependent on their remaining important political figures. This is particularly so given that the bodies charged with implementing such policies – the Local Criminal Justice Boards – are comprised of criminal justice administrators who are more concerned with system efficiency than victims' needs *per se*. Where the government has provided funding, it has usually been in the name of getting witnesses to give evidence (under the *No Witness, No Justice* scheme), which boosts system efficiency and ultimately *cuts* the cost to the central purse. In addition, while victims are given information about the system – such as the presence of special measures, facilities and so on – this is all information that would convince them to come to give evidence, rather than a full and realistic overview of the infrequent highs and persistent lows of being a witness.

At the centre, after many years victims now finally have their own minister, but this position seems to be one of spokesperson rather than agent of reform and therefore the appointment is sparse indication of the government taking responsibility for victims. Indeed, there is a real question as to whether the true audience for these reforms is the victims at all; it may instead be the wider (and rather mystical) 'law-abiding community'. The greater part of this community apparently does not have to deal with the criminal justice system on any kind of regular basis, but they do appreciate the suffering of victims who must do so: especially if these victims meet with stereotypical notions of vulnerability. On the latter issue, we can again note the government's proposal to reduce state compensation for non-serious injury, based on alleged BCS findings that such victims would prefer services. In fact, no BCS sweep has ever asked victims to choose directly between the two, and it may be asked – in a victim-centred system – why should these be mutually exclusive options? As such, from the government's perspective, the *appearance* of assisting victims may be all this policy needs to achieve. It has to be said that the public also appreciates cost-cutting, hence some very clear statements in more recent policy documents that the government is attempting to reduce costs and boost efficiency in criminal justice (Home Office 2006a).

While many of the measures intended to help victims have therefore had questionable results – and their implementation raises questions as to the government's real motives – other reforms linked with improving victims' lot in criminal justice seem to have little to do with victims (or even the narrower group of victim witnesses) at all. This is particularly true of more punitive reforms such as the hearsay and bad character provisions under the Criminal Justice Act 2003. Indeed, more recently, clamping down on offenders has been linked directly in the rhetoric with supporting victims, as if the former necessarily implies the latter (Home Office 2004e). This has all the appearance of a political strategy designed to appease perceived punitive values amongst victims, albeit the evidence suggests victims are not as vindictive as this implies (Erez 2004). Hence, once again the audience for such measures is not the victims, but the public at large in an era of populist punitiveness.

Of course, the positive views expressed by victims and vulnerable and intimidated witnesses regarding court facilities and special measures clearly indicates that many victims have benefited from some aspects of these policies, including the advent of special measures, the extension of the Witness Service and even the Effective Trial Management structure. In addition, with the introduction of victims' advocates, a small percentage of (possibly ideal) victims are being afforded some measure of party status.

Nevertheless, there remains much doubt as to whether the victims themselves have been the true focus of this policy, especially as most measures only benefit victims *as witnesses*. Since 2007, the new Ministry of Justice has taken the lead role in developing reforms of the criminal justice system. Time will tell how this new arrangement will impact on victims in policy-making. Initial indications give a sense of business as usual, with the Ministry pledging to 'deliver a more effective, transparent and responsive criminal justice system for victims and the public' (Ministry of Justice 2008). Of course, many victims have benefited from such policies. Nevertheless, the fact remains that an analysis of the underlying influences behind such reforms indicates that this has often been more by accident or happy coincidence rather than specific design. For this reason – as argued in the last chapter and above – the government has not gone far enough in any of its reforms to genuinely bring victims to the heart of this system. As such, the next chapter will begin discussing one possible mechanism by which this could be achieved.

Notes

1 As has recently been suggested (Home Office 2003a).
2 Wide-scale social and political changes.
3 The explanatory notes accompanying the Domestic Violence, Crime and Victims Bill 2003 called the *new deal* 'the first national strategy for victims and witnesses' (Her Majesty's Stationery Office 2003: 4).
4 For convenience, the term 'policy chain' will be retained as a reference to the chronological advent of such developments over time.
5 Based on probably fallacious notions of (unenforceable) rights (Fenwick 1995).
6 For the more long-term history see Spencer and Flin (1993).
7 It was announced in 1996 that all Crown Court centres now had a Witness Service. Funding to expand the Service to all magistrates' courts came in 2001 with an increase of Victim Support's grant to £22.7 million.
8 *The Times*, 19 June 2008.
9 See Chapter 2.
10 A Victims Fund was however established later that year, the government pledging to channel £4 million from the proceeds of crime into the fund over the next two years to develop services for victims of sexual offending.
11 Which again suggests a somewhat ulterior political motive and a vengeful characterisation of victims.
12 The issue of targets will be returned to below.
13 See p. 56.
14 Which largely remains true in the statutory era.
15 For example, waiting rooms and TV links were introduced at Court C on the initiative of an usher (interview with a court clerk at Court C).
16 As was evident in the area under review.
17 In the Glidewell (1998) Report.
18 Presently around £30 million (Victim Support 2007).
19 See Rock (2002). For a wider discussion of how policy-makers use definitions see Macleavy (2006).
20 'Survivor' is becoming the established term to refer to this group (Rock 1998).
21 More recently, the government has been called upon to tackle the issues facing victims in *civil* proceedings (Casey 2008).
22 Section 143 of the Serious Organised Crime and Police Act 2005.
23 Which links with the development of the multi-agency approach discussed below and again seems to be part of broader trends towards 'horizontal' policy-making (Matheson 2000; Milbourne *et al.* 2003).
24 Although the 2003 Act still restricts rape itself to non-consensual penetration of the penis into the vagina or anus.
25 Although in practice the high percentage of guilty pleas means that in many cases CJS professionals presume the opposite (Carlen 1976).

26 Most recently, the government is responding to calls from the media to address a perceived escalation in knife crimes and stabbings (see BBC 2008).
27 See Lindblom and Woodhouse (1993) for a discussion of how interest groups adapt their strategies to retain influence in policy-making.
28 See p. 84.
29 This is clear from its Annual Reviews (Victim Support 2004, 2005, 2006, 2007). Victim Support schemes also had representation on the JUSTICE Committee (1998).
30 On which, see below.
31 Owing to a last-minute change of plea to guilty, witness reluctance or other factors (see Chapter 5).
32 *The Times*, 19 June 2008.
33 And in other policy areas (Ryan 1999).
34 Young (1996) discusses how victimhood has been overtaken by citizenship, meaning victimhood is now equated with 'all of us' (Walklate 2007: 21).
35 Case Progression Officers (CPOs) were introduced as part of the new Case Management Framework and are intended to facilitate effective pre-trial review hearings (Home Office 2004d). See Chapter 5.
36 Although, subsequent evaluation seems to avert these fears (Crawford and Newburn 2003).
37 The government had difficulty getting its Criminal Justice Bill though the House of Lords due to this provision (BBC 2003).
38 Part 10.
39 See Chapter 6.
40 Including free legal aid where warranted.
41 It is questionable whether relevant reforms have been put in place to meet these latter requirements, especially on the issue of mediation.
42 Recommendation 1450 (2000).
43 Para. 1.3.
44 Walklate (2007) discusses how this reflects the relationship between the state and the law.
45 This policy-maker clearly found it unusual that victims, or lay people generally, should be allowed to talk to politicians.
46 In the upcoming Law Reform, Victims and Witnesses Bill the government is focusing increased attention on victims of crimes involving guns and other offensive weapons (Office of the Leader of the House of Commons 2008).
47 See Egeberg (1999).
48 Walklate (2007) adds the development of research linking gender with victimisation.
49 Whereas Rock (2004) is concerned only with national policy processes rather than international, local or regional policy-making.
50 See Chapters 5 and 6.

Chapter 4

A narrative-based model of victim-centredness in criminal trials

Having compiled and assessed the policy and political background behind the government's pledge to put victims at the heart of the criminal justice system, this chapter will put forward one possible model (or an important component of a model) for victim-centred criminal justice. The chapter will draw upon the concept of 'narrative' from the sociological and psychological literatures to suggest that putting victims at the heart of criminal justice necessitates a more detailed appreciation of the roles victims' own stories might play within the substantive trial process. Examples are given from the literature to illustrate the social functions and therapeutic benefit of storytelling for sufferers of many traumas, and for crime victims in particular. Under the proposed model, criminal trials themselves are viewed in terms of a collection of stories and interpretations of stories.

Storytelling and narrative

It has often been suggested that people are natural storytellers and that all human beings share this fundamental capacity (Coles 1989). Recent years have witnessed an explosion of academic interest in the way human beings interpret and ascribe meaning to disturbing life experiences by recounting them in the form of stories (Maines 1993; Orbuch 1997). With the realisation that stories play such a key role in people's lives has come the widespread application of concepts like storytelling, account-making and narrative to a vast array of issues across the social sciences, humanities, and even the physical sciences (Maines 1993). Pioneering the use of life stories in social research, Ken Plummer describes these developments in the following terms:

> Recently, from all kinds of different theoretical perspectives in the human studies ... there has been a convergence on the power of the metaphor of the story. It has become recognised as one of the central roots we have into the continuing quest for understanding human meaning. (1995: 5)

Given such endorsement, applying this metaphor of the story to victims in criminal trials might well prove advantageous when attempting to identify features of a victim-centred system. As such, this chapter is chiefly concerned with the place and roles of account-making within the substantive criminal trial procedure.

Orbuch *et al.* provide one concise definition of account-making:

> [P]eople's story-like constructions of events that include explanations, descriptions, predictions about relevant future events, and effective reaction. (1994: 250)

While the breadth of this definition must be conceded, it does illustrate that account-making goes beyond the simple retelling of events in a 'story-like' way. Account-making is thought to have important psychological and social implications for storytellers. In particular, it is argued that account-making improves a person's understanding and acceptance of the specific events being recounted and can also help one cope with future life challenges (White and Epston 1990).

It should be stressed that 'narrative', 'story-telling' and 'account-making' are not necessarily synonyms. For example, while there is a clear overlap in the literature between narrative and account-making, Orbuch (1997) draws two main distinctions between the two. Firstly, he argues that narrative implies a public recounting of events, usually delivered orally to an audience. Account-making, on the other hand, can include private activities like writing diaries or self-reflection. As a second distinction, Orbuch emphasises that account-makers are usually troubled by specific stressful or imposing events, whereas such events do not necessary feature in narratives. An additional distinction is made by Kellas and Manusov (2003), who view accounts as a subgroup of narratives which set out to make sense of or explain life events.[1] While such debates are interesting and important, this chapter will focus less on the semantics and more on the overarching point that narrative as a concept is a useful means of understanding how crime victims deal with their traumatic experiences.

The benefits of account-making

The literature on the impacts of crime confirms that victimisation can indeed represent a stressful or imposing event (Shapland and Hall 2007). The hypothesis being put forward in this chapter is that victims would benefit from the opportunity to construct story-like accounts through the criminal trial procedure. As such, before drawing specific connections between account-making and trials it is first necessary to illustrate the apparent benefits of narrative account-making in a general sense.

If human beings are indeed natural storytellers then it perhaps comes as little surprise that account-making seems to bring therapeutic benefits. As such, a trip to any health services library will uncover a whole host of therapeutic texts – written by and for practitioners – emphasising the benefits of patients externalising such experiences and helping the individuals who experience them to tell their stories. In particular, it is argued that account-making improves a person's understanding and acceptance of specific events and can also help one cope with future life challenges (White and Epston 1990; Kellas and Manusov 2003). Here, 'trauma' is often understood as reflecting discontinuity in a person's life story. Under this construction trauma is damaging precisely because it robs sufferers of the ability to make sense of their ongoing experiences in a coherent narrative (Sewell and Williams 2002).

Such ideas have been most developed in the medical field, where Bury (1982) argues that chronic illness represents a biographical disruption in a person's life that causes them to rethink their self-concept. Williams (1984) develops this idea further to describe the conceptual strategies people employ to create a sense of stability and order in their lives following such disruption. In a similar vein, Giddens (1979) has argued that major life events undermine taken-for-granted aspects of the social fabric. Many researchers and clinical practitioners have thus provided evidence that account-making can bring therapeutic benefits to those suffering trauma of various kinds (Kleinman 1988; White and Epston 1990) and to crime victims specifically (Dalgleish and Morant 1992; Riessman 1992).

The clinical observations of practitioners have been substantiated by researchers (and vice versa). For example, Harber and Pennebaker

(1992) refer to developments in schema theory to illustrate how traumatic events represent a disparity between the learned schemas people develop over the course of their lifetimes in order to live and operate in their environment, and new (traumatic) experiences. As such, victimisation can affect a person's underlying assumptions concerning, for example, orderliness and justice in the world (Herman 2003; Shapland and Hall 2007). Harber and Pennebaker suggest that, in order to resolve such 'significant disparities between expectations and events' (1992: 362), trauma victims must confront the troubling memories and that:

> This confrontation is best accomplished by translating the chaotic swirl of traumatic ideation and feelings into coherent language. (p. 360)

According to the authors, the therapeutic benefit of such narratives (to use their terminology) will be enhanced when these narratives are organised and have a clear beginning, middle and end.

Harber and Pennebaker (1992) back up their assertions with their own detailed review of practical experiments conducted in this area. One category consists of so-called 'writing experiments' in which a group of respondents are asked to write about emotions and facts surrounding traumatic events in their lives over a number of days, and are then compared to a control group (Pennebaker and Beall 1986; Pennebaker *et al.* 1988; Pennebaker *et al.* 1990). In their review of the findings of these projects, Harber and Pennebaker (1992) note that writing such stories seems to bring genuine (if temporary) health benefits to the participants as well as self-perceptual and moral-enhancing advantages. It should be noted that the research participants in some of these experiments were university students (as is common in psychological studies). This of course leaves the work open to criticism that the results should not be applied to society in general. It is also clear that these authors are largely reviewing their own research, which always raises questions of objectivity. Nevertheless, the findings do seem indicative of wider trends and at least on the first point it is worth bearing in mind that student victimisation rates are unusually high – especially in relation to burglary (Barberet *et al.* 2003) – compared to the general population.

The fact that such benefits are accrued from *writing* about traumatic incidents is particularly interesting for the purposes of the present research, which is based on a criminal trial procedure still firmly grounded in the orality principle (Ellison 2001). Indeed, Harber and

Pennebaker (1992) go on to emphasise the additional therapeutic benefits that writing about an experience may bring to victims of trauma, because it is a constructive activity that yields a tangible product.

In another excellent review of the wider evidence, Orbuch (1997) discusses how communicating narrative accounts can help people cope with major life events, while failure to engage in an account-making process can lead to chronic problems. The notion that an absence of successful account-making is actually detrimental to health is a consistent theme running through the literature (Pennebaker and Beall 1986; Harber and Pennebaker 1992; Sewell and Williams 2002).

Kellas and Manusov (2003) studied the effect of account-making on people's adjustment to relationship dissolutions and, once again, this involved respondents providing written narratives. While accepting some methodological limitations (again including the use of student respondents) their results nevertheless confirm that the coherence of an account and the maker's ability to put it in episodic or sequential order are positively related to their adjustment to relationship dissolution. Furthermore, the results indicate that people who can communicate complete accounts may have a greater sense of self-worth compared to those who are unable to do so.

Notions of account-making also appear in the literature on victims of crime, although sometimes only by implication. For example, Kenney (2003) argues that homicide survivors[2] have a greater sense of coping when they engage in activities enabling them to 'compartmentalize their thoughts and deal with them one at a time' (p. 25). In a subsequent paper, Kenney expresses another telling point:

> Subjects [homicide survivors] were very clear that coping is not recovering completely, returning to 'normality', or going back to the way they were before the murder. Instead, subjects referred to the ability to live their lives 'around it' and 'go on'. (2004: 244)

This seems closely akin to the view that victims must find ways to resolve traumatic events from their pasts through ongoing coping strategies or schemas, which allow such events to be successfully incorporated into their wider life narratives (Harber and Pennebaker 1992).

Criminal victimisation has been linked more specifically with narrative account-making in relation to sexual abuse. Dalgleish and Morant (1992) suggest that the manner in which people tell their stories shapes their claims concerning their own positions and lives. Linking this with accounts of sexual abuse, Riessman (1992) emphasises the value of narrative in the transitional process from victim to survivor of rape. As such, Riessman argues that victims of sexual abuse can construct a 'surviving self' through telling their story. The findings of Orbuch *et al.* (1994) also demonstrate the value of narrative account-making activities in the context of sexual abuse, the authors summarising the forms and benefits of account-making as:

> [E]xpressing emotions about the assault; cognitively clarifying aspects of the assault; resolving some of the resultant anger, fear, and paralysis of action; and actually moving on with one's life constructively. (p. 261)

This construction illustrates both short- and long-term benefits derived from successful account-making.

Of course, much of the above literature does not focus on victims of crime specifically and none of it draws links with the criminal trial process. The methodological limitations of these studies have been described, and it is also clear that a relatively small core of researchers are working in this area. Nevertheless, the evidence supports the basic proposition that account-making and narrative are generally beneficial to crime victims, which means commentators must consider their place (or lack thereof) in a victim-centred system.

Stories in criminal trials

Given the apparent therapeutic benefits of narrative account-making the next logical question is whether, in the context of the government's pledge to put victims at the heart of the criminal justice system, it might be desirable to apply some of these benefits to victims in criminal trials and how this could be achieved. Thus, to begin addressing the issues of primary interest here, this section will first investigate the present role of narratives in criminal trials.

The preceding paragraphs have concerned themselves with stories told by victims of crime and other traumas in isolation or, at most, communicated to specific researchers and/or therapists. When examining the implications of account-making for criminal trials, however, it is vital to consider the impact of multiple narratives. The adversarial justice model of England and Wales revolves around a competition between the prosecution and the defence. In a contested trial both sides therefore have their own version or versions of events to convey, their own stories to tell.[3] Nevertheless, Van Duyne's (1981) psychological analysis of sentencing differences suggests that the picture is actually even more complex.

Among numerous important issues raised by Van Duyne is the author's contention that information presented in court during a criminal trial (whether in oral or written form) is far from objective. In fact, such information always allows a certain leeway for differing interpretations by different actors involved in the process. As such:

> We may regard the total information in a case as a 'story' concerning one or more criminal offences in which the reporting officers, defendants and witnesses express their findings and views, and which may contain contradictions and points which are unclear, this can result in different interpretations of one and the same file. (Van Duyne 1981: 15)

Effectively then, these differing interpretations create a whole collection of narratives. For example, as Van Duyne illustrates, a prosecutor's professional experience (among other factors) will shape the case files he or she produces for the court. McConville *et al.* (1991) have emphasised the role of the police and prosecution working together in the construction of cases before they even reach court, to the extent that:

> The reality of Crime Control (in which, whatever their public postures to the contrary, police and Crown Prosecutors join hands) means that courts do little more than endorse constructions according to the quality of workmanship, the combativeness of the defence lawyer and the hand of Fate. (p. 172)

Indeed, to draw a parallel with the defence side of the equation, we might refer to McConville *et al.*'s (1994) study of the work of defence solicitors and how they adopt a confrontational attitude to clients as a means of enforcing standardised case theories in individual cases:

> Certainly at the magistrates' court stage, if not beforehand, solicitors and their staff adopt a confrontational approach to clients, challenging them to deny the police evidence against them and virtually to prove their own innocence. (p. 276)

As such, defence solicitors effectively compel defendants to accept a version of their story that corresponds to lawyers' stereotypical impressions:

> Like the police, defence solicitors and their staff frequently work on the basis of standardised case theories and stereotypes of the kinds of people who become involved in events leading to arrest and criminal charge, whether these be fights outside pubs, domestic burglaries or car thefts, or incidents of shop-lifting. These people are commonly seen by their legal advisers as feckless and dishonest, and such images are allowed to structure the way in which their cases will be handled from the outset. (p. 277)

Hence, it seems that by the time a case has reached the court, the stories involved will already have gone through a substantial process of interpretation by both sides. The stories are then reinterpreted by judges based on their own experience and 'knowledge of the world' (Van Duyne 1981). Judges, juries, clerks and magistrates will likewise interpret the oral or written evidence of victims, witnesses and police officers – who similarly develop their own versions of the story. Thus, in addition to the two versions presented by the opposing sides in the adversarial process, a criminal trial will typically involve a whole host of other stories, including those stories participating actors tell themselves in interpreting the information. Thus, a criminal trial can be understood in terms of a collection of stories.

Victims' narratives and account-making at the heart of criminal justice

In Chapter 1 it was suggested that the criminal trial is the most symbolically powerful component of the criminal justice system (Tyler 1990). As such, if trials are typified by a collection of stories, it makes sense to suggest that in a victim-centred system the accounts made by victims would be afforded particular distinction within the trial process. It is not the specific goal of this present chapter to argue for or against the instrumental impact of such narratives on criminal procedure, either before or during the sentencing stage. While such effects might well prove a significant feature of a victim-centred system overall, the contention here is simply that incorporating victims' accounts within trials is an important feature of such a system. In other words, a normative argument is submitted based on the view that the trial *procedure* is equally or more important to members of the public compared with instrumental *outcomes*. This approach is well grounded in established literature, with Ashworth (1993), Erez (1994) and Tyler (1990) all emphasising the view that 'normative issues matter' (Tyler 1990: 178). So, for example, the 2002 Witness Satisfaction Survey indicates that witnesses' feelings that they have been taken for granted is a strong predicator of overall dissatisfaction with their experience (Angle *et al.* 2003).

Aside from these purely normative concerns, however, the above discussion implies that incorporating victims' account-making within criminal trials will bring more tangible benefits in the form of therapeutic effects. It is not being suggested that these benefits could replace the benefits derived from professional counselling[4] or even the less structured reflection and retelling of stories in the longer term. It might, however, constitute a means by which victims take something positive away from the criminal justice system, and it is submitted that this is an important goal for any victim-orientated process.

In fact, the notion that criminal justice can and should afford participants therapeutic outcomes is the subject of a growing literature (Wexler and Winick 1996; Stolle 2000). Rottman and Casey (1999) introduce the notion of 'therapeutic jurisprudence' in the following terms:

> Legal rules, legal procedures, and the roles of legal actors (such as lawyers and judges) constitute social forces that, like it or not, often produce therapeutic or antitherapeutic consequences. Therapeutic jurisprudence proposes that we ask whether the law's antitherapeutic consequences can be reduced, and its therapeutic consequences enhanced, without subordinating due process and other justice values. (p. 14)

So far, therapeutic jurisprudence has been associated mainly with restorative and community justice initiatives, and with wider problem-solving strategies, often adopted through the creation of specialist courts (such as domestic violence or drug courts) (Rottman 2000). Nevertheless, it is clear that, provided other justice values are not infringed (a point returned to in Chapter 7), therapeutic account-making as part of the criminal trial process would be commensurate to the goals of this approach.

To summarise, the argument here is based on the idea (or ideal) of a criminal justice system which genuinely holds victims at its heart. While accepting the existence of other attributes, two desirable features of such a system are submitted. Firstly, because the system revolves around a process constituted by multiple stories, to put the victim at the heart of that system implies that the victim's story should be highlighted within that process, not excluded, marginalised or reinterpreted to the extent that it is no longer the victim's own narrative. Secondly, the notion of a victim-centred system implies that some form of benefit will be accrued to victim participants. The relevant literature suggests that account-making is one way to inject such benefits – achieving a more therapeutic jurisprudence – while this would also be consistent with the first feature.

Victims' narratives in present criminal trials

Within the current system in England and Wales, victims contribute to the trial process in three main ways: witness statements, victim personal statements and the process of giving evidence. Each of these will be taken in turn with a view to establishing why – in principle and based on guideline documents and literature – all three fail to produce true narratives or account-making from the perspective of the victim. These arguments will then be backed up by reference to the empirical findings of the present research in the next two chapters. This section also demonstrates how account-making can be used as a tool in assessing the victim-centredness of the criminal justice system.

Witness statements

The taking of witness statements is usually one of the first steps in the process that culminates in a criminal trial. It is largely based on such statements that lawyers from the Crown Prosecution Service make their decisions on whether to pursue a prosecution, guided by public interest and evidential criteria (CPS 2004). Witness statements therefore form the core of the case file assembled by a prosecutor and subsequently presented to the court.

The witness statements of crime victims contain what is purported to be their own version of events or, from the lawyers' perspective, their evidence. There has been little investigation into the manner in which witness statements are taken, although generally it appears that they are not usually written out by the victims themselves, but are instead compiled by police officers based on an interview. The 2004 edition of the *Prosecution Team Manual of Guidance* seems to envision the police filling in most of the relevant (MG11) form and the language employed is always one of police 'taking' witness statements rather than victims 'giving' their evidence (Home Office 2004h). Graham *et al.* (2004) note that this police-led method is the traditional way of gathering witness statements.[5] Victims are given the opportunity to read their statements and make corrections before signing each page. Subsequently, a typed version of the statement is produced and the victim is again asked to sign each page to confirm its accuracy (Home Office 2004h).

Two main distinctions can be drawn between genuine account-making on the one hand and the process of giving a witness statement on the other. Firstly, the fact that witness statements are apparently compiled by police officers means the victims themselves will be somewhat removed from the process. This seems to detract from the established norms of therapeutic account-making – as described in the literature above – in which respondents are usually asked to physically write about stressful or imposing events themselves. Hence, in the case of witness statements, victims miss out on any benefits derived from engaging in the constructive exercise of physically writing out their accounts.

The second distinction between witness statements and narrative account-making lies in the fact that police officers are under pressure to take statements from victims as soon as possible after an alleged offence (Home Office 2004h). Narrative, on the other hand, is usually conceived in terms of a story being told some time after the events and following reflection and interpretation. Indeed, according to Orbuch *et al.*'s (1994) definition, this is largely the point of any account-making exercise. Of course, giving the victim time to reflect and interpret events is precisely what the police, the courts and lawyers are seeking to avoid by taking statements as soon as possible, because from their perspective the statements are taken for evidential purposes. The issue then is whether victims themselves have this same purpose in mind when they give their statements, or whether they view the procedure more in terms of account-making. It is submitted that the latter possibility is more likely considering that everyone is to some extent a storyteller whereas few civilian victims are likely to think in terms of evidential rules.

Of course, it could be argued that – regardless of what the officer actually writes down – the victim is in fact participating in an account-making exercise just by reporting the information. That said, the lack of time to reflect on the events in most cases, coupled with victims not actually writing the accounts physically and in their own words, seems to distance this process from true account-making.

Furthermore, even if providing statements did afford victims some of the therapeutic benefits associated with account-making, if such narratives are not fully recorded they will never form part of the trial procedure. It is submitted that, given the evidential priorities of police officers, it is unlikely that victims' full and unedited accounts are in fact recorded in witness statements, and the ethnographic evidence for such a proposition will be examined in Chapter 6. If this hypothesis proves correct, then considerable doubt would be cast on the notion that victims are presently being brought to the heart of the criminal justice system. On the contrary, this would suggest victims' narratives are kept very much at the periphery.

Even if victims did write out their witness statements themselves – based on account-making rather than evidential criteria – following Van Duyne (1981) this would still be subject to the prosecutor's interpretation of that statement. Such interpretation will clearly influence the presentation of the information by prosecutors, in their opening speeches and also in the way they conduct a trial generally.

Victim personal statements

We have seen that victim personal statements were rolled out as a national initiative in October 2001, following two major evaluations of pilot schemes (Hoyle *et al.* 1999; Morgan and Sanders 1999). Their apparent purpose is to give victims of crime the opportunity to submit another statement in addition to their regular witness statements. Within such statements, victims are invited to comment on how a crime has affected them 'physically, emotionally, psychologically, financially or in any other way (Home Office 2001e: 2).

In terms of providing victims with a vehicle for narrative account-making, victim personal statements boast a number of advantages over traditional witness statements. Firstly, it seems that victim personal statements are intended to be written in the victim's own words, and, perhaps in the victim's own hand. Some qualification is necessary here because the language used in the relevant guidance note for practitioners (Home Office 2001c) is somewhat vague, again referring to police officers 'taking the statement' but also clearly maintaining that victims 'will be free to say what they wish'. The *Manual of Guidance* is similarly vague on this point (Home Office 2004h). The leaflet produced for the victims themselves is more consistent, advising victims:

> The police will ask if you want to fill in a victim personal statement when they have finished filling in the witness statement. (Home Office 2001c: 5)

In practice, qualitative analysis has suggested that the VPS statements are completed in a number of ways. These can be placed on a continuum ranging from self-completion methods – where victims write out their own statements with a low level of police control – to 'police checklist' methods, where the police elicit victim personal statements in a similar way to witness statements (Graham *et al.* 2004). The lack of any quantitative data[6] makes it impossible to know which methods are most commonly utilised by the police, but techniques which involve victims writing their own VPS statements obviously seem more consistent with account-making principles. As such, if the system is to become truly victim-centred, clearer guidelines to this effect are required. In addition, victims' awareness of the existence and purpose of the scheme needs to be increased, as Graham *et al.* found their awareness on both counts to be very low.

The above extract refers to so-called 'stage one' victim personal statements, which are taken at the same time as the traditional witness statement. According to the *guidance note* and the *Manual of Guidance*, stage one victim personal statements should be taken on the same form (form MG11) as the main witness statement, 'with a clear separation between the evidential part of the statement and the VPS' (Home Office 2004b: 138). This is a puzzling definition, as a victim personal statement is itself evidence, a point we will return to in a moment. What is perhaps more interesting for present purposes is that victims can also make subsequent 'stage two' victim personal statements on separate MG11 forms. A stage two VPS can be used to record the more long-term effects of crime or simply update/supplement a previous personal statement. The VPS guidance for victims assures them they can update their personal statements 'at any stage before the case gets to court' (Home Office 2001b: 9).

This is clearly significant from the perspective of narrative, as it seems to give victims the freedom to develop the information initially presented, allowing time for the reflection and interpretation associated with genuine account-making. As such, it seems likely that stage two victim personal statements have the greatest potential to elicit therapeutic benefits for victims compared with witness statements, or even the stage one VPS. Once more, however, the accrual of such benefits is reliant on victims being informed about the scheme, an issue on which Graham *et al.*'s findings are again telling:

> There was low or no awareness of the option of making a later VPS. (2004: 54)

Of course, even if stage one or two VPS statements are made, at this stage the victim personal statement encounters the same limitations as the traditional witness statements discussed above. While producing such a statement (or statements) through methods involving low levels of police control might constitute account-making, the question becomes whether – in the context of the government's pledge on victims – these narratives are being readily incorporated within the trial process itself.

This is a question for Chapter 7, but the difficulty here is clearly that – just like the stories presented in witness statements – the use and interpretation of victim personal statements are in the hands of the prosecutor presenting the case. Unlike the equivalent schemes in several US states (Erez 2000), the English and Welsh version of victim personal statements does not allow the victims themselves to read a VPS orally in court (JUSTICE 1998).[7] Thus, the victim must rely on the prosecutor presenting the statement to the court, referring to it in a speech, eliciting information contained within it during the victim's examination in chief or simply handing it in to the judge, who is under no obligation to refer to it. Roberts and Erez (2004) therefore argue that the communicative function of a victim impact statement is curtailed by prosecutors, who take away the uniqueness of a victim's story and emphasise different aspects of it than the victim would. Once again, therefore, the victim's own interpretation of the story may easily be subjugated by that of the prosecutor and judge.

Even assuming the full text of a VPS was faithfully reproduced during a trial in a manner true to the victim's own interpretation, meaning and understanding, in such a case the victim's story is still subject to the interpretation of those who hear it. In the trial context such interpretation may well involve the exclusion of a lot of the information due to restrictive interpretations of how victim personal statements can be used. So, at the pilot stage Morgan and Sanders (1999) concluded that victim statements were seen primarily as an aid to sentencing by criminal justice professionals but that in practice they still had little if any impact on most sentencing decisions. This is because the vast majority of cases were – from the court's perspective – unremarkable as opposed to novel, and therefore sentencers felt they did not require the VPS, because it did not tell them anything they did not already know about the impact of the crime.

As we have already seen, soon after the national rollout of victim personal statements the then Lord Chancellor's Department published a Practice Direction that drew attention to the VPS scheme, but also set out some fairly restrictive limitations. The text of that Direction is worth repeating here:

> The court must pass what it judges to be the appropriate sentence having regard to the circumstances of the offence taking into account, so far as the court considers it appropriate, the consequences to the victim. The opinions of the victim or the victim's close relatives as to what the sentence should be are therefore not relevant … [if] opinions as to sentence are included in a statement, the court should pay no attention to it. (Lord Chancellor's Department 2001)

This statement firstly confirms that the court's consideration of victim personal statements should be confined to the sentencing stage following conviction. More significantly, however, the Direction suggests that if criminal justice actors consider a victim's 'VPS made' account to be 'inappropriate' or contain 'irrelevant' elements then the account should be wholly or partly excluded. Either way, this results in a brand new interpretation of the victim's story.

Giving evidence

Giving evidence in court is still the most visible and obvious contribution made by victims of crime during the trial procedure. Unlike witness statements or victim personal statements, the process of giving evidence represents victims' sole opportunity to communicate information to the court firsthand. Further to this, the evidence itself can often sound very much like a story being told by the victim. Nevertheless, a number of significant features seem to distinguish the evidence-giving procedure from true narrative account-making. These will be discussed now and illustrated with practical examples in Chapter 6.

The main difference between accounts and court-based evidence is that while the former are made the latter is elicited by questioning lawyers. Of course, counsellors might also elicit accounts from clients by prompting them to participate in an account-making exercise. In such cases, however, the counsellor is not attempting to actively control the information provided (as is arguably the case with lawyers) but is instead acting in the capacity of a receptive audience (Sewell and Williams 2002).

To make the point concisely, in the present system victims giving evidence in courtrooms are not there to tell stories, but to answer questions. This immediately renders the victims subservient to the procedure because the stories they tell are thereby constrained by the logical scope and reasonable interpretation of the questions being asked, with lawyers/judges possessing the exclusive right to determine what such 'logical and reasonable interpretations' entail. Thus, if victims' answers stray beyond the scope of the information lawyers intended to elicit from a question, they are likely to be halted. Even when the questioning lawyer employs relatively open language – 'tell the court what happened' – there is still an implicit limitation to the scope of the answer being called for, beyond which victims are not permitted to stray. The consequence of this is that, once again, the victim's own narrative is distorted in favour of an alterative version of the story.

The notion that questioning lawyers effectively control the evidence presented by witnesses is supported by established literature. Luchjenbroers (1996) has provided a detailed content analysis of barrister–witness dialogue during a six-day Supreme Court murder trial in Australia. Although based on a single trial, the results clearly illustrate the questioning strategies employed by barristers to effectively control the information provided by witnesses. The wording of Luchjenbroers' conclusion makes it particularly suitable for inclusion here:

> [W]itnesses can hardly be thought to tell their own stories in their own words. (1996: 501)

Indeed, in direct contrast to notions of account-making as rewarding and therapeutic, the wider literature is almost unanimous in its portrayal of the evidence-giving process as a difficult and uncomfortable experience (Carlen 1976; Shapland *et al.* 1985; Jackson *et al.* 1991; Rock 1993; Ellison 2001).

This last observation pre-empts another important distinction between account-making and evidence, which reflects a contrast between natural and unnatural modes of expression. As noted already, narrative account-making usually involves account-makers telling their stories in their own way, based on personal reflection on past events. Aside from the specific experiments that have been carried out in this area, this can often be achieved privately through notes and diaries (Orbuch 1997). Even when account-making is carried out in the context of an experiment or therapy – where respondents/clients may be specifically asked to present their accounts in written form – there are usually few further stipulations as to how exactly this must be done. For example, in some written experiments, respondents are told not to concern themselves with spelling, punctuation or grammar (Harber and Pennebaker 1992). Hence, as pointed out at the beginning of this paper, genuine account-making seems to reflect a very natural way of imparting information through stories.

In contrast, when victims give evidence during criminal trials they are asked to relay information in a very unnatural, unfamiliar way. A courtroom is an unfamiliar environment for most people and can be frightening and intimidating (Hamlyn *et al.* 2004a). The evidence is itself elicited from witnesses in a very unnatural manner, with witnesses usually being told to present their answers towards the bench or jury while simultaneously receiving the questions from a lawyer standing in another direction (Rock 1993). In addition, the fact that notes of a witness's evidence must be taken by hand by more than one person in the room means that witnesses are required to present the information at an unnatural speed and volume: persistently being interrupted in their flow and asked to slow down or speed up or speak more loudly. In summary, Jackson (2004) observes:

> It is seldom appreciated just what a wide array of cognitive, social and emotional skills the legal system demands of witnesses. (p. 73)

Furthermore, it is not just the procedure of giving evidence that may be difficult to victims and other witnesses. In many cases victims will be asked to cope with some very unfamiliar concepts: hearsay being a prime example on which witnesses of all kinds receive no information or guidance in published materials.

Of course, as with written statements, witnesses giving evidence may be asked to elaborate on what they consider to be very small details while passing over what they view as important ones. Not only is this all highly frustrating, it is also likely to compromise witnesses' ability to present their narratives in what they consider a logical and consecutive order, another important characteristic of account-making emphasised above (Kellas and Manusov 2003). In addition, and particularly during cross-examination, questions may be confusing, coercive or insulting (Temkin 1987). Overall then, the evidence-giving procedure seems far removed from the very natural process of therapeutic account-making.

Ellison (2001) places some of the blame for the problems faced by witnesses (specifically vulnerable and intimidated witnesses) on the system's continued reliance on the orality principle (the notion that evidence should typically be presented out loud). Certainly this seems at odds with our understanding of account-making, which embraces written accounts. Of course, even if the orality principal were not so dominant, the preceding discussion of witness statements and victim personal statements suggests that presently it would still be difficult to ensure that a written version of the victim's account was incorporated within the trial procedure.

The final distinction to be drawn between account-making and evidence is that the latter is not necessarily a voluntary exercise.[8] It has already been noted that therapists might try to convince their clients to engage in an account-making process. Such persuasion is, however, far removed from the position of some victims in criminal trials: summoned to give evidence on pain of arrest and imprisonment. At present, the clearest examples can be drawn from cases of domestic violence, which traditionally have been very difficult to prosecute. Some blame for this can be attributed to the prevailing police professional culture which is to a large extent uninterested in such crimes, dismissing them in favour of 'real' police work (Reiner 2000). More specifically, however, the difficulty of attaining prosecutions for domestic violence lies in the fact that many of its victims are unwilling to report the matter or provide evidence (Cretney and Davis 1997; Temkin 1999). When such cases are reported, it is still very common for victims to subsequently withdraw their complaints and submit so-called 'retraction statements'.

The reaction of the Crown Prosecution Service to poor conviction rates for domestic violence has been to initiate a policy of driving forward these prosecutions. The full details will be reviewed in Chapter 5 but, essentially, this policy involves treating domestic violence victims as parties with reduced capacity who – unable to make 'rational' decisions as to whether they should support a prosecution and give evidence by reason of their relationship with the defendant – need to be saved from themselves.[9] In principle, this policy will remove any influence the victim might exert over whether or not a case is proceeded with (albeit this influence is generally quite minor to begin with). The consequence is that if a case of domestic violence is brought to court against a victim's wishes, it is open for prosecutors to summon them to attend or – if a summons has failed to secure attendance – to request a warrant. One can see this as a strange reversal: from the victim's perspective there is no story to tell but the system itself demands one. Of course, such a forced narrative would be limited by the factors already discussed while – most likely – any remaining benefits to the victim would be further eroded by the mandatory nature of the exercise.

Victims' narratives in criminal trials: a summary

The limitations placed on victims' capacity to tell their stories through the criminal trial procedure can be broadly summarised by reference to the disparity alluded to earlier between the system's evidential criteria and the account-making requirements (or natural expectations) of the victims themselves. The implications of this are illustrated on a diagram.

Figure 4.1 depicts a horizontal timeline running from point T1 (the point of victimisation) through point T2 (when a victim gives evidence to the police in the form of a statement) and ending at T3 (the trial, when a victim gives evidence in court). As has already been observed, the police usually take a victim's witness statement as soon as possible after the initial incident. Subsequently, however, many victims will face a prolonged wait between stages T2 and T3 while the case is brought to trial. This waiting period (T2–T3) can be anything from a year to 18 months for offences of violence, and possibly even longer in complex cases (Bari 2006).

The question raised by this is whether victims' stories remain static in their own minds during this prolonged waiting period. The use people make of stories to bring order and ascribe meaning to past experiences (especially troubling experiences) has already been discussed. Taking this into account, it seems fairly unlikely that many victims arrive at court at stage T3 prepared to tell exactly the same story they told at stage T2. This is because, in the intervening period, the victim's ongoing attempts to story the experience of victimisation

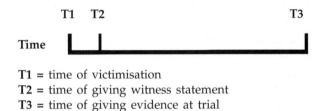

T1 = time of victimisation
T2 = time of giving witness statement
T3 = time of giving evidence at trial

Figure 4.1 Timeline of victims' narratives

will result in extensive thought, reinterpretation and development of that story.

Hence, the narrative that victims are prepared to present when they arrive at court at stage T3 may be quite different from that given at stage T2. Such differences might include new details occurring to the victim in the intervening period, links drawn with other experiences prior to or following stage T1 and variation in the language used to relay these events. In a more general sense, different aspects of the story may – by stage T3 – seem important to the victim and worthy of inclusion, exclusion, or emphasis. It is crucial to appreciate that this is not a case of victims 'carelessly' allowing their minds to slip, but is instead representative of the natural way people deal with these kinds of experiences, Plummer's root to understanding human meaning (1995: 6).

The problem faced by victims at trials, however, is that the process restricts them to the version of the story given in their witness statements at point T2, because this is the version the lawyers are expecting and will be seeking to elicit. The difficulty here may lie in the fact that the system presently has no way of making any version of the story between T2 and T3 available to prosecutors, as the CPS usually only has the T2 statement to work with. This is because later witness statements are generally not taken (as they would be considered unreliable) while stage two victim personal statements are still rare. Hence, what prosecutors are left with is the T2 story that – as noted earlier – is largely constructed by the police. This implies that the accounts victims are allowed to make though the criminal justice are effectively set in stone at the earliest stage of the justice process.

In sum, criminal trials effectively restrict victims to the T2 version of their stories that – in their own minds – might well constitute an outdated narrative. This of course suggests that the accounts victims are permitted to make will have less relevance to them than the more reasoned and considered (T3) version, which is born from a prolonged period of self-reflection, interpretation and developments in understanding (T2–T3). The victims themselves can hardly be blamed for engaging in such activities – given our understanding of the natural ways people use stories – nor can they be criticised for wishing to give what they view as the most up-to-date and relevant narrative. In contrast, the system compels victims to cast their minds back many months to a version of the narrative from which they themselves may now derive little meaning, effectively excluding the fruit of the prolonged period of self-reflection and development.

Fundamentally, therefore, a genuinely victim-centred trial procedure must be capable of incorporating more developments between points T2 and T3, thus allowing victims to tell their full stories and derive therapeutic benefits from so doing. Many questions are raised by this proposition, including how it would operate and whether it would be legitimate to impose any limits on victims' accounts in a victim-centred system. Most importantly, there is a real question as to whether such a system would lead to unfair proceedings and prejudice defendants, this will be addressed in Chapter 7.

Clearly these questions overlap with issues raised in previous chapters, especially the notion of victim rights and the incessant objections of the due process perspective. In Chapter 2 it was argued that the conception of an automatic zero sum game between victim and defendant rights may be flawed but, before moving on to address how the narrative-based model would operate, it is first necessary to substantiate what role (if any) victims' narratives play (or could potentially play) in existing criminal procedures. This will be done in the next two chapters by examining the empirical evidence gathered for this research. We will then be in a position to conclude whether or not accounts could be incorporated into the existing justice model and thus into an overall model of victim-centredness to be presented in the final chapter.

Notes

1 In this case, the dissolution of relationships.
2 That is, the indirect victims of homicide.
3 See below.
4 Although joint CPS, Home Office and Department of Health guidelines indicate that child witnesses should not receive any form of therapy which involves the detailed recounting of experiences prior to giving evidence at trial, as a guard against witness coaching (CPS 2001).
5 Evidence from the present research also supports this view (see Chapter 6).
6 Which were rendered unviable by low take-up rates.
7 Even if they could – as might be possible under the victims' advocate scheme (Home Office 2005b) – the statements themselves would still be subject to the same limitations as the existing VPS.
8 Although, unlike Scotland, the general theory in England and Wales is that a witness's evidence is based on their voluntary attendance at court.
9 See pages 143–146.

Chapter 5

Victims in criminal trials: victims at court

The main empirical results from this study will be split between this chapter and the following chapter, pending a detailed discussion and analysis in Chapter 7. The data are organised in a chronological fashion, following the victim through the trial process. In this chapter we will examine the support and facilities available to victims and other witnesses before the trial, before moving on to the trial itself (especially the evidence-giving process) and then the position of the victims after the trial in Chapter 6.

The Witness Service

The funding for a permanent Witness Service run by Victim Support at all three courts under review had been in place since 1995, making the area among the first in the country to have a Witness Service at all of its magistrates' courts. The Service at all three courts had its own office and prosecution witness waiting rooms, although at the magistrates' courts these were small and not purpose built. All waiting rooms contained seating, a coffee table and magazines. At Court B the waiting room had its own tea-/coffee-making facilities, whereas at Court A Service volunteers would visit the cafeteria three floors below on the witnesses' behalf (with the witnesses' own money).[1] It is ironic that a service often snubbed as offering 'the tea and sympathy routine' (as described by one defence solicitor working at Court B) was in this case unable to provide such services themselves due to a lack of (local) funding.

At Court B, Witness Service volunteers would usually be telephoned by security personnel to collect newly arrived victims and witnesses from the court reception desk. At Court A, it was more usual for the security personnel to escort witnesses directly to the Witness Service room. At Court C, the Witness Service manned their own reception, which would be pointed out by security staff. Security staff were a victim's first point of contact on arrival at all three courts and, as such, had a significant role in conveying information and first impressions of the court.

Court C, the Crown Court centre, had multiple purpose-built witness waiting rooms similar to the suites used by police to interview rape victims and conduct pre-recorded examinations in chief. These rooms contained sofas, televisions, board games, toys and video players for which child witnesses were encouraged to bring videos. The rooms also had desks, power and internet points, a facility one witness told me had been extremely useful to her, having waited in these rooms for many hours on several previous court visits. At Court C, the witness waiting rooms were situated in their own area of the courthouse – with their own toilets – away from the main concourse. This differed from both Courts A and B, where the waiting rooms were adjacent to the main concourse and witnesses were forced to leave this 'safe area' to visit a lavatory shared with all other court users.

Figures published by Victim Support and what was then the Local Magistrates' Court Committee (2004) reveal that the Witness Service at all three courts came into contact with and offered support to a high percentage of victims and prosecution witnesses. Observations recorded outside courtrooms and the surveys distributed at Court B confirmed this. None of the courts had separate areas for defence witnesses and no observations were recorded of support being offered to them, although the Service co-ordinator at Court B said such support would be provided on request. In practice, however, one legal adviser[2] at Court B believed that Witness Service volunteers would be 'horrified' by such a prospect and such requests from the defence were rare. Another legal adviser explained this concentration on prosecution witnesses in terms of their increased vulnerability to intimidation. The argument was that defence witnesses often know and support the defendant, meaning there is less chance of intimidation. Of course, contrary to this, it can be argued that defence witnesses will still need information and facilities even if they are happier to give evidence and less intimidated than the 'average' prosecution witness.

The support offered by the Witness Services at all three courts appeared initially to involve 'settling the witness down' in the witness waiting room and then offering them a tour of the courtroom. Courtroom familiarisation visits were carried out at all three courts prior to the commencement of the day's business, with the Witness Service at Court B seeming especially consistent in offering such visits. The coordinator at Court B noted that they had never had a witness coming for such a visit in advance of the trial date who did not return on the day to give evidence.[3]

Pre-trial familiarisation sessions usually lasted around 10 minutes. Witnesses would have the different parts of the court pointed out and named for them, with particular emphasis on where witnesses would be giving evidence. In the magistrates' court, witnesses would usually be told that they could ask to sit down once their evidence had begun. The usher was almost always present and would assist the volunteer, also taking the opportunity to ask adult witnesses what kind of oath/affirmation they wanted to take. Volunteers would also tell witnesses the order in which they would be asked questions from prosecution, defence and the bench.

Some volunteers went further to offer advice on the evidence-giving process. This would often involve preparing the witness for difficult questions with anecdotes like 'You can only tell them what you know.' On a few occasions, lawyers setting up in the courtroom expressed unease over this, especially when a volunteer's layman translation of the adversarial system did not meet with the strict black-letter reality. Such concerns were expressed by defence solicitors especially:

> I sometimes wonder whether they go outside the bounds of what we would deem to be acceptable in their efforts to reassure. (a defence solicitor appearing at Courts A and B)

Volunteers would typically end a pre-trial visit by answering questions from the witness and their families. The most common question at this point was 'Where's *he* going to be?', referring to the defendant.

Keeping victims and other (prosecution) witnesses apart from defendants and their witnesses before a trial was not always straightforward. On several occasions volunteers would lead victims past defendants on their way to view the court. The general feeling among prosecutors, court staff and Witness Service volunteers was that time spent out of the waiting room was – for a prosecution witness – 'vulnerable' time to be restricted at all costs. Indeed, there was a degree of truth to this, as demonstrated by one solicitor advocate:

> We had five prosecution witnesses from the same family coming into court, and what does the defence lawyer do but bring the defendant in with his witness! And they're all looking at each other; that's not very good for people about to give evidence. (a solicitor advocate appearing at Courts A and B)

Following the courtroom familiarisation visit the Witness Service would send volunteers into the courtroom to get updates on the running (or non-running) of the trial. This information would usually be provided by the legal adviser in the magistrates' court, but sometimes by the lawyers, especially the prosecutor. In the Crown Court, however, barristers tended not to spend as much time in the courtroom before a trial. This often left just the clerk, who was not kept up to date with developments outside the courtroom to the same extent as a magistrates' legal adviser. Moreover, volunteers seemed less comfortable approaching Crown Court clerks directly compared to their magistrates' court equivalents, relying much more on CPS caseworkers to relay information back and forth from the court.

It was much more common for legal advisers in the magistrates' courts to ask prosecutors especially whether witnesses had been given information compared with Crown Court clerks. That said, interviews with clerks suggest they do keep witnesses in mind, especially in the case of vulnerable and intimidated witnesses:

> We're the lines of communication to ensure that the usher in charge of the witness area where that witness is waiting is aware of what's going off, so that they can let the witness know. The CPS clerk in court will be aware of the situation … and the overall responsibility for the [prosecution] witnesses lies with them. (a court clerk at Court C)

Notably, this response excludes the Witness Service entirely, while emphasising the role of CPS 'clerks', by which the respondent means CPS caseworkers.

Even in the magistrates' courts, there was little consistency between individual legal advisers, some of whom would periodically telephone the Witness Service room with updated information while others did relatively little. Generally, however, the flow of communication between the Witness Service and courtroom staff seemed smoother at Court B compared with Courts A or C.

The success of Witness Service volunteers in acquiring information for witnesses at all three courts often seemed determined by how pushy they could be. A minority of lawyers expressed frustration at being 'badgered' by the volunteers:

> I think the Witness Service has probably got a bad reputation, a reputation for being busybodies. (a legal adviser at Court B)

Nevertheless, most court staff and legal practitioners at all three courts said that the Witness Service had been accepted as a normal and integral part of the court process, and did fine work:

> They [witnesses] would relate better to members of the Witness Service than they would to me or many of my colleagues, however friendly we are ... it does form a link in many ways between the lay person and the court system. (a barrister appearing at Courts A, B and C)

> As a prosecutor you very rarely have time to see everybody [witnesses] to the full degree you would wish, especially when they turn up late ... I can't see that the Crown could operate efficiently without it [the Witness Service]. (a solicitor advocate appearing at Courts A and B)

This second extract is interesting, as it suggests a degree of unity between the Witness Service and the prosecution. In addition, it is clear that the presence of the Witness Service concentrated the minds of magistrates' court legal advisers on witness issues. Elements of dissent did however persist in the minds of several respondents. The view was expressed several times that volunteers gave witnesses a biased view of the trial process:

> I am occasionally concerned – when I'm in court and they're showing people around – at the sort of things they say to the witnesses ... talking as if the defendant is clearly guilty. (a legal adviser at Court B)

One barrister thought the Witness Service played an important role, but was concerned by a lack of consistency between Services at different courts:

> [T]he Witness Service in one court system are far better than the Witness Service in another ... one specific court has a Witness Service who are absolutely fantastic ... who will phone around to trace missing witnesses, who have always phoned the day before or a few days before to just double check that they are still coming ... who are thoroughly pleasant and helpful and give tours of the courtroom. Now they all try and do that, my experience is that they don't all achieve it. (a barrister appearing at Courts A, B and C)

Notably, this barrister focuses on the role of the Witness Service in helping get witnesses to court. This has been a developing role for the Service at all three courts, especially following the introduction of case progression officers (CPOs) to flag up witness (and other) problems in advance of a trial (Home Office 2004d). At Court C, the CPO would hold a meeting with the Service, the CPS, and the police trial unit to discuss the readiness of upcoming cases. The implications of this may be that the Witness Service is becoming an instrument of promoting system efficiency, as discussed in Chapter 3.

Prosecutors and victims

The clearest disparity in witness treatment between the two magistrates' courts and the Crown Court was in the degree of direct contact victims and witnesses had with prosecutors. Most prosecutors at the magistrates' court would go and meet victims and other prosecution witnesses early on, before the trial began (or was adjourned or resolved in some other way). The CPS confirmed this as their policy:

> At the magistrates' court, our solicitors and our lawyers and agents – I would hope – would always try to introduce themselves to the victims and witnesses. (the Chief Crown Prosecutor)

Many barristers and CPS prosecutors saw this as an integral aspect of their role:

> My role as an advocate for the Crown is to at least attempt to put them [witnesses] at their ease. (a solicitor advocate appearing at Courts A and B)

Hence, most prosecutors in the magistrates' courts would introduce themselves, and offer such reassurance and as much explanation as they felt able, as well as a copy of the witnesses' statement. Seeing copies of their statements before giving evidence seemed an important concern for many witnesses, and Witness Service volunteers would often appear promptly to request them from the prosecutor if they were not provided.

Barristers in the Crown Court relied to a far greater extent on CPS caseworkers to pass information to and from witnesses. It was nonetheless clear that this was a limitation of current occupational cultures among barristers rather than a direction of policy by either the Bar Council or the CPS:

> I know for a fact that [barristers in the Crown Court are] encouraged to have rather more contact with witnesses than they normally do. (a barrister appearing at Courts A, B and C)

> We require barristers to go and introduce themselves to victims and witnesses and the professional standards document reflects that that is what they should do. (the Chief Crown Prosecutor)

Despite this, a number of advocates remarked that it was often difficult to fit in a discussion with victims and witnesses, especially when dealing with a number of cases at once in the magistrates' court. Furthermore, there were definite culturally imposed limits placed on these exchanges, many prosecutors feeling obliged to ask the defence lawyer for permission before straying too far beyond the standard greeting and explanations. One younger barrister admitted that he would prefer that witness care was not part of his job:

> I'm still not entirely sure of what [witness care] means because you've got to be careful – you've got to maintain a level of – well – I don't believe that you should be too 'pally' with the witnesses, I don't believe that they should be encouraged to refer to you as being on 'their side'. (a barrister appearing at Courts A, B and C)

Nevertheless, prosecutors in general seemed far more willing to converse with their witnesses in the magistrates' court than is suggested by previous studies, and most prosecution witnesses giving evidence at Courts A and B had clearly met the prosecutor before. In the Crown Court there was more evidence of the traditional barriers between witnesses and barristers. While prosecution barristers were going to meet witnesses, they would usually do so quite late on, just before a trial was about to start (or not). It was also clear from watching the evidence of prosecution witnesses that some of them had not met the prosecution barrister directly before coming into court. When questioned on this issue, one barrister maintained that highly experienced Crown Court counsels did not need to speak to witnesses beforehand in order to 'build up a rapport', but could do so very quickly during the evidential process itself. This seems to betray a view that witness contact before a trial is intended to assist counsel.

As already noted, an important element of Crown Court witness care was the activities of CPS liaison officers, which have received almost no attention in existing literature. At Court C, the liaisons played a vital role as the prosecuting barrister's link with the CPS, and were often the ones going back and forth keeping witnesses informed and relaying information back to the prosecuting barrister. This appears to be a new role for the CPS, perhaps mirroring the apparent decline in the role of police officers, who previously were often on hand at court to perform such roles (Shapland *et al.* 1985). That said, representatives of the CPS maintained that Crown Court caseworkers had always carried out such duties.

Wider facilities and information at court

All three courts had a clearly marked reception desk and, at Court C, the Witness Service manned an additional reception. All three courts also had signposting, case listings near the entrance, a public announcement system to call witnesses and lawyers to court and a cafe. There were also numerous informative booklets and leaflets on hand at all three courts. Court C had abundant seating and Court A also had high-quality seating outside most courts.[4] Court B struggled to some extent in this regard, having only limited plastic seating outside the courtrooms and in the cafe.

The first and second waves of the court users survey distributed for this project at Court B indicate that (prosecution) witnesses were generally satisfied with the Witness Service. All respondents who answered or partially answered the relevant questions thought the Service was a good or satisfactory source of information, and 21 per cent indicated it was the most useful source of information.[5] Security staff and court ushers were also rated 'good' sources of information by over half the respondents. Conversely, Table 5.1 suggests that respondents did not make much use of leaflets, the court PA system or case listings.

Survey respondents were also asked whether they had received the *Witness in Court* booklet (Home Office 2003g). Out of the 46 who answered the question and said they had attended to give evidence (for prosecution or defence), 19 (41 per cent) said they had received the book before coming to court, 20 (43 per cent) said they had not received the book, six (13 per cent) said they could not remember and one (2 per cent) said he had received the book but had not had the chance to read it. Overall, the results indicate that prosecution witnesses and victims are more likely to receive the *Witness in Court* booklet before coming to court than those on the defence side, probably because the police will hand out the booklets directly to prosecution witnesses and victims. These figures are considerably lower than those from the 2000 Witness Satisfaction Survey, where 74 per cent of witnesses recalled receiving information through the *Witness in Court* booklet or some other leaflet (Whitehead 2001). The 2002/03 British Crime Survey confirms that receiving information about the criminal justice system in the form of a booklet can increase victims' confidence in that system, albeit here 20 per cent of respondents said they had not had time to read it (Salisbury 2004).

Table 5.2 details results from the first and second waves of the survey concerning users' views of court facilities. The majority of respondents (n=57) considered the facilities either 'good' or 'satisfactory'.

Respondents were also asked to assess their overall satisfaction with court facilities and the provision of information to them prior to the trial, and on the day (see Table 5.3).

Most respondents were satisfied with the provision of information and court facilities, although the 48 per cent of respondents who were only 'quite satisfied' with facilities at court suggests room for improvement.

Waiting at court

This section will examine issues relating to the efficiency of the courts and legal professionals in getting trials up and running, and how this impacted upon victims.

Table 5.1 Court users' rating of different sources of information at Court B*

	Rating							
	0 No answer	1 Good	2 Satis-factory	3 Unsatis-factory	4 Poor	5 Didn't use	Most useful	Least useful
Reception	1 (2%)	32 (56%)	15 (26%)	0 (0%)	0 (0%)	9 (16%)	3 (5%)	1 (2%)
Witness Service	7 (12%)	32 (56%)	6 (11%)	0 (0%)	0 (0%)	12 (21%)	12 (21%)	0 (0%
Signs	7 (12%)	24 (42%)	23 (40%)	0 (0%)	0 (0%)	3 (5%)	1 (2%)	0 (0%)
Courtroom plans	9 (16%)	23 (40%)	14 (25%)	1 (2%)	0 (0%)	10 (18%)	0 (0%)	3 (5%)
Security	3 (5%)	30 (53%)	20 (35%)	1 (2%)	0 (0%)	3 (5%)	0 (0%)	0 (0%)
Leaflets from court on day	10 (18%)	6 (11%)	8 (14%)	0 (0%)	2 (4%)	31 (54%)	0 (0%)	30 (5%)
Leaflets received before day	11 (19%)	12 (21%)	11 (19%)	1 (2%)	2 (4%)	20 (35%)	0 (0%)	0 (0%)
Public announcement system	12 (21%)	8 (14%)	15 (26%)	0 (0%)	0 (0%)	22 (39%)	0 (0%)	3 (5%)
Case listings	6 (11%)	25 (44%)	15 (26%)	0 (0%)	0 (0%)	11 (19%)	1 (2%)	1 (2%)
Usher	11 (19%)	29 (51%)	12 (21%)	0 (0%)	0 (0%)	5 (9%)	3 (5%)	0 (0%)
No answer to most or least useful question							37 (64%)	46 (80%)

*Percentages are of respondents answering any part of these questions (n=57).

Table 5.2 Court users' rating of the facilities at Court B*

	Rating					
	0 No answer	1 Good	2 Satis- factory	3 Unsatis- factory	4 Poor	5 Didn't use
Seating	3 (5%)	27 (47%)	24 (42%)	2 (4%)	0 (0%)	1 (2%)
Cafeteria/ refreshments	4 (7%)	20 (35%)	24 (42%)	9 (16%)	0 (0%)	0 (0%)
Witness waiting area	8 (14%)	24 (42%)	20 (35%)	1 (2%)	0 (0%)	4 (7%)
Toilets	2 (4%)	20 (35%)	24 (42%)	3 (5%)	2 (4%)	6 (11%)
Car parking[6]	5 (9%)	8 (14%)	19 (33%)	5 (9%)	6 (11%)	(25%)
Proximity to public transport	9 (16%)	22 (39%)	20 (35%)	1 (2%)	0 (0%)	5 (9%)

*Percentages are of those respondents answering any part of these questions (n=57).

The running of trial proceedings

Table 5.4 breaks down all observed trial proceedings (that is, proceedings originally scheduled to be full trials) into full, adjourned and otherwise resolved trial proceedings. Consistent with previous research, the majority of these cases were resolved in another way or adjourned on the day they were scheduled to run as full trials. More cases were otherwise resolved than run as full trials at all three courts, reflecting national targets which emphasise reducing postponements. The present national target for adjourned trial rates is 19.5 per cent in the magistrates' courts and 16.5 per cent in the Crown Courts (Avon and Somerset Criminal Justice Area 2006). The postponement rates in Table 5.4 compare to the 20.3 per cent national average in the magistrates' courts, and the 12.3 per cent average at the Crown Courts (Home Office 2006a). Naturally, national figures and targets relate to *all* criminal trial proceedings rather than proceedings selected specifically because civilian victims are involved.

Table 5.3 Overall satisfaction with court facilities, the provision of information before the date of trial and the provision of information at court on the day at Court B

	n*	Extremely satisfied	Very satisfied	Quite satisfied	Quite dissatisfied	Very dissatisfied	Extremely dissatisfied
Facilities at court	58	11 (19%)	17 (29%)	28 (48%)	1 (2%)	0 (0%)	1 (2%)
Information available before the date of trial	49	11 (22%)	17 (35%)	17 (35%)	3 (6%)	0 (0%)	1 (2%)
Information available at court on the date of trial	46	15 (32%)	17 (37%)	13 (28%)	0 (0%)	0 (0%)	1 (2%)

*Number of survey respondents answering the relevant question.

Table 5.4 Full, adjourned and otherwise resolved trial proceedings

	Number of trial proceedings	% of this/these courts' trial proceedings
Court A		
Full trials	50	45
Adjourned trials	26	23
Otherwise resolved trials	36	32
Total trials	112	100
Court B		
Full trials	50	43
Adjourned trials	27	23
Otherwise resolved trials	39	34
Total trials	116	100
Court C		
Full trials	12	63
Adjourned trials	2	11
Otherwise resolved trials	5	26
Total trials	19	100
Magistrates' courts (A and B)		
Full trials	100	44
Adjourned trials	53	23
Otherwise resolved trials	75	33
Total trials	228	100
All courts (A, B and C)		
Full trials	112	45 *
Adjourned trials	55	22 *
Otherwise resolved trials	80	32 *
Total trials	247	100

*Figures do not add up to 100 per cent due to rounding.

The vast majority of trial proceedings began later than scheduled.[7] Long delays were especially common in the Crown Court centre, where the average trial proceeding began over five hours late, compared to around one hour late at both magistrates' courts. Generally the longer delays in the Crown Court may be explained by the increased complexity of cases and the presence of more witnesses and evidence. Culturally, the observation sessions also revealed a reduced sense of urgency among professionals in the Crown Court to resolve or begin trial proceedings compared with the lower courts.[8] The Crown Court

Table 5.5 Number of full, adjourned and otherwise resolved trial proceedings starting late

	Total number of trial proceedings*	Number late	% late	Number more than 30 minutes late	% more than 30 minutes late	Number more than 60 minutes late	% more than 60 minutes late	Number more than 120 minutes late	% more than 120 minutes late
Court A	111	110	99	70	63	37	33	7	6
Court B	113	112	99	60	53	24	21	8	7
Court C	18	18	100	17	94	17	94	12	67
Magistrates' courts (A and B)	224	222	99	130	58	61	27	15	7
All courts (A, B and C)	242	240	99	147	61	78	32	27	11

*Excludes 5 cases where start time was unknown

Table 5.6 Lateness averages*

	Average lateness (HH:MM)	95% Confidence intervals (HH:MM)		
		Lower bound	Upper bound	Range
Court A	00:54	00:45	01:03	00:18
Court B	00:43	00:36	00:49	00:13
Court C	05:08	01:27	08:50	07:23
Magistrates' courts (A and B)	00:48	00:43	00:54	00:11
All courts (A, B and C)	01:08*	00:50	01:26	00:36

*Excludes 5 cases where start time was unknown

also seemed more capable of varying listing schedules and resource allocations at the last minute compared with the lower courts.

Late-running trial proceedings

A total of 62 reasons were recorded to explain why different proceedings began late. These have been grouped into 12 categories on Table 5.7.

Listings issues and witness problems were most commonly responsible for delaying the start of proceedings at the magistrates' courts. Time taken for lawyers to reach agreements (or not) was also a common delay at all three courts. Legal arguments delayed proceedings in over half the observed Crown Court cases, whereas magistrates' court proceedings usually raised few legal issues.

Table 5.8 breaks these four categories down into their component reasons for lateness. Here, 'resolving listings issues' usually meant deciding which of two cases listed in the same courtroom at the same time should take precedence. These results – taken alongside the cases where another trial had to be dealt with first – reveal the extent of the delays caused by the system of 'double-listing' at all three courts.

Double-listing occurs when more than one trial is scheduled to take place at the same time in the same court, based on the assumption that one or more will not proceed. Many advocates remarked that the

Table 5.7 Categories of reasons why proceedings started late and percentage of trial proceedings starting late for each category of reason at Courts A, B and C*

	% of Court A trial proceedings	% of Court B trial proceedings	% of Court C trial proceedings	% of Court A and B trial proceedings	% of all trial proceedings (Courts A, B and C)
Listings issues	48	44	21	46	44
Witness problems (witness reluctance etc.)	54	38	11	47	39
Agreements and deals (plea bargains,[9] bind overs[10] etc.)	28	28	32	28	28
Evidential issues	21	13	26	17	17
Defendant problems	16	15	11	15	15
Legal arguments	8	9	53	8	12
Equipment problems and logistics	11	9	0	10	9
Administrative errors and delays	7	7	0	7	6
Lawyer problems (availability etc.)	6	2	0	4	4
JP/judge problems (availability etc.)	2	5	11	4	4
Errors made by lawyers	2	1	5	1	2
Other	6	15	11	11	11

*More than one reason for lateness allowed for each trial

double-listing system confused issues at the beginning of the court day, leading to mistakes being made. Nevertheless, observations suggested it was practically impossible for a busy magistrates' court to operate without double-listing. Interviews with practitioners confirmed that the system was in place at most magistrates' and Crown Courts, with some courts scheduling five or six cases in one courtroom. In Court A, listings officers actually abandoned the system for several weeks during the observation sessions. It was subsequently reinstalled when it became clear that the court's facilities were insufficient to deal with its caseload.

Table 5.8 also reveals the time taken in a significant number of magistrates' court cases to persuade, chase up, or convince absent/ reluctant witnesses to give evidence.[11] Such problems often only came to light on the day of the trial. It will be seen below that the widespread opinion among lawyers and court staff was that one simply cannot know in advance whether a witness will arrive to give evidence. That said, in many cases the lawyers immediately knew from a note on the case file that a witness was reluctant. Prosecutors seemed especially prepared for witness reluctance and other problems prior to domestic violence trials, which are discussed at the end of this chapter.

In the Crown Court, last-minute witness reluctance was less of a problem. Possibly this is because fewer Crown Court cases are dismissed as unimportant by witnesses or because more time is spent beforehand ensuring witnesses will attend, especially with the advent of case progression officers, discussed below. Witnesses in the Crown Court may also become more concerned about the consequences of refusing to give evidence, as in one chance observation of a CPS caseworker talking to a reluctant witness outside court in which the caseworker heavily implied that the judge could send the witness to prison if she refused to give evidence.

Non-running trial proceedings

It was also possible to collect 31 reasons why listed trials were adjourned or resolved in other ways, these are grouped into categories on Table 5.9.

The two prevailing categories of reasons why trials failed to proceed were agreements/deals and witness problems. These categories have been broken down into their component reasons on Table 5.10.

These results tell a similar story to those on trial lateness, indicating that many trials failed to proceed at all three courts due to

Table 5.8 Breakdown of the main categories of reasons why proceedings started late and percentage of trial proceedings starting late for each reason at Courts A, B and C*

	% of Court A trial proceedings	% of Court B trial proceedings	% of Court C trial proceedings	% of Court A and B trial proceedings	% of all trial proceedings (Courts A, B and C)
Listings issues	**48**	**44**	**21**	**46**	**44**
Another case dealt with first	24	22	16	23	23
Resolving listings issues	24	22	5	23	21
Witness problems	**54**	**38**	**11**	**41**	**39**
Trying to get a civilian witness to court and/or persuading to give evidence, or debating what to do about absence (summons, warrant etc.)	38	30	11	34	28
Trying to get a police witness to court	1	3	0	2	2
Prosecution advocate needed to speak to prosecution witnesses	13	4	0	9	8
Waiting for prosecution witness to finish breast-feeding baby	1	0	0	<1	<1
A witness has childcare issues	1	0	0	<1	<1

Table 5.8 continues overleaf

Table 5.8 continued

	% of Court A trial proceedings	% of Court B trial proceedings	% of Court C trial proceedings	% of Court A and B trial proceedings	% of all trial proceedings (Courts A, B and C)
Agreements and deals	**28**	**28**	**32**	**28**	**28**
Discussions about bind over	6	9	0	7	6
Negotiations on plea bargain	15	17	21	16	17
Defence advocate trying to convince defendant to plead guilty (with no bargain)	4	2	11	3	4
Trying to agree on facts in a Newton hearing	1	1	0	1	1
Coming to a deal that is not a plea bargain involving other civil proceedings	1	0	0	<1	<1
Legal arguments	**8**	**9**	**53**	**8**	**12**
General legal argument	5	4	21	5	6
Legal adviser wanted to check authorities	0	1	0	<1	<1
Late special measures application	1	0	11	<1	1
Debate about need for special measures or additional special measures	0	1	0	<1	<1

Bad character application under the Criminal Justice Act 2003	0	2	16	1	2
Debate over bad character application under the Criminal Justice Act 2003	2	1	5	1	2

*More than one reason for lateness allowed for each trial

Table 5.9 Categories of reasons why proceedings were adjourned or resolved in another way and percentage of trials adjourned/otherwise resolved for each category of reason at Courts A, B and C*

	% of Court A trials	% of Court B trials	% of Court C trials	% of Court A and B trials	% of all trials (Courts A, B and C)
Agreements/deals	**23**	**31**	**26**	**27**	**27**
Witness problems	21	17	0	19	17
Evidential issues	7	3	5	5	5
Listings issues	1	5	0	3	3
Practical and administrative problems	**2**	**2**	**5**	**2**	**2**
Illness/death	4	1	0	3	2
Professional embarrassment	2	3	0	2	2
Defendant problems	1	2	0	1	1
Magistrate/judge problems	1	2	0	1	1

*More than one reason for failure to run allowed for each trial

last-minute plea bargaining, or because of witness reluctance (at least at the magistrates' courts).

Effective trial management

The Effective Trial Management Programme (ETMP) was introduced into Courts A, B and C in 2003 as part of the Criminal Case Management Framework[12] with the goal of increasing court efficiency. A key feature of the ETMP is the appointment of Case Progression Officers (CPOs). Their purpose is to stay in contact with the CPS, police, solicitors, Witness Service and other relevant agencies to identify issues and problems *before* the trial date. Such issues – including bad character,[13] special measures[14] applications, witness availability[15] or reluctance – would be recorded on certificates of readiness presented to the court at case progression hearings. As such, every court, CPS branch, police area and solicitors firm should have a named CPO.

The case progression officer at Court C would usually start working on a trial about two weeks before its scheduled start date because,

Table 5.10 Breakdown of main categories of reasons why proceedings were adjourned or resolved in another way and percentage of trials adjourned/otherwise resolved for each reason at Courts A, B and C*

	% of Court A trials	% of Court B trials	% of Court C trials	% of Court A and B trials	% of all trials (Courts A, B and C)
Agreements/deals	**23**	**31**	**26**	**27**	**27**
Bind over	3	9	0	6	5
Guilty plea following plea bargain	12	15	16	13	13
Guilty plea (without plea bargain)	8	7	11	7	8
Facts agreed on day in Newton hearing	0	1	0	<1	<1
Case dropped following deal that is not a plea bargain but involves dropping civil charges	1	0	0	<1	<1
Witness problems	**21**	**17**	**0**	**19**	**17**
Witness does not come due to reluctance, or arrives but does not want to give evidence	17	16	0	16	15
Police witness not present	1	1	0	1	1
Witness arrives at pre-planned time but could not come back when the trial is adjourned for later in the day	2	0	0	1	1
Witness not here, unknown reason	1	1	0	1	1

*More than one reason for failure to run allowed for each trial

in her words, she knew solicitors would not begin 'sorting it out' before then. The CPO would then telephone all the relevant agencies and solicitors to enquire whether they were ready for trial. Unlike at magistrates' Courts A and B, agencies were not sent the certificates of readiness to complete themselves, but rather these were filled in by the CPO personally, based on telephone discussions. The rationale here – which came from the presiding judge at Court C – was that a verbal-based system would ensure solicitors applied their mind to the issues and did not simply 'tick a box'. The CPO also held a weekly meeting with representatives of the police, CPS and the Witness Service to discuss upcoming cases and any problems arising the previous week.

Generally, the ETMP was received with cautious optimism. Nevertheless, many solicitors dismissed it as fruitless bureaucracy. One solicitor considered the system a 'joke' because, from his perspective, completing the forms made little difference to benches:

> I say I've got no instructions, the district judge says, 'Well, we'll just have to see what happens on the day, it'll go ahead' … what is the sanction to it? (a defence solicitor appearing at Courts A and B)

This issue of sanctions was raised a number of times during interviews. Many believed that magistrates' court benches (including district judges) were not strict with the administration of case progression hearings:

> The pre-trial review process, I think, is the real problem we have in the magistrates; I don't think enough people have enough information about the files on the day … the pre-trial review should be conducted far more harshly. (a barrister appearing at Courts A, B and C)

The impression of this barrister was that issues like the number of witnesses and the scope for plea-bargaining were not sufficiently finalised at these hearings due to lack of information on all sides. The criticism was that magistrates and district judges are prepared to let such matters pass, to be resolved on the day of the trial. The same respondent contrasted this position to that of the Crown Court equivalent, which he considered far more robust. Some interviewees felt that the inadequacies of the ETMP system were down to a lack of organisation or resources in various organisations. The need for proactiveness was another common theme in discussions on the ETMP, leading some to admit that a blame culture had arisen between the different justice agencies, witnesses and practitioners.

The 'inevitability' of adjournments and otherwise resolved trial proceedings?

Underlying much of what staff, administrators and legal practitioners said about the ETMP was the widespread view that, ultimately, it was *impossible* to eliminate many of the problems causing last-minute delays and adjournments:

> It is part of the trial process that trials don't go ahead on the day ... it is an unavoidable part. (a barrister appearing at Courts A, B and C)

Much of the blame here was placed with the unpredictability of witnesses. Many interviewees also commented on the general unreliability of defendants, who did not keep appointments and often would not express any opinion on their case before the day of the trial. As one solicitor noted:

> [T]o be able to batter the criminal mind with common sense takes a little bit of time. (a solicitor appearing at Court B)

This solicitor also confirmed that defendants often base their decisions on pleading guilty or not on whether or not witnesses turn up on the day of the trial.

Witness waiting times

Tables 5.11 to 5.14 indicate the percentage of magistrates' court trial proceedings which started late with witnesses waiting at court to give evidence at the listed start time. Table 5.11 shows that civilian witnesses were kept waiting in the majority of cases at both magistrates' courts, with Court B fairing slightly better in terms of civilian victims and non-victims. Tables 5.12 and 5.13 indicate that a markedly smaller percentage of proceedings at Court B involved keeping any witness waiting for longer than 30 or 60 minutes compared with Court A.

Nationally, the Victim's Code of Practice guarantees that victims should wait no more than two hours before evidence at magistrates' or Crown Courts. This standard was largely met at Courts A and B.

It was clear that lawyers running trials at all three courts preferred having witnesses physically present in court buildings before any decisions were made. Most disliked the idea of introducing staggered calling times; hence all witnesses were called to attend court just before the theoretical start time of the trial:

> You could be very brave and timetable the witnesses, but I'm afraid witnesses are often as disorganised as defendants ... they're in that sort of pool where trouble happens. (the Clerk to the Justices at Court B)

Table 5.11 Trial proceedings starting late in which witnesses were on time and waiting

	Total Number of proceedings*	Civilian victims	Civilian non-victims (excluding defendants, including experts)	Any civilian (excluding defendants)	Police
Court A	111	72 (65%)	59 (53%)	86 (77%)	57 (51%)
Court B	113	66 (58%)	68 (60%)	87 (77%)	56 (50%)
Magistrates' courts (A and B)	224	138 (62%)	126 (56%)	173 (77%)	113 (50%)

*Excludes 4 cases where start time was unknown

Table 5.12 Trial proceedings starting over 30 minutes late in which witnesses were on time and waiting

	Total Number of proceedings*	Civilian victims	Civilian non-victims (excluding defendants, including experts)	Any civilian (excluding defendants)	Police
Court A	111	51 (46%)	42 (38%)	61 (55%)	41 (37%)
Court B	113	36 (32%)	32 (28%)	45 (40%)	37 (33%)
Magistrates' courts (A and B)	224	87 (39%)	74 (33%)	105 (47%)	78 (35%)

*Excludes 4 cases where start time was unknown

Table 5.13 Trial proceedings starting over 60 minutes late in which witnesses were on time and waiting

	Total Number of proceedings*	Civilian victims	Civilian non-victims (excluding defendants, including experts)	Any civilian (excluding defendants)	Police
Court A	111	29 (26%)	24 (22%)	34 (31%)	25 (23%)
Court B	113	13 (12%)	16 (14%)	19 (17%)	12 (11%)
Magistrates' courts (A and B)	224	42 (19%)	40 (18%)	53 (24%)	37 (17%)

*Excludes 4 cases where start time was unknown

Table 5.14 Trial proceedings starting over 120 minutes late in which witnesses were on time and waiting

	Total Number of proceedings*	Civilian victims	Civilian non-victims (excluding defendants, including experts)	Any civilian (excluding defendants)	Police
Court A	111	4 (4%)	4 (4%)	6 (5%)	3 (3%)
Court B	113	3 (3%)	3 (3%)	4 (4%)	4 (4%)
Magistrates' courts (A and B)	224	7 (3%)	7 (3%)	10 (4%)	7 (3%)

*Excludes 4 cases where start time was unknown

This alludes to the fact that many victims of crime have also faced criminal charges themselves (and vice versa) and hence were not considered reliable. Several lawyers added that one could never be sure in advance whether a trial was going to run at all, or of the order in which witnesses would need to be called. Many lawyers also emphasised the difficulties of estimating how long a witness would take, most seemed to be working on a presumption of around 20 minutes per witness, a rather conservative estimate according to the observation results (see Chapter 6).

While staggered calling was generally frowned upon, it was clearly accepted practice in the Crown Court not to call witnesses to the first day of a trial (as listed) if it was known that the trial proper would not begin that day, or if it was known – to a high degree of certainty – that a witness would not be reached that day. Thus, staggered calling was used to a limited degree. In court C, police witnesses could be given pagers to allow them to leave the court building till they were needed. At the magistrates' court, the reason for not embracing this system for use with civilian witnesses was clear:

> In some courts they're given pagers. We've stayed clear of that because some of the victims are offenders themselves. (the Clerk to the Justices at Court A)

The implication here is obviously that many victims were judged to be criminals and therefore liable to steal court equipment. This clearly raises questions concerning the treatment of non-ideal victims and whether some victims are more equal than others in this new victim-centred system.

It has been noted that court staff would generally have witness waiting times in mind at the beginning of the day, if only because national targets required that these be reduced. In the magistrates' courts, the district judges were clear that witness waiting times had become an issue of concern for the bench:

> I'm much more inclined now to say, 'Are all the witnesses here?' and perhaps ask one or two preliminary questions about that, particularly if there's been a delay of an hour or two. (a district judge sitting at Court A)

There were many examples in the magistrates' courts of benches enquiring about witnesses and asking whether they were being kept informed. In one case at the Crown Court, on being asked for more time to resolve a legal point, the judge remarked:

> Yes, but I'm just thinking about the poor old victim. (a circuit judge sitting at Court C)

Bringing the witnesses into court to offer first-hand explanations from the bench was less common. There was often a conflict here between new ideas of victim involvement displayed by a magistrates' bench and more traditional attitudes on the part of some prosecutors. In several cases magistrates were talked down by lawyers from directly addressing witnesses, implying that the working practices of the lay bench are more developed along the lines of witness care than some of the professionals before them.[16] In the Crown Court, judges were generally less inclined to enquire about the position of witnesses waiting outside, although it was occasionally mentioned.

Domestic violence: 'one on its own'?

Over a third (34 per cent) of magistrates' court trials which were late in starting partly or wholly due to witness reluctance involved domestic violence. The challenge faced by prosecutors pursuing domestic violence charges is that complainants often retract their police statements and become unwilling to give evidence at a late stage, leading to collapsed cases (Cretney and Davis 1997). As such, many lawyers considered domestic violence trials singularly problematic. As one barrister put it:

> Domestic violence is one on its own, I'm afraid, there is no set pattern to that. (a barrister appearing at Courts A, B and C)

The CPS has recently initiated a policy to bring more of these cases to justice. This is a national policy which has received some publicity (CPS 2005b), albeit very little detailed information has been forthcoming regarding its implications. Perhaps for this reason, prosecutors and other practitioners were somewhat confused by the policy.

The policy has two elements. Initially, the aim is to ensure the police collect as much evidence as possible in order to build cases which are not entirely dependent on the complainant's evidence (see Association of Chief Police Officers 2008). The role of the CPS when reviewing the case file is to ensure every possible avenue of investigation has been exhausted.

Confusion, however, existed among lawyers regarding the second aspect of the policy, concerning the public interest criterion. The Chief Crown Prosecutor explained this aspect of the policy in the following terms:

> So the policy recognises it is not as simple as a woman saying, 'I don't want to give evidence, I've forgiven him' … It's often not as simple as that; there will be all sorts of drivers, which might be financial – 'Where am I going to live if I leave?' – a lack of confidence that victims of domestic violence can often have; a very, very low self-esteem. So that actually that individual might not be capable of making any major decisions about their life because they're just totally undermined, feel pretty useless and downtrodden. (the Chief Crown Prosecutor)

One interpretation of this is that domestic violence victims are being treated as parties with reduced capacity, somewhat akin to children or the mentally ill. The Chief Prosecutor indicated some agreement with this proposition and many lawyers were clear in their view that such victims must be 'protected from themselves' (a barrister appearing at Courts A, B and C). Some lawyers took a slightly less sympathetic, more politicised view of the policy, pointing out that the CPS was concerned about the public backlash if domestic violence victims came to harm or were killed following cases against their abusers being dropped.

Examples of lawyers' confusion on the CPS policy were common. One solicitor went so far as to suggest that the policy rendered the public interest test redundant. Even a district judge described the policy as follows:

> [The CPS] have guidelines as to how they approach domestic violence cases, and the general thrust of it is 'prosecute every case'. (a district judge sitting at Court A)

Domestic violence trials were still considered a very problematic issue at the courts under review. In many cases the Crown were indeed seeking to rely on the evidence of one reluctant complainant. When such witnesses did attend court, it was common for them to arrive in the company of the defendant, sometimes holding hands. These points would be raised at the case progression hearing, although again such issues were often considered inherently unpredictable. The Local Criminal Justice Board had resisted piloting new specialist domestic violence courts to deal with these pre-trial hearings (cjsonline 2005b) on the grounds that it was thought that effective processes were already in place, and that the term 'specialist courts' had a tone of prosecution bias.

On the morning of a domestic violence trial most prosecutors seemed prepared for difficulties in most cases. There was often a clear note on the file[17] that the complainant was reluctant to speak and/or a copy of her retraction statement. Many prosecutors showed reluctance to implement the letter of the CPS policy, often claiming there was 'no point' given the witness's reluctance and the reconciliation of the parties. This was especially common among agent barristers or solicitor advocates working on behalf of the CPS. Indeed some agent prosecutors believed they were purposely given the more 'difficult' cases to deal with; 'difficult' not in the sense of the legal and factual issues to be adduced, but in the sense of needing to deal with a generally 'messy' and emotionally charged situation which they considered different from their more regular work.

The Chief Crown Prosecutor made it clear that the 'proper' course of action under the policy would be to compel the witness to attend court through a witness summons and, if that failed, to obtain a warrant and have the complainant brought to court. It was fairly common in these cases for victims to have a witness summons served upon them before the date of the trial. Nevertheless, while prosecutors often *spoke* about the possibility of taking further steps (a warrant), in practice they would usually redouble their efforts to negotiate an alternative solution with the defence, which was usually achieved. A number of lawyers admitted that the only purpose of discussing a witness warrant was to compel the defendant to plead guilty or accept a lesser charge.

Throughout the observations, no domestic violence complainants were compelled to give evidence, save by the prosecutor's powers of persuasion. Nevertheless, a more forceful approach was sometimes taken:

> I've had domestic violence cases where the witness has been summoned ... I've had to make her a hostile witness so I can actually lead her on her statement to get the evidence in ... it doesn't give very much credibility in a case. (a solicitor advocate appearing at Courts A and B)

The Chief Crown Prosecutor was also clear that witness warrants had been used in many such cases, although she was prepared to admit a more practical reality:

> There's a limit to how far you can push … when you get to court – you've taken out your witness summons – if people are still absolutely adamant they're not going to give evidence, in a number of cases we have to leave it, we have to accept that and drop the case. (the Chief Crown Prosecutor)

It was expected that data from this study would reflect the complex issues that come with prosecuting domestic violence, and the clear perceptions among practitioners that these are problematic cases. In fact, however, this was not the situation, as is demonstrated by comparing the number of full running trials, adjourned and otherwise resolved cases observed in this research with the equivalent categories of domestic violence cases as a distinct group on Table 5.15.

The interesting result here is the similarity between the overall full, adjourned and otherwise resolved trial rates at Courts A and B[19] and those specifically of domestic violence trials. Another interesting result is derived from comparing the average lateness figures for all trials with those of domestic violence trials, shown on Table 5.16.

Given the problems described above, it might be expected that domestic violence trials would run (or not run) later than trials in general. Clearly, though, this was not markedly the case, albeit the confidence intervals for the smaller number of domestic violence trials are wider.

Surprisingly, these findings indicate that domestic violence proceedings do not run significantly differently from other trials. One explanation might be that cases of domestic violence[20] concentrate the minds of lawyers such that negotiations are carried out more efficiently at the pre-trial stage compared with other types of case. As such, impressions like those given above of domestic violence as a particularly difficult kind of trial to run may be based on a minority of unusual cases that stick in the minds of practitioners.

Victims at court

The above discussion has highlighted the key issues encountered at the three courts under review relating to the practical running of trials involving civilian victims. It is clear that recent reforms have

Table 5.15 Full, adjourned and otherwise resolved trial proceedings/ domestic violence (DV) trial proceedings

	Number of trial proceedings/ DV trial proceedings[18]	% of courts' trial proceedings/ DV trial proceedings
Court A		
Full trials/DV trials	50/12	45/48
Adjourned trials/DV trials	26/6	23/24
Otherwise resolved trials/DV trials	36/7	32/28
Total trials/DV trials	112/25	100/100
Court B		
Full trials/DV trials	50/7	43/30*
Adjourned trials/DV trials	27/4	23/17*
Otherwise resolved trials/DV trials	39/12	34/52*
Total trials/DV trials	116/23	100/100
Court C		
Full trials/DV trials	12/4	63/80
Adjourned trials/DV trials	2/0	11/0
Otherwise resolved trials/DV trials	5/1	26/20
Total trials/DV trials	19/5	100/100
Courts A and B (magistrates')		
Full trials/DV trials	100/19	44/40*
Adjourned trials/DV trials	53/10	23/21*
Otherwise resolved trials/DV trials	75/19	33/40*
Total trials/DV trials	228/48	100/100
All courts		
Full trials/DV trials	112/23	45*/43
Adjourned trials/DV trials	55/10	22*/19
Otherwise resolved trials/DV trials	80/20	32*/38
Total trials/DV trials	247/53	100/100

*Figures do not add up to 100 per cent due to rounding

achieved a degree of operational impact on matters such as victim and witness care, reduced waiting times, information provision and support. Nevertheless, the practical reality of a busy court with limited resources inevitably complicates the ideal model of victim care espoused in policy documents. Hence, courts have had difficulty achieving the levels of efficiency envisioned by new case management

Table 5.16 Lateness averages for all trial proceedings/ domestic violence trial proceedings*

	Average lateness (HH:MM)	
	All cases	DV cases
Court A	00:54	00.54
Court B	00:43	00:41
Both courts	00:48	00:48

*Excludes 5 cases where start time was unknown

procedures. The picture is further complicated by divergent opinions and practices among legal practitioners and court staff. Resistant occupational cultures and practices among professionals within the system may ultimately prove the more significant barrier to achieving victim-centred criminal justice, a fact which will become increasingly apparent as I turn in the next chapter to look at the criminal trial itself.

Notes

1 At least one volunteer had been scalded on these hot drink runs.
2 A magistrates' legal adviser is similar to a Crown Court clerk except that he or she is charged with informing and guiding magistrates on the law. Unlike a court clerk, it is therefore a legal position and all new legal advisers must be qualified barristers or solicitors (a few of the older advisers at Courts A and B had started before this was a requirement, but they were very much in the minority).
3 Obviously witnesses prepared to come to court before the trial may also be more likely to turn up on the day.
4 The exception being the old wooden benches outside the Youth Courts, although here posters of recent films adorned the walls.
5 Of the 12 respondents who did not use the Service, five were defence witnesses, one was a defendant and five were not directly involved in the proceedings. Only one was a prosecution witness.
6 None of the courts had public car parking facilities.
7 The start of proceedings was deemed to be when the bench entered the court to deal with the case formally, rather than the beginning of negotiations and requests for time beforehand.
8 General sorting out of evidence delayed the start of trials in 21 per cent of cases at this court.

9 The term 'plea bargain' is used here to describe the process whereby prosecution and defence advocates agree that an alternative, lesser, charge to that originally levied against a defendant will be acceptable to both sides, and the defendant agrees to plead guilty to this charge. The term itself was not popular among advocates, who preferred phrases like 'reaching an understanding'.

10 A bind over is a very old form of case disposal whereby the defendant assures the court that he or she will not commit any crimes within a given period of time, on pain of forfeiting a given amount of money. A bind over does not count as a criminal conviction as it does not involve a formal admission of wrongdoing.

11 Locating absent defendants was also a common delay; for 12 per cent of trials at Court A; 14 per cent at Court B; 11 per cent at Court C; 13 per cent at the magistrates' courts overall and 13 per cent at all three courts.

12 See Chapter 2.

13 Criminal Justice Act 2003.

14 Youth Justice and Criminal Evidence Act 1999.

15 The MG11 witness statement form completed by police officers now has a question regarding witness availability (Home Office 2004h).

16 It was more common to see this happen in Court B than Court A, and it never occurred in Crown Court C.

17 The CPS flagged up domestic violence cases with a prominent yellow sticker on the case file.

18 A case was classified as domestic violence when it involved intimidation or violence between members of the same family, partners or other persons in a domestic setting.

19 The number of domestic violence trials observed in Crown Court C (n=5) is not sufficient to draw meaningful comparisons.

20 Replete with bright yellow stickers on the case file.

Chapter 6

Victims in criminal trials: the trial itself

This chapter picks up where Chapter 5 left off to discuss the place of victims in the trial process itself. The process of calling and questioning witnesses will be examined, as well as their reactions to the process and their use of any special measures facilities. The chapter also briefly examines the support afforded to victims after a trial.

Calling witnesses

The vast majority of the 342 witnesses (103 civilian victims) observed giving evidence in this project did so from a witness box at the Crown Court or (adult) magistrates' courts. At Court C, the witness boxes faced the jury, with the defendants positioned beyond the direct eye line of the witness. In the magistrates' courts, however, docks were usually directly opposite the witness box such that the witness would be looking at the defendant. In some courtrooms at Court A (the oldest of the three buildings) the witness box was situated within arm's length of the open dock.[1] In the earlier observation sessions, witnesses were generally expected to give evidence this close to the defendant. As time went on, however, court legal advisers began suggesting alternatives, including having the defendant sit as far away as possible from the witness within the dock, or behind his lawyer for the duration of the witnesses' evidence. In the Youth Courts at Courts A and B, witnesses would sit behind a desk at Court B and simply on a chair in the middle of the room at Court A.

The procedure for calling witnesses was fairly standardised across the three courts. Witnesses would be led into the court and directed to stand in the witness box (or sit in the case of Youth Courts). Occasionally witnesses would sit immediately in the adult courts and were asked to stand. This was followed by the oath or affirmation, which the usher would administer and sometimes guide the witnesses through if they had problems with speech or literacy. In almost all cases the calling lawyer would then introduce him/herself and offer some explanation and pointers, including asking the witness to keep their voice up[2] and to face either the magistrates or the jury:

> Even though it's going to be me asking the questions, they're the ones who have to hear what you're saying. (a crown prosecutor to a witness at Court B)

On this point, one solicitor advocate noted:

> Witnesses are rubbish at looking at the bench; they just revert to type, you just look at the person you're talking to … it's not a worry, it's more of a courtesy. (a solicitor advocate appearing at Courts A and B)

Nevertheless, lawyers would often express their appreciation for the unusualness of the situation. In the magistrates' court witnesses were told that notes had to be taken, meaning there was a need to proceed slowly and that the lawyer asking questions 'might have to stop you occasionally'. Witnesses were often tipped to 'watch the legal adviser's pen' so when he/she stopped writing they would know to continue speaking. At this point magistrates would in most cases invite the witness to sit. At Court C, judges seemed more averse to witnesses automatically sitting through their evidence, but would usually invite the witness to 'speak up' if they wanted to sit or needed a break. Magistrates would sometimes do the same, although it was more common for breaks to be offered later by the bench.

When witnesses (usually children) at the magistrates' courts gave evidence via live video-link they would already be sitting in the video-link room when the equipment was activated. The court legal adviser – who always ran the equipment – would speak to the witness first, introducing himself then switching the witness's view to introduce one by one the prosecutor, defence lawyer and magistrates. When a district judge was sitting, the bench would usually host these introductions, and also provide similar advice about speaking slowly and clearly.

The video-link equipment at all three courts was usually sufficient to allow witnesses to be easily seen and heard in the courtroom, and apparently for the witness to hear questions easily and see the lawyers. Nevertheless, achieving this often required a degree of trial and error, whereby witnesses would be asked to adjust the microphone. Loud feedback was a recurring problem at Court B especially, despite the equipment at this court being more modern than at either of the other courts.

At the Crown Court, video-link equipment and screens were built into the courtroom. Consequently, the court clerks who operated the equipment had no difficulty setting up or operating special measures. In the lower courts, however, video-links had to be specially set up by porters before a trial. At both magistrates' courts it would usually take legal advisers some time to (re)familiarise themselves with the equipment, which would often involve calling a porter into the court to get it working, or consulting with other legal advisers. While relatively little time was wasted on such activities, there was an impression that knowledge about the equipment was passed on more through word of mouth than by specific training. All legal advisers observed operating such equipment did so smoothly and effectively during the trials themselves.

Most magistrates' courtrooms had portable screens that would be manoeuvred into position when needed by a combination of the ushers, legal adviser and lawyers. This need to organise the screens manually at Courts A and B reflects the practical difficulty of courtrooms incorporating special measures equipment for which they were not designed. This was a particular challenge for the ageing 1960s building at Court A, where former offices and consultation rooms had been converted into (prosecution) witness waiting rooms and video-link rooms. A problem often remarked upon by lawyers and magistrates at both Courts A and B was that the video monitors used for special measures blocked the magistrates' view of the courtroom when they were in position on the bench. Magistrates complained about this at both courts, and chief administrators openly acknowledged the problem and were critical of what they viewed as the centre imposing cheap equipment on them through a national contract.

The majority of victims and witnesses of all kinds gave evidence with no specific supporters in the courtroom, albeit having a supporter was not a rare or unusual occurrence. More civilian witnesses came into the courtroom at Court A with a non-Witness Service volunteer compared with Court B, where a volunteer supporter was more common than a friend or family member. Witness Service volunteers were more frequently brought into court by all categories of witnesses at Court B compared with Court A. This may reflect the generally more relaxed attitude exhibited towards the Witness Service by court staff and lawyers at Court B compared with Court A. As such, while overall the more popular option seemed to be for witnesses to bring their own supporters into the courtroom, this apparently did depend on the court. Civilian *non*-victims were rarely supported by volunteers in the courtroom at Court A, whereas this was far more common at Court B. This suggests that the Witness Service at Court A was concentrating much of its attention and support on victims themselves, whereas at Court B the Service considered their role more in terms of all (prosecution) witnesses. In Court C, observations suggested that supporting victims through volunteers accompanying them into the courtroom was more common than using them to support civilian witnesses who were not victims. Most witnesses bringing supporters into the courtroom at Court C were victims.

When special measures were operating, the practice of allowing Witness Service or other supporters into the video-link room varied between courts. At Court C the presiding judge took the view that volunteers should not sit with witnesses in the video-link rooms, only a court usher was permitted to do so. At Courts A and B, however, both Witness Service and non-Service supporters were allowed to sit with the witness, along with an usher. It is important to emphasise the key role played by court ushers – especially at the magistrates' courts – in supporting victims and witnesses giving evidence via live video-link. In practice ushers were also often responsible for conveying information to witnesses before the start of the trial, and were one of the few sources of information available to defence witnesses.

Giving evidence

Table 6.1 provides details of the average length of questioning, including and excluding any breaks afforded to witnesses. Civilian victims giving evidence at all three courts were on average kept answering questions longer than other witnesses. In the magistrates' court, most witnesses in this study gave all their evidence without a break, the process lasting an average of 52 minutes.

Table 6.1 Average length of questioning with and without breaks at Courts A, B and C*

		Average length of questioning (HH:MM)	
	n**	Excluding breaks	Including breaks
Civilian victims			
Examination in chief	100	00:24	00:26
Cross-examination	97	00:29	00:43
Total questioning	103	00:52	01:08
Defendants			
Examination in chief	77	00:13	00:14
Cross-examination	77	00:14	00:15
Total questioning	77	00:28	00:30
Police			
Examination in chief	50	00:11	00:11
Cross-examination	43	00:08	00:09
Total questioning	50	00:19	00:20
All civilians (excluding defendants and experts)			
Examination in chief	206	00:18	00:19
Cross-examination	195	00:20	00:28
Total questioning	209	00:38	00:46

*Excluding cases where an average length of questioning was not calculated. Refers to number of examinations in chief/cross-examinations rather than number of witnesses

Table 6.2 displays the results of timing witness's speech during the evidence-giving process and calculating the percentage of time they actually spoke for. The remarkable thing about this data is how similar the results are for each category of witness. Existing literature indicates that advocates exercise a great deal of control over the evidence-giving process (Luchjenbroers 1996). These figures seem to suggest that lawyers on both sides conduct this process in a standard way, regardless of whom they are questioning. This means that, firstly, victims are not contributing in any more significant way to the process than any other person giving evidence and, secondly,

Table 6.2 Average percentage of time speaking during different components of evidence at Courts A, B and C (percentage of *component*)

	n*	Average percentage of time speaking in each component of evidence
Civilian victims		
Examination in chief	100	37
Cross-examination	108	27
Examination in chief and cross-examination	208	32
Defendants		
Examination in chief	78	37
Cross-examination	80	29
Examination in chief and cross-examination	158	33
Police		
Examination in chief	47	37
Cross-examination	38	29
Examination in chief and cross-examination	85	33
All civilians (excluding experts, including defendants)		
Examination in chief	279	37
Cross-examination	285	28
Examination in chief and cross-examination	564	32

*Excludes cases where no percentage was calculated. Refers to number of examinations in chief/cross-examinations rather than number of witnesses

that they are not being treated in any special way by criminal justice practitioners.[3]

Of particular interest to the present study is the question of whether the presence of special measures assists victims and other witnesses to give evidence. Tables 6.3–6.5 present timing figures for victims and other civilians who used special measures to give evidence. Initial comparisons between these results and those in Table 6.2 indicate that special measures did not impact a great deal on the percentage of time a witness spoke during the different components of the process.

Employing T-test analysis – with the percentage of time speaking during the different components of evidence as the test variable and the presence or absence of special measures as the grouping variable – generally confirms that for most classes of witness at all three courts

Table 6.3 Average percentage of time speaking during different components of evidence with special measures at Courts A, B and C (percentage of *component*)

	n*	Average percentage of time speaking in each component of evidence
Civilian victims		
Examination in chief	26	40
Cross-examination	31	24
Examination in chief and cross-examination	57	31
All civilians**		
Examination in chief	37	37
Cross-examination	44	23
Examination in chief and cross-examination	81	30

*Excludes cases where no percentage was calculated. Refers to number of examinations in chief/cross-examinations rather than number of witnesses
**No experts gave evidence through special measures and defendants are unable to under the Youth Justice and Criminal Evidence Act 1999

there was no statistically significant difference between the average percentages of time spoken with or without special measures. The exception to this was with cross-examination of civilian witnesses at all three courts taken together (t=3.010, df=283, p=0.003) and just at the magistrates' court (t=2.886, df=254, p=0.004):

Interestingly, these tables seem to suggest that the presence of special measures for these witnesses actually led to them speaking for a slightly lower proportion of the time. Certainly, the findings of this research prohibit any conclusion that special measures offer any guarantee that witnesses will be able to express themselves more easily during evidence.

Comparison of the means revealed more significant differences between the percentage of time victims and civilian witnesses spoke with and without pre-recorded examination in chief specifically and these results are set out on Tables 6.8 and 6.9.

Comparison of the means here indicates a 15 per cent average increase in the time speaking while giving evidence with pre-recorded examination in chief for civilian victims (t=–3.937, df=99, p<0.000) and a 12 per cent increase for civilians in general (t=–4.915,

Table 6.4 Average percentage of time speaking during different components of evidence with special measures at Courts A and B (percentage of *component*)

	n*	Average percentage of time speaking in each component of evidence
Civilian victims		
Examination in chief	21	37
Cross-examination	22	25
Examination in chief and cross-examination	43	31
All civilians**		
Examination in chief	30	34
Cross-examination	34	23
Examination in chief and cross-examination	64	29

*Excludes cases where no percentage was calculated. Refers to number of examinations in chief/cross-examinations rather than number of witnesses
**No experts or defendants included (see Table 6.3)

Table 6.5 Average percentage of time speaking during different components of evidence with special measures at Court C (percentage of *component*)

	n*	Average percentage of time speaking in each component of evidence
Civilian victims		
Examination in chief	5	51
Cross-examination	9	23
Examination in chief and cross-examination	14	33
All civilians**		
Examination in chief	7	49
Cross-examination	10	24
Examination in chief and cross-examination	17	34

*Excludes cases where no percentage was calculated. Refers to number of examinations in chief/cross-examinations rather than number of witnesses
**No experts or defendants included (see Table 6.3)

Table 6.6 T-Test comparison of mean percentage of time speaking by civilians during cross-examination with and without special measures at Courts A, B and C

	Mean % of time speaking during cross-examination	Standard deviation	n
Civilians cross-examined at Courts A, B and C *with* special measures	23%	9.99	44
Civilians cross-examined at Courts A, B and C *without* special measures*	29%	11.27	241

*No experts or defendants included (see Table 6.3)

Table 6.7 T-Test comparison of mean percentage of time speaking by civilians during cross-examination with and without special measures at Courts A and B

	Mean % of time speaking during cross-examination	Standard deviation	n
Civilians cross-examined at Courts A and B *with* special measures	23%	9.11	34
Civilians cross-examined at Courts A and B *without* special measures*	29%	11.08	222

*No experts or defendants included (see Table 6.3)

df=562, $p<0.000$). Coupled with first-hand observation of this process, pre-recorded examination in chief seems to increase the percentage of time a witness speaks during evidence to a more significant degree than special measures in general. This is to some extent unsurprising, as evidence through live links or behind screens remains very similar in content and style to traditional questioning. The advent of a free narrative phase during pre-recorded examination in chief (in which witnesses are not interrupted) is probably the most significant break

Table 6.8 T-Test comparison of mean percentage of time speaking by civilian victims during examination in chief with and without pre-recorded evidence at Courts A, B and C

	Mean % of time speaking during cross-examination	Standard deviation	n
Civilian victims giving evidence during examination in chief with pre-recorded evidence at Courts A, B and C	50%	16.538	14
Civilian victims giving evidence during examination in chief with special measures *other than* pre-recorded evidence or *without* special measures at Courts A, B and C*	35%	12.321	87

*No experts or defendants included (see Table 6.3)

Table 6.9 T-Test comparison of mean percentage of time speaking by civilians during examination in chief with and without pre-recorded evidence at Courts A and B

	Mean % of time speaking during cross-examination	Standard deviation	n
All civilians giving evidence during examination in chief with pre-recorded evidence at Courts A, B and C	32%	15.722	20
All civilians giving evidence during examination in chief with special measures other than pre-recorded evidence or without special measures at Courts A, B and C*	20%	12.421	544

*No experts or defendants included (see Table 6.3)

with traditional questioning procedures yet seen, and the closest to true account-making.

In most cases the degree of control that questioning lawyers, magistrates' court legal advisers and benches have over the evidence-giving process was underlined by the prevalence of interruptions endured by many witnesses during the observed sessions, mapped out on Table 6.10.

An interruption was counted here in any instance when a questioning lawyer asked a question or made a statement before the witness had completed something they were saying. In other words, any instances in which the lawyer cut the witness short.

Table 6.10 Number and percentage of witnesses interrupted during different parts of evidence, Courts A, B and C*

	Examination in chief	Cross-examination	Examination in chief and cross-examination**
Civilians (including victims and experts but excluding defendants)	153 (72%)	58 (27%)	161 (76%)
Police (including police victims)	25 (49%)	6 (12%)	26 (51%)
Civilian victims	82 (79%)	34 (33%)	85 (82%)
Civilian non-victims (including experts but excluding defendants)	71 (65%)	24 (22%)	76 (70%)
Defendants	55 (71%)	26 (34%)	56 (73%)
All prosecution witnesses	78 (33%)	63 (27%)	167 (71%)
All defence witnesses	66 (61%)	27 (25%)	76 (70%)
Total witnesses (including experts and defendants)	222 (65%)	90 (26%)	243 (71%)

*Percentages are out of the total number of each type of witness observed
**That is, witnesses interrupted during both components of evidence

Civilian victims were interrupted more often than any other category of witness during the whole evidential process, and examination in chief specifically, whereas they were second (by 1 per cent) only to defendants for cross-examination. It is also interesting to note that interruptions during examination in chief were more common than interruptions during cross-examination. This may seem peculiar given that cross-examination is intended to challenge a witness's evidence, whereas examination in chief is the closest witnesses come to telling their version of the story. The most likely explanation lies in the fact that, during examination in chief, lawyers had to be very specific about eliciting the information they wanted; usually that which was recorded in the witness statement. During cross-examination, however, many lawyers employed a strategy of allowing witnesses to speak in the hope that they would say something contradictory to their previous evidence.

The most common reason in both examination in chief and cross-examination for witnesses being interrupted at all three courts was the questioning lawyer asking another question (48 per cent of witnesses). This was also true of cross-examination taken alone (22 per cent). During examination in chief, however, pausing for lawyers and court staff to take notes was the most common reason for witnesses being interrupted, with 45 per cent of all witnesses interrupted during examination in chief for this reason, dropping to just 2 per cent during cross-examination. This again implies that examination in chief is more restrictive than cross-examination for witnesses.

Breaking down the data on Table 6.10 to examine civilian victims specifically, the same broad pattern emerges whereby asking another question and pausing the victim to take notes are prominent. It is, however, notable that the percentage of victims interrupted this way was generally higher than for witnesses in general. There was also a greater prevalence of interruptions to stop hearsay and 'excessive' information for civilian victims compared to other civilians. This again demonstrates the limits placed on the accounts of victims.

One question taken up in interviews was whether lawyers had adapted their style of questioning over time to better account for the needs and perspectives of crime victims. Responses often emphasised that the approach taken by lawyers eliciting evidence was very much down to each individual's style of advocacy. Although many were loath to generalise further, respondents generally agreed that older barristers and defence solicitors were usually more willing to take a confrontational tone with witnesses:

> I have noticed – now compared to twelve years ago – you do get less intimidation and twisting of arms of witnesses when they're in the box than you did 12 years ago, but it seems to be with the newer barristers ... I can't say that I've noticed with any of the 'old school' barristers that there's been any noticeable change. (a court clerk at Court C)

One legal adviser saw the perceived differences between older and younger advocates as reflecting changes of emphasis in their training over time:

> You can get by more [now] on legal knowledge rather than really good advocacy skills. (a legal adviser [originally trained as a barrister] at Court B)

Several practitioners lamented what they viewed as a general decline in the quality of cross-examinations:

> The younger generation of lawyers – particularly the solicitors – I don't think cross-examination skills are as keen as they used to be; I think sometimes witnesses aren't put under the sort of pressure they should be. (a legal adviser at Court B)
>
> By and large the cross-examination is less robust. (a district judge sitting at Court A)

In addition, some lawyers argued that – given the adversarial nature of the system – it was important that the process did not become too easy for victims and witnesses:

> I don't think things should be too fluffy ... I don't like intimidating, because it does smack of probably not properly respecting human rights, but certainly it should be formal. (the Clerk to the Justices at Court B)

This view reflects the observation made in court that lawyers exercised control over the evidential process mainly through a formal tone and style of questioning rather than an overtly hostile manner, and this applied to all victim and non-victim witnesses. That said, one solicitor advocate noted that harsher forms of cross-examination could sometimes 'wind the victim up such that they actually strengthen their resolve and give better evidence' (a solicitor advocate appearing at Courts A and B). This view did seem to be confirmed (at least anecdotally) in some observation sessions, where witnesses appeared extremely confident and motivated following fairly hostile questioning, if only because they felt compelled to prove the questioning lawyer wrong. On the other hand, it was noted several times by interviewees that the 'best' lawyers don't need to take a hostile tone to elicit evidence from witnesses:

> If a barrister is good at his job then he could probably elicit the information without using that sort of attack. (a court clerk at Court A)

In questioning one barrister on how he decided on the style of questioning he was going to employ with witnesses, it became clear that this depended very much on the individual witnesses:

> It's all very complicated, because no two witnesses are the same … often you can gauge a lot by how they take the oath. (a barrister appearing at Courts A, B and C)

Hence, for this barrister, each new witness necessitated a careful and speedy assessment exercise to gauge a witness's intelligence, confidence, level of intimidation, and so on, and this would affect how he asked questions. Of course, this view contradicts the findings given above, which suggest that lawyers are asking questions in a standardised way for all witnesses.

Data were also recorded as to the manner in which lawyers would indicate to witnesses that their evidence might be untrue. Lawyers went about this in three main ways: suggesting or implying the witness was 'mistaken'; openly confessing the belief that witnesses were 'misleading' the court; and directly labelling witnesses as liars. Victims were most commonly subject to the misleading strategy, more commonly than civilian witnesses in general, more of whom had no such strategy applied to them at all. This reflects the fact that the victim's evidence is often key, and defence advocates will be more inclined to test it forcefully. Wider references to witnesses' character were relatively rare, but more common during cross-examination.[4] Once again, a greater proportion of victims had to face questions about their characters during cross-examination than defendants. Many advocates considered it a bad tactical move to bring in the characters of witnesses – or to treat them too harshly – for fear of appearing to bully them in the eyes of magistrates or juries.

In calling a witness, it was clear that the basic goal of an advocate was to elicit from that witness the details recorded in that witness's statement, which most advocates would have in their hand and work through during the examination in chief process. Conversely, during cross-examination, victims especially were quickly brought up on any derogation from their witness statements by defence lawyers. Such derogations were often used to support defence claims that the victim was unsure, could not remember, or may be lying. This chimes with the discussion in Chapter 4 as to how victims are restricted to the old version of their story.

One frequent criticism made by witnesses themselves was that information had been reported by them to the police but had not been recorded in their statements. Defence lawyers would usually respond by pointing out that the statement had been signed and therefore presumably read and checked by witnesses at the time. One explanation for these reported discrepancies is that while such information *was* reported to the officer by the victim for the purposes of an *account-making* exercise, it was not recorded by that officer because it was of little use to the *evidence-building* exercise.[5] As for victims' failure to spot such omissions when signing their statements, the distractions of very recent victimisation might be explanation enough. In addition, as the victim does not approach the exercise with the same evidential priorities as lawyers or police officers, it is unsurprising that they miss the evidential significance of smaller details in favour of what is important to them in the construction of a narrative. Given that one of the fundamental features of a narrative is that victims *develop* it over time, they may be unaware that once a statement is made and signed it cannot be changed to reflect developed interpretations of events. Indeed, the impression was that many witnesses did not appreciate the evidential significance of detracting from their original statements. Some witnesses appeared to believe that the purpose of coming to court was to add details not previously mentioned.

Reactions to evidence

As witnesses progressed through examination in chief and cross-examination any emotional reactions they displayed would be noted. This was a subjective exercise, but one which has resulted in a large amount of data in the form of some 37 different apparent emotional reactions to giving evidence in court (see Table 6.11).

Table 6.11 Witnesses' apparent reactions to examination in chief and cross-examination at Courts A, B and C (all witnesses)*, **

	Examination in chief		Cross-examination	
	n***	%	n***	%
Calm	339	99	306	89
Confident	339	99	307	90
Nervous	36	11	30	9
Tearful	17	5	30	9
Angry at defendant(s)	9	3	16	5
Defensive	2	1	30	9
Angry (generally)	5	1	30	9
Angry about questions being asked	2	1	32	9
Confused	6	2	24	7
Frustrated	1	<1	15	4
Determined	1	<1	2	1
Irritated or annoyed by lawyer asking questions	1	<1	11	3
Upset (generally)	4	1	6	2
Embarrassed	3	1	1	<1
Excited	1	<1	0	0
Restless/fed up/bored	3	1	3	1
Tired	3	1	1	<1
Vindictive or bitter against the defendant	3	1	5	1
Angry about incident	4	1	3	1
Upset about incident	7	2	5	1
Upset by questions	0	0	1	<1
Flustered	0	0	3	1
Angry at another witness	5	1	4	1
Uncomfortable	1	<1	0	0
Depressed	1	<1	1	<1
Remorseful	1	<1	2	1
Unsure what to say	2	1	3	1
Tongue-tied	0	0	1	<1
Professional	1	<1	0	0
Anxious	1	<1	1	<1
Animated	1	<1	1	<1
Angry at police	0	0	1	<1
Argumentative	0	0	2	1
Tense	1	<1	1	<1
Concentrating	0	0	1	<1
Determined	2	1	1	<1

*Percentages are of all witnesses observed for this research (n=342)
**Multiple reactions allowed for each evidential component
***Number of witnesses experiencing this reaction sometime during examination in chief/cross-examination

By way of clarification, Table 6.11 shows us that 36 witnesses (11 per cent) appeared nervous at some point during the course of their examination in chief while only 30 (or 9 per cent) displayed this reaction during cross-examination. This again seems to problematise the assumption that cross-examination is always the harder aspect of giving evidence. Almost all witnesses appeared calm and confident *at some point* during both components of the evidential process, even if this was for a relatively low percentage of the whole experience. Most of the apparent emotional reactions recorded in this research were 'negative' (angry, tearful, vindictive and so on).[6] Apart from calmness and confidence, other positive reactions include 'determined', 'professional' and 'concentrating'. Overall, witnesses tended to experience a wider range of emotions during cross-examination.

Table 6.12 gives the emotional reaction data just for those witnesses who gave evidence through special measures (n=39). Given that these were deemed vulnerable or intimidated witnesses it is no surprise that a greater percentage of this sample demonstrated negative reactions compared with other witnesses, although the figures are still low. Of course, the fact that the witnesses still displayed such negative reactions indicates that special measures do not wholly negate their effect. Notably, there is also a higher prevalence of confusion on this table compared to Table 6.11. Certainly the observation sessions indicated that some young witnesses found giving evidence through video-link confusing. This was especially so when the questioning lawyer (who was all the witness could see) broke off to speak to the magistrates or when opposing lawyers made an objection, as in such cases the witness could neither see, nor hear, the source of the interruption. The other key point to draw from this table is that the emotional reactions displayed during examination in chief compared to cross-examination are very similar. Indeed, the figures are identical for all reactions excluding 'calm', 'confident' and 'nervous'. This implies that the difference between the two key components of evidence is less obvious for witnesses giving evidence through special measures, and therefore their emotional reactions are more consistent throughout the entire process.

In the court user surveys conducted at Court B (see Table 6.13), witnesses were asked directly how they felt while giving evidence.

The first table indicates that many witnesses are not left feeling especially 'bad' emotionally after giving evidence. These results broadly reflect Shapland *et al.*'s (1985) finding that most victims felt they had succeeded in taking steps to get over initial difficulties with the evidence-giving process, and that 47 per cent of victims

Table 6.12 Apparent reactions to examination in chief and cross-examination of witnesses giving evidence through special measures at Courts A, B and C (all witnesses)*, **

	Examination in chief		Cross-examination	
	n***	%	n***	%
Calm	36	92	34	87
Confident	36	92	35	89
Nervous	8	21	9	23
Tearful	9	23	9	23
Angry at defendant(s)	3	8	3	8
Defensive	7	18	7	18
Angry (generally)	6	15	6	15
Angry about questions being asked	3	8	3	8
Confused	4	10	4	10
Frustrated	3	8	3	8
Irritated or annoyed by lawyer asking questions	1	3	1	3
Upset (generally)	2	5	2	5
Embarrassed	2	5	2	5
Excited	1	3	1	3
Restless/fed up/bored	2	5	2	5
Tired	1	3	1	3
Vindictive or bitter against the defendant	2	5	2	5
Remorseful	1	3	1	3
Tense	1	3	1	3

*Percentages are of all witnesses observed for this research giving evidence through special measures (n=39)
**Multiple reactions allowed for each evidential component
***Number of witnesses experiencing this reaction sometime during examination in chief/cross-examination

in that study (the largest percentage) were 'satisfied' with the court proceedings. The 15 per cent of respondents feeling 'intimidated' during evidence in the present research compares to the 21 per cent reporting that they felt 'intimidated by the process' in the 2002 Witness Satisfaction Survey (Angle *et al.* 2003). In contrast to the observation data, the bulk of the survey respondents recalled negative emotional

Table 6.13 Questionnaire 4, witnesses' reported feelings during and immediately after giving evidence at Court B*

How do you feel now?**	Number and percentage	How did you feel during evidence?**	Number and percentage
Relieved	10 (37%)	**OK**	7 (26%)
OK	6 (22%)	**Worried**	6 (22%)
Satisfied	4 (15%)	**Frustrated**	4 (15%)
Angry	4 (15%)	**Angry**	4 (15%)
Worried	3 (11%)	**Intimidated**	4 (15%)
Scared	2 (7%)	**Calm**	3 (11%)
Unhappy	2 (7%)	**Confused**	2 (7%)
Happy	1 (4%)	**Confident**	2 (7%)
Frustrated	1 (4%)	**Unhappy**	1 (4%)
Confused	0 (0%)	**Scared**	1 (4%)
Other	2 (7%)	**Other**	1 (4%)

*n=27, multiple answers allowed
**Answers selected by respondents from a closed list

reactions while giving evidence. The suggestion could therefore be made that witnesses do tend to react badly to giving evidence, but in keeping with the observed data they prepare themselves sufficiently to keep this concealed, possibly because they know the importance of *appearing* calm and confident. Alternatively, it may be that witnesses tend to focus on and report the negative aspects of giving evidence more readily than the positive (or neutral) aspects such as a sense of vindication or satisfaction at holding one's own.

Overall, the results indicate that a sizeable proportion of witnesses – and even victims – give evidence with little apparent difficulty, albeit victims of crime may be more negatively affected by giving evidence than witnesses in general. While the literature in this area tends to emphasise the plight of those witnesses and victims especially affected (or even damaged) by the evidential process, it is important to realise that many victims and witnesses give their evidence in fairly sedate tones. Indeed, in the fourth version of the witness survey distributed at Court B, out of the 27 respondent witnesses (all of whom had given evidence) 10 said it had been easier than expected, another 10 said it had been about the same as expected, which left only seven saying evidence had been a more difficult experience than expected. This all suggests that practical issues – such as allowing victims to finish speaking when giving evidence – may be just as important as

Table 6.14 Questionnaires 1–3, percentage of all witnesses who answered questions on how they felt during evidence at Court B*, **

	During prosecution questions							During defence questions						
	0	1	2	3	4	5	6	0	1	2	3	4	5	6
Calm	10	10	5	35	15	20	5	15	15	5	30	10	15	10
Confident	25	10	0	30	20	15	5	20	10	0	30	15	15	10
Intimidated by the defendant	20	30	15	25	0	5	5	15	30	20	15	10	5	5
Intimidated by the lawyer asking questions	25	15	30	20	0	5	5	25	20	20	15	5	10	5
Intimidated by the courtroom setting	25	15	25	35	0	0	0	20	15	40	25	0	5	0
Worried	25	20	20	15	15	0	5	20	25	30	20	0	5	0
Scared	25	40	10	15	0	0	10	20	40	15	15	0	5	5
Angry	25	35	15	20	0	5	0	20	45	15	15	0	5	0

*n=20
**Respondents were asked to rate each reaction on a closed list from 1 (didn't feel this way at all) to 6 (felt extremely like this). A 0 here indicates that no answer was given for this reaction

addressing issues like intimidation and fear of the courtroom. It also seems to back up the contention that the adversarial system may not need reforms of a fundamental nature to achieve victim-centredness.

Interestingly, most of the more experienced practising lawyers and court staff had failed to note any difference in the average witness's demeanour over time in terms of confidence or preparedness:

> I don't particularly recognise a different attitude to the court … In terms of whether they're better prepared, I suspect there are an awful lot to whom all these changes haven't made that much difference … I'm not sure that I've noticed a huge difference in the demeanour or preparedness of witnesses. (a district judge sitting at Court B)

One respondent believed that the reason for this lack of appreciable change in witness preparedness was the continued lack of information provided to them:

> They don't appear to be much more understanding of the system ... the leaflets are about what's going to happen in court ... but do they really paint a realistic picture? Do they say, 'You're likely to be listed with another trial'? Whether they give them the real story is another thing. I think it would be better to prepare them by giving them a bit of background about the court system as a whole. (a legal adviser at Court B)

This suggests that many sources of information provided to victims and witnesses fail to provide a truly frank view of the system, omitting issues like waiting times and possible intimidation.

Special measures

A total of 39 witnesses were observed giving evidence via special measures, most of them children. Seven adults were observed giving evidence through special measures, all of them women[7] and four of them victims (the other three being prosecution witnesses). Four of these adult witnesses gave their evidence behind screens and three gave evidence via live video-link. These latter three were all giving evidence in a single Crown Court trial involving multiple sexual offences.

Views on the advent of special measures were mixed. Most practitioners agreed it was a good thing to provide facilities for 'genuinely' vulnerable or intimidated witnesses, especially children:

> The live link is probably getting better evidence out of the youngsters ... we used to have a lot of youth trials with people crying in them ... they don't seem to be getting as upset as often [now]. (a legal adviser at Court A)

Some lawyers also felt special measures (especially video-link) brought advantages to advocates:

> You do have a bit more time to build up a rapport. (a barrister appearing at Courts A, B and C)

> It can work equally well for the person calling that person as a witness ... because they sit and reflect, they're not overpowered by the situation. (a district judge sitting at Court B)

Nevertheless, several interviewees saw a problem in what they perceived to be a blanket application of special measures to any witnesses who could be considered remotely vulnerable or intimidated:

> Special measures directions are good if they assist a particular witness. The blanket introduction of them in the Youth Courts for under-17s, violent or sexual offences, I don't necessarily agree with that. Whilst one can see the logic behind it there are some mature young people that might be quite comfortable to give their view in a court setting and may not like to give their evidence in another room to a camera. (a legal adviser at Court B)

This question of what to do when a witness is automatically entitled to special measures but does not wish to use them arose several times. In one case a trial was adjourned because the video-link equipment was not working, even though the young witness was quite happy to give evidence in the courtroom and had missed school – and his mother, work – to be at court. One legal adviser gave her view that vulnerable and intimidated witnesses did not have to give evidence via special measures if they did not want to, and remarked on how lawyers never seemed to give witnesses the choice:

> I don't remember any case where they [lawyers] said, 'Well, we'll go and show them [witnesses] what a courtroom setting is like [then] we'll go and show them the [video-link] room where they'll have to sit and see what they'd prefer' … the wording [of the Act] is ambiguous, it can be argued either way … but it's not set in stone. (a legal adviser at Court B)

The same respondent went on to describe one recent consequence of such attitudes:

> We also had a case a fortnight ago, a young lad giving evidence on the link who didn't want to give evidence on the link … he started giving his evidence via live link and then something arose as he was talking – a legal point – so the judge started asking the advocates questions about this legal point. The lad ended up storming out of the room saying he wasn't going to give evidence any more … because he felt that people were discussing the case round him, that it was confusing for him

> because he could hear advocates talking but didn't know who was saying what. And he actually ended up refusing to give evidence, because he felt peed off. (*ibid*.)

Hence child witnesses can clearly find it confusing not being able to see other people in the courtroom aside from the person asking questions. On a wider point, it was quite common to see lawyers discussing legal points around witnesses both during video-link evidence and when the witness was standing live in court.

This also relates back to an account-making point, in that victims are not being permitted to tell their stories in the manner in which they feel most comfortable, and may actually find it difficult to make an account when they are distanced from the audience for that account. Many respondents noted problems associated with video-link rooms in particular:

> Take this court [Court A]. Have you been down to the video-link rooms? It's like a dungeon! How can that be witness-friendly for a young person to go down there? Honestly, it looks as if you're going into a cell ... When you're there all day waiting to come on, it's a long time for you to be cooped up in a room like that, and it can have an effect upon them in the way they give their evidence. (a solicitor advocate appearing at Courts A and B)

These points echo the observation that witnesses can feel 'locked up' inside witness waiting rooms.

Aside from the impact on witnesses themselves, defence solicitors in particular argued that what they saw as the automatic granting of special measures applications to prosecution witnesses was manifestly unfair, especially given that defendants cannot apply for special measures.[8] Certainly no applications for special measures were refused during the course of these observations, even when they were made on the morning of the trial (which was common despite prior case management hearings) and therefore outside the time limit for such applications under Criminal Procedure Rules.[9] That said, one district judge raised the important point that – without generalised rules – the only alternative would be to spend time carefully assessing each individual witness, which was bad for the court and the witnesses.

Not all respondents believed that special measures had become an automatic right, certainly not in the Crown Court:

> I would say that of the applications that are made now, probably a smaller percentage of them are granted than the percentage of those made 12 years ago … there's a lot more applications made where they're just 'trying it on' because they know that they can make the application. We had one this morning where the prosecution were making an application for screens for two mature men in their 40s and 50s. That sort of application probably wouldn't have been even considered 12 years ago. (a court clerk at Court C)

Implicit in this quotation is an underlying view that certain kinds of victim witnesses are 'right' for, or 'deserving' of, special measures and some are not:

> Two of the witnesses had got referral orders, ISPs [Intensive Supervision Programmes], supervision orders, they'd been in and out of the court like yo-yos. And these buggers [the prosecution] want special measures for them! I said, 'You are joking!' (a solicitor appearing at Court B)

Of course, the research indicates that a large proportion of victims of crime have criminal convictions (Dignan 2005). Even respondents who were broadly in favour of special measures were still wary of applying them to adult witnesses.

Some defence advocates in particular felt that the system could be abused, with witnesses requesting special measures to attract sympathy from the bench or jury. This leads us to the very important question of whether the use of special measures has any impact on the findings of magistrates or jurors. Interview respondents were divided in their opinions although, generally speaking, most thought that special measures did not influence verdicts, especially now benches had grown accustomed to them:

> I've seen 100 special measures, half of them have been guilty and half of them have been not guilty. (a legal adviser at Court A)

> The magistrates are more used to it now, and so it's nothing out of the ordinary, and so it perhaps doesn't affect them as much as it might have done when these things first came around. (a legal adviser at Court B)

> I would hope juries would perceive now that this is a normal state of affairs, it's not an indication that there's something nasty or unpleasant about the defendant and therefore we can be satisfied about his guilt. I think people know now – they've see it on TV – it's part of the system. (a district judge sitting at Court B)

Nevertheless, another district judge was of the view that special measures might sway the results of a case:

> I find it harder to assess the evidence from someone who's giving evidence over a video-link ... From colleagues in the Crown Court who deal with cases involving abuse of children and so on, they have also got the impression that juries probably find it harder to convict on evidence given over a video-link, because it's somehow more remote; you get more of a feel of what's going on if the witness is in front of you. I think in many ways it doesn't probably serve the ends of justice, although I can see why it's much more comfortable for the witness. (a district judge sitting at Court A)

There is a very significant implication in this quotation that making witnesses comfortable is opposed to the ends of justice. In a victim-centred system, however, it is surely the case that victim comfort would be prioritised (albeit perhaps not to the extent that the process becomes easy) because such comfort would improve the quality of the evidence (and, importantly, the *narrative*) and this would be considered in the interests of justice.

Some lawyers were concerned that prosecution witnesses giving evidence via video-link were more likely to be believed than defendants, who could not:

> If I was defending in those circumstances and we had complainants there I wouldn't like it because you know, of course, that your defendant then is going to be there in court for all to see. I just think it distances them [the witnesses], it almost puts them on a pedestal; little kids – depending on what they're saying – are often believed. (a barrister appearing at Courts A, B and C)

One solicitor advocate was not so concerned about video-links, but was worried about screening off witnesses in the courtroom itself:

> [T]he downside of screens is it's very overt, particularly from a bench's point of view, so they're bound to be influenced by it to some degree, [they] think, 'If this person is sufficiently intimidated, what kind of a nasty character is the defendant?' (a solicitor advocate appearing at Courts A and B)

Prosecution and defence lawyers also raised some of the more traditional criticisms of video-links: that they distorted information such as the relative size of defendant and victim and prevented juries and magistrates from judging the body language or demeanour of witnesses, which almost all respondents agreed was vital to the process both for the bench or jury and for the lawyer asking questions.

> If you've got everybody in court to give live evidence I think it's much better, because you can see the demeanour of them. (a solicitor advocate appearing at Courts A and B)

Indeed, in one trial at Court A the defence lawyer was so adamant on this point that the court usher was asked to go to the video-link room and stand next to the victim giving evidence to provide some sense of scale (with dubious results). Other lawyers admitted that they found cross-examination more difficult through video-links, especially because they could not tell if they were 'on to something' with the witness.

Another district judge pointed out that it was also hard for the witness not to be able to judge the lawyer's demeanour:

> I suppose they have no relationship with you either, because you're just a face on the screen, they can't see how *you're* reacting to something. (a district judge sitting at Court A)

The final issue to be discussed relating to special measures is pre-recorded examination in chief. Owing to the inclusion of a free narrative phase by interviewing police officers (see Chapter 2) this is probably the closest a victim's evidence comes to true account-making in the present system. As such, results relating to the percentage of time witnesses are permitted to speak when giving evidence in this manner have already been noted.[10]

During the observation sessions, 16 witnesses aged from eight to 16 years old were seen giving evidence through pre-recorded examination in chief. The evidence would be conducted in broadly the same way as regular video-link evidence, in that it would begin with the young child live on the screen being introduced to everyone in the courtroom by the bench, or by the legal adviser when sitting with lay magistrates at Court A or Court B. The video would then be played while the witness watched from the video room. On the videos, a child would be interviewed by a specially trained police officer in suites with the appearance of a typical front room. The officer would begin by pointing out the microphones that would record what the child said. This would be followed by a few settling down questions about the child's hobbies and school. Next would follow the free narrative phase where the child was able to present his or her narrative account without any interruptions from the interviewing officer. Such accounts were usually short, taking five to 10 minutes. The officer would then question the child in a more traditional (but non-intimidating) manner about the account, and this formed the longest component of the process. This was all broadly in accordance with official guidelines (Home Office 2001a). Overall, pre-recorded evidence interviews lasted an average of 52 minutes,[11] although they ranged from 13 minutes to two hours and 13 minutes. At this point, the lawyer calling the witness would usually ask a few supplementary or clarification questions – after which the bench would usually offer a break to the witness watching from the video-link room. Cross-examination would then follow in the same manner as regular video-linked evidence.

Pre-recorded evidence provoked differing views among respondents. Interestingly, the same district judge who was sceptical of video-linked evidence above was greatly in favour of pre-recorded examination in chief for children:

> I'm actually quite used to that particular system because I used to do a lot of family work in practice ... so I represented a lot of children and did a lot of public law children cases, and so there were an awful lot of video interviews involved in that. (a district judge sitting at Court A)

This extract indicates that relevant training and experience can change engrained cultural view among lawyers even on fairly contentious issues. A second district judge (with a defence solicitor background) also considered pre-recorded examination in chief beneficial to the system, allowing important evidence to be heard which would have previously been excluded.

Nevertheless, one might argue that such questioning is controversial in the sense that – certainly in these observation sessions – many details which fell outside the strict rules of evidence were nonetheless presented in open court. This was described as very problematic by at least one legal adviser:

> I think the pre-recorded evidence that the police do is awful! It doesn't follow the rules of evidence. It's horrible! I just think it's worrying; the police need to be trained on evidence … things can come out in that evidence, most of the time it's just, that's totally irrelevant. (a legal adviser at Court B)

Other respondents also expressed reservations at the skills and level of training among police officers carrying out such interviews. There were also concerns about the perceived inability in the magistrates' courts to edit the recordings or skip past 'irrelevancies'. Magistrates and district judges were therefore being trusted to put such details from their minds.

Overall, however, pre-recorded examination in chief did not promote as much controversy among lawyers as anticipated:

> Some interviews are better than others … [but] my experience is that in most instances they [police interviewers] are pretty well trained. (a district judge sitting at Court A)

> I think video-recorded examination in chief is very helpful. (a barrister appearing at Courts A, B and C)

In sum, the occupational culture of legal practitioners was generally approving of special measures in principle, but often wary of them in practice. Given the degree of control lawyers exert over witnesses during evidence, it was somewhat ironic to note the disgruntlement of many lawyers when they felt they were losing part of that control to special measures. Nevertheless, the issue of *who* should be afforded such protection seemed more controversial than the measures themselves. Hence, 'undeserving' witnesses (by reason of past convictions) were not considered suitable for the measures. Adults too were generally believed not to require this level of protection in most cases. As such, the barriers to allowing victims to make their accounts in this way during trials are not so much *evidential* or *procedural* obstacles – based on perceptions of justice or legal rules – as they are cultural restrictions on lawyers' understanding of victimhood and vulnerability.

The impact of crime in criminal trials

For the vast majority of criminal justice practitioners and personnel, the impact of offences on victims had little place in the trial procedure, and should be reserved entirely for the sentencing stage. Nevertheless, impact information would occasionally arise in the trial itself, sometimes during the prosecutor's opening speech and sometimes during the evidence of victims. In both instances these tended to be restricted narratives, confined to the immediate (usually physical) impact of a crime on the individual victim.

Generally speaking, prosecutors sought to describe or elicit from victims the impact of crime only to the extent that it was necessary to prove the case. For example, in cases of common assault it is necessary to prove that a victim apprehends imminent unlawful violence. As such, it was fairly common for a prosecutor in such a case to ask victims how the incident made them feel. Similarly, when trying to prove a case of assault occasioning actual bodily harm, the prosecutor must show that actual bodily harm was indeed inflicted on the victim. Consequently, it was equally common in such cases for a prosecutor to ask about injuries and, ideally, this questioning would be backed up by photographs of said injuries or a doctor's report. As such, 73 per cent of all victims observed giving evidence in this research were asked something about the impact of the crime.

Questioning about the impact of a crime would also sometimes come from defence lawyers during the cross-examination of victims. This occurred in 34 per cent of all victim cross-examinations. Here the goal would be to demonstrate the *lack* of impact, the absence of any injuries, for example. To this end, the most common section of the trial in which the impact of crime on victims was discussed was the defence advocate's closing argument.

When asked specific questions about the impact of crime during evidence, victims would occasionally attempt to describe the more wide-ranging impacts, including long-term physical complaints or fear. Such instances were, however, generally the exceptions rather than the rule, and were usually curtailed by the questioning lawyer either through asking the question in a restrictive manner in the first place, or through halting the victim in the witness box.

Magistrates, district judges and juries therefore did not receive a great deal of information regarding the impact of crime on victims during the trial process itself. When such information did arise, it came in piecemeal fashion from the evidence of various witnesses, medical evidence and the victims themselves. Clearly there is no specific part of a criminal trial in which the impact of the crime on the victim is voiced. The underlying concern that such information would sway a jury or bench is of course a reasonable one. Nevertheless, this does detract from account-making notions of victim-centred criminal justice, in that the stories told by victims during trials are thereby missing a very important component, the effect of the incident upon them.

As described in previous chapters, victim personal statements were introduced nationally in October 2001 in an attempt to convey the impact of crime on victims to sentencers. Again, because these were clearly viewed as a *sentencing* exercise among practitioners, very little mention of them was made during the trials themselves, and they were never called for during a trial by the bench at any court. On one single occasion a solicitor advocate from outside the local area substantially quoted a victim personal statement directly during his opening speech. On being questioned informally after the proceedings, the solicitor expressed some surprise that victim personal statements are not usually heard from during trials in the area under review. This hints that the exact use made of victim personal statements may vary between areas.

In the present study, most respondents agreed that many more victim personal statements were being taken by police officers than had previously been the case. If victims did not want to make such a statement, a clear note was usually made on the relevant form that the victim had been given the opportunity to do so:

> I've seen a lot of them recently; conversely, I've seen a lot of 'I've been explained the VPS system but I don't wish to make a statement at this time'. We are seeing them increasingly. (a barrister appearing at Courts A, B and C)

> More recently it's becoming clear that the police are remembering to do it. (a legal adviser at Court B)

Discussions with police officers largely confirmed this view:

> We've linked it to the MG11, the sample weeks that we've done, we've actually been monitoring VPS take-ups, and it's still low in the force but – although I don't have any comparison with other forces – I suspect we do quite well at it. At least it's offered to people ... at least the rates have improved. (a police chief inspector)

The MG11 is the standard witness statement form filled in by police officers and signed by witnesses. Here, the officer was referring to the fact that the VPS is now completed on the same form. This respondent was very clear on the point that, while many victims still did not choose to complete a victim personal statement, the VPS was usually being explained and they were usually being given the option to submit one. In addition, the back of the printed MG11 now had its own witness needs assessment form so the officer could flag up at an early stage whether special measures might be needed in court. According to the chief inspector, these were being completed in 78 per cent of cases.

In describing victim personal statements, respondents said that they followed on from the witness statement, usually in the same style of language and in the same handwriting. Consequently, the statements taken in this area were usually completed by the police along with the substantive witness statements:

> From the victim personal statements that I have looked at, I'm convinced that as many of them as have come from the individuals have also come from the police officer's input … I've never seen one written by the victim, it's a continuation of their statement. (a defence solicitor appearing at Courts A and B)

This again implies that the victim's account is being replaced with that of the police.

On the court user's survey distributed at Court B, respondents who categorised themselves as victims of crime were asked questions about victim personal statements. The answers given were often confused and contradictory, suggesting a general lack of knowledge and understanding by victims on this issue. In a discussion on the equivalent questions on the WAVES survey, one OCJR representative noted that respondents nationally have been confused by such questions, not knowing exactly what a victim personal statement is or the difference between this and a witness statement.[12] This may reflect the practice just described of having the VPS follow directly on from the witness statement on the same MG11 form.

So far this section has been referring to initial VPS statements made at the time of giving a witness statement. Interestingly, very few lawyers or practitioners realised that victims could make a subsequent – stage two – victim personal statement and none had seen one. Conversely, however, the local witness care unit was very clear that the witness care officers had been proactive on this issue:

> We're actually encouraging people to make the VPS … by explaining that just because [a victim] says no initially … we can get someone to you right up till the day of court, or when you want to do one. (the manager of a witness care unit)

A common criticism made of many victim personal statements by respondents was that they were taken too early:

> It's usually done right at the very start of the process, when victims and witnesses have perhaps other issues at the forefront of their minds. The officers have other issues because they'd rather like to catch the person that's been involved in this offending behaviour. So for me it's a little bit too early and maybe the wrong line of attack in terms of who takes that statement. Someone like a dedicated victim/witness support officer – not a police officer who has other priorities – should be dealing with that kind of issue, maybe a week or so after the incident when people's recollections, people's thoughts, have become a bit clearer. When you're traumatised the last thing you want to do is write about it [the impact of crime]; you don't really know what you're thinking at that stage, do you? (the District Legal Director at Court A)

This mirrors closely a point made in Chapter 4 regarding victims' narratives, in that the present system does not allow any time for the natural reflection on and development of the story from the victim's perspective.

The last quotation also raises the issues of whether the police are the best people to be completing VPS statements. The broad consensus among lawyers held that while VPS statements were appearing more in the files, they were often short and did not provide a great deal of information. A lack of training and understanding of the scheme among police officers was often blamed. One solicitor advocate described the typical VPS statement as:

> Bland, predictable and not much use … clearly a postscript, it's an afterthought, what you'd call a tick box from the bobby's point of view. (a solicitor advocate appearing at Courts A and B)

This respondent was very keen to present full details of the effect crime had on victims to the court at the sentencing stage, but was frustrated by the lack of detail he described in most VPS statements and the fact that – by the sentencing stage – victims were no longer on call to give evidence to this effect themselves. Of course, making the victim give evidence twice is hardly conducive to a victim-centred system.

The above notwithstanding, at trial many advocates said they would now routinely make some reference to the victim personal statement, even if the information therein was fairly limited (and assuming there was one):

> I would highlight the stuff in it [the VPS] ... and read [it] out and say what the victim says about the matter, otherwise they never get a voice, do they? (a solicitor advocate appearing at Courts A and B)

> I've noticed more references ... more recently – yeah – I think the prosecution are getting more adept at remembering to adduce this evidence when it's available. (a legal adviser at Court B)

This raises the question of how the courts have received victim personal statements and what impact they have on sentencing. Many of the interview respondents were convinced that this impact was significant:

> There is no doubt the VPS statement has a powerful impact upon sentencing. (the District Legal Director at Court A)

In the Crown Court, one clerk described how judges were now asking for details from the VPS. He also described several occasions where the survivors of homicide victims had written letters to the judge, detailing the impact of the crime upon them, and how these had been taken into account. Certainly among younger advocates, the notion of including victim impact details at the sentencing stage was largely accepted:

> If someone's the victim of an assault I think it's very important, a judge will need to know for sentencing purposes what effect this has had on someone. I don't think it's as important for somebody to write 'and I think they should be made to pay' or 'they should go to prison for a very long time', I'm not sure where that takes us, but that does appear. What you want from a victim impact statement[13] is '79-year-old Doris has been

> burgled', I want to know and I want to be able to tell the judge that her wedding ring that was taken – from her late husband – is something that she will never get over. And that is something I would say, because I think it's important. Likewise, you would want to be able to tell the judge that, yes, he got a bang to the head and has received treatment and has found it very difficult to sleep since. (a barrister appearing at Courts A, B and C)

This extract reveals a great deal about the occupational practices and beliefs of at least one young barrister. While the respondent was obviously very concerned about communicating victim impact details to the court, the hypothetical example he draws on is clearly a textbook ideal victim. It is also clear that the barrister was not supportive of victims having any kind of influence over sentencing, although this quotation does indicate that victims' opinions as to the proper sentence are finding their way into the statements. Sentencers themselves were clearly seeking out victim personal statements, at least in some cases:

> Quite frequently I have them read out to me, and I quite frequently ask, because there are obviously types of cases – cases of violence or dishonesty affecting elderly people; offences of violence in general I think it's useful to have a victim personal statement. And, yes, it can be of significance … it can make the difference between a custodial and non-custodial sentence. (a district judge sitting at Court B)

This suggests VPS statements can make a significant difference to sentencers. Nevertheless, shades of the ideal victim are again surfacing here. It became obvious through talking to several lawyers and practitioners that judges and magistrates would first make a determination as to whether the type of case in issue was one in which a victim personal statement would be useful, and *then* move on to ask questions about victim impact. The drawback of this approach from the victim's perspective is that the cases in which victim personal statements will be called for by the bench will be limited by the understanding of judges and magistrates present of how different crimes may impact upon different victims. Hence, as one solicitor advocate pointed out:

> The magistrates do their utmost to *try* and take account of the effect on the victim. But there are two factors there. Firstly, I

> think the magistrates can imagine for the most part what the effects on the complainant would be … but they become case-hardened; they've heard so many cases of assault, they've heard so many people, that the effects of the assault tend to lessen on them. (a solicitor advocate appearing at Courts A and B)

The local Magistrates' Court Committee (as it was then) had endeavoured to train magistrates in the impact of crime on victims. In particular, the Justices' Chief Executive described an exercise by which a drama group had acted out the stages a victim goes through with the criminal justice system and the impact of different crimes. This had apparently galvanised enthusiasm within the local area to pilot the *No Witness, No Justice* witness care units.

In fact, the widespread view was that Crown Court judges – as opposed to magistrates – were better at taking account of or seeking out the impact of crime on victims, and were also better at making it clear that they had done so:

> I can't say that the magistrates do [make enquiries about victim personal statements]. A judge would want to know. I've heard judges ask in the past, 'Is there a victim impact statement?' They want to know and they will actually ask that. I think you'll find most judges are on top of that … They do get it in [to sentencing remarks], which I think is important as well, and this is probably the purpose behind them, that you want the judge to turn round and say, 'This must have been terrifying for the victim; indeed they can't go out on their own any more. You think about that while you go away for the next eight or nine months'. (a barrister appearing at Courts A, B and C)

That said, in the magistrates' court, one district judge referred back to the lack of detail one tends to find in many victim personal statements as a limitation of their use in sentencing:

> The only thing is, I don't know if they're prepared by police officers [but] they all sound a bit the same in the sense that they're all a bit obvious. If, for example, you've had your nose punched, then you're going to say it was very upsetting, I felt pain, it was a shock, I was off work two days. And you think – well – yes I sort of guessed that. They're very obvious things

> that they're saying – whether they could say any more I don't know, but I just get the feeling that it's somebody asking them. (a district judge sitting at Court A)

This seems to confirm that the manner in which victim personal statements are being taken by the police has a negative impact on their usefulness as sentencing tools. Indeed, given that many VPS statements seem to be more representative of a *lack* of impact on victims, one defence solicitor advocate said he would sometimes use them *in mitigation*. The view of this district judge also seems to mirror that of the defence solicitor quoted earlier, to the effect that VPS statements sometimes seem to be coming as much from the police officers as from the victims themselves.

For their part, a representative of the police revealed that there had originally been talk of creating a template VPS for police officers to follow, but this had been abandoned on the advice that it would be restrictive for victims. In practice, however, it seems that VPS statements are still being completed in a standardised way, just as lawyers themselves seem to conduct their own questioning in quite a prescribed, formulised manner.[14]

Finally in this section, some respondents expressed reservations about proposals (now being piloted) to introduce victims' advocates. One defence solicitor branded them 'a dangerous extension' of the victim personal statement, especially in relation to victims speaking themselves in court. A particular concern voiced by lawyers on this point was the inequality such a system would produce between more articulate and less articulate victims. Several advocates were also of the view that working for victims in this way would be a very unpopular job professionally.

Overall there was little argument among most practitioners that the increased focus on victim impacts was a positive development in theory. Once again, however, the real debate came with the practice: both in terms of how VPS statements should be taken and the use made of them in court. Lawyers from both sides of the adversarial system were very wary of allowing emotionally charged details or opinions into the sentencing process, and certainly the trial process. More generally, there was again an impression that victim impact is mainly being emphasised in cases involving stereotypical victimisation. This can only reinforce sentencers' traditional notions of the impacts of crime.

Victims and witnesses after trials

After giving evidence, it was common practice at all three courts for either the magistrates or the judge to thank witnesses, albeit the proportion of defence witnesses (especially defendants themselves) being thanked was markedly lower than for prosecution witnesses or victims. Victims and witnesses were then usually informed that they were free to observe the remainder of the proceedings from the public gallery. Very few witnesses elected to do so and this was, if anything, less common among victims themselves. In fact, usually the only reason witnesses would wait in the public gallery was to see/support a relative or friend about to give evidence, after which both parties would leave. Only a handful of victims or witnesses stayed in court to watch the trial through to its conclusion. Slightly more defence witnesses did so, but again this largely seemed to be a way of supporting the defendant.

One particular practice among advocates relating to victims giving evidence through special measures is worth recalling here. Having watched witnesses or victims giving evidence from behind a screen or through a video-link, on the few occasions where it occurred, many advocates were somewhat nonplussed to see the witness or victim coming into court to observe from the public gallery. This was usually pounced upon by the defence as evidence that the victim could not have been as intimidated as she claimed. This is interesting because it provides an example of a measure intended to assist victims and vulnerable witnesses being adapted for use *against* them.

The fact that the victim is so rarely present at the end of a trial raises the question of how they are to be informed of the outcome. Indeed, even if victims were present, they might well need some degree of explanation. One representative of Court B made it clear that – in his view – passing on information should not be the courts' responsibility as it would prejudice their impartiality. Responsibility for contacting victims and witnesses had essentially been turned over to the CPS and the joint police/CPS witness care units. As such, when victims – or other prosecution witnesses – were still present at the end of proceedings at the magistrates' court, most prosecution advocates said they would usually explain the results to them, and such explanations were observed taking place many times. This was particularly important after trials were adjourned or otherwise resolved, as such cases raised puzzling concepts like bind overs or plea bargains. Not all advocates took this role gladly:

> As a barrister briefed just for that trial you can often be perceived as a scapegoat – 'You're the person who can go and explain this'. Now I've never liked doing that, I've never liked going and explaining [to victims and witnesses] and saying, 'Look, really it isn't your decision but this is what has happened, and what do you feel about it?' but we're encouraged to do so. (a barrister appearing at Courts A, B and C)

As noted above, this view regarding scapegoating was common among disgruntled agents working on behalf of the Crown. The feeling seemed to be that the CPS reserved for agents the cases in which a high degree of victim or witness contact work would be necessary, rather than having the Crown prosecutor who had dealt with the case from the beginning face the victims herself. This same respondent was also very clear that the same task would not fall to him in the Crown Court, where he would rely on CPS caseworkers. There is also a clear view expressed here that the form of disposition a trial takes on the morning is not the victim's decision.

Nevertheless, many criminal justice practitioners were accepting of the idea that victims and witnesses should receive information and full explanation of the outcomes of their cases, even if they had not been present for the whole trial:

> One of the things I do think might be helpful is the feedback to victims or to victims' relatives, so that as well as explaining to people before coming to court how they will be in court and how they will be asked questions, they also get proper feedback at the end. (a district judge sitting at Court A)

In the case of dropped charges, adjourned, or otherwise resolved trial proceedings, it was confirmed by the CPS Chief Prosecutor that they would send a letter to the victim soon afterwards explaining the decision. These letters were written by staff at the CPS victim information bureau based on notes left by the prosecutor. While such letters would contain some fairly standard paragraphs, they were not pro forma letters. Before being sent, such letters would be forwarded to the relevant prosecutor for amendment and a signature, hence the letter did come directly from the relevant prosecutor. In some cases this was also a bone of contention, as in one adjourned trial where the complainant had arrived at court heavily intoxicated, the Crown prosecutor expressed some frustration at being obliged to write her a polite letter explaining why the case did not proceed.

In addition, all witnesses would receive a letter from the joint CPS/ police witness care unit informing them of the outcome of the case. The witness care unit also referred victims on to organisations that could provide victims with further help and support if necessary.

Victims at the heart of criminal justice: principles or practice?

During the course of this research there was often a stark contrast between how lawyers *spoke* about victims and their *actions* during actual criminal trials. This seemed to reflect a conflict between new ideas of victim-centredness and more engrained notions of how criminal trials ought to operate, as well as what is and is not the lawyers' job. Take, for example, these two extracts from notes at two different magistrates' court trials and concerning different lawyers:

> The defence lawyer is saying again quite forcefully that the 12-year-old witness (female) shouldn't be made to give evidence → even through video-link → [the lawyer] notes that there is always a problem finding witnesses for domestic violence cases. (note taken at trial 157)

> During the break the prosecution lawyer said [that] breaking down into tears was the only 'good thing' the prosecution witness did for the case. (note taken at trial 59)

In the first extract, the defence lawyer's concern for a vulnerable witness demonstrates a degree of sympathy largely unseen in previous studies. Through multiple observations like this it became apparent that legal occupational cultures have altered to the extent that lawyers are now willing to *talk* about victims and show sympathy to them more readily than appears to have been the case previously. When it came to actual trials, however, the *practice* of many lawyers seemed to frustrate such sentiments, and opinions like that demonstrated in the second extract were prominent, with the tactical reality of winning the case overshadowing any concern the prosecutor might be feeling for the prosecution witness.

As with any body of professionals, departing from established practices could result in a lawyer being ostracised by colleagues. This was demonstrated on one occasion when – following a change of plea on behalf of the defendant – an agent prosecutor arranged for the defendant and victim to shake hands. The agent defence counsel clearly disapproved, and was subsequently heard passing the story on (replete with disapproving sentiments) at several future trials. A similar fate befell any lawyer who departed too greatly (or 'eccentrically') from established trial norms, which helps to illustrate why traditional and deeply engrained notions of legal practice – which are non-conducive to victims' needs – are difficult to eliminate from lawyers' individual occupational cultures. On the one hand, this may be attributed to the very close-knit nature of the social world this research encountered at individual courts, and the only slightly wider social/cultural network of legal practitioners in the geographical area as a whole. In the wider sense, however, such actions on the part of individual lawyers would have been contrary to the established tenets of legal culture as a whole.

Of course, some respondents admitted that – as professionals – they were probably unable to see the system from the perspective of victims or witnesses:

> I don't know how it comes across, because I sit on the other side – it's normal to me because that's how it was done. I've never been a witness in court proceedings; if I was a witness in court proceedings I'd have a different view. (a legal adviser at Court A)

Like this final respondent, academics and policy-makers might question the ability of seasoned court professionals to put themselves in the place of victims coming to court to give evidence. Nevertheless, we might also pre-empt the conclusions draw in Chapter 7 by observing that if the occupational culture of advocates, administrators and other legal personnel has in fact adapted to the point where they at least *attempt* to take a victim's eyes view of the criminal justice system, this can only bode well for the achievement of a truly victim-centred system. The possible characteristics of such a system will be discussed in the final chapter.

Notes

1 The docks used in most trials at Courts A and B were simple benches with no barrier between the defendant and the rest of the court.

2 On two occasions in the Crown Court, witnesses became confused by a device resembling a microphone built into the witness box. The device was intended for use with the court's hearing aid loop system but did

not in fact amplify the voice. The witnesses therefore had to be advised against speaking into the object.

3 Splitting these results down to examine the three courts individually produced similar findings.

4 The majority of these observations were carried out before the bad character provisions in the Criminal Justice Act 2003 were in force.

5 Advocates confirmed that witness statements are usually written by police officers rather than by victims or other witnesses themselves.

6 Although one might argue that anger, for example, may help a witness deal with the process and compel them to get their points across more clearly.

7 No lawyer spoken to for this research had experience of adult males giving evidence via special measures.

8 Confirmed in the case of *R (on the application of S)* v. *Waltham Forest Youth Court* [2004] 2 Cr App R 21.

9 See Rule 29.1(1)(4).

10 See Tables 24 and 25 above.

11 Standard deviation = 30.96.

12 This respondent also reported that early WAVES figures confirm that more VPS statements are now being taken.

13 Despite the scheme being renamed 'victim personal statement' in 2001, the term 'victim impact statement' appeared to have stuck with many lawyers and court workers.

14 See pages 153–164.

Chapter 7

Victims 'at the heart' of criminal justice: a discussion

The goal of this book has been to cast light on the government's contention that it is putting crime victims at the heart of the criminal justice system in England and Wales, with a particular focus on what this pledge means for the criminal trial. In Chapter 1, this investigation was broken down into three key questions:

1 What would it mean to have a victim-centred criminal justice system?
2 What factors have driven this 'policy'?
3 What has putting victims 'at the heart' of the system meant so far in practice?

This chapter will examine how the issues and results presented in all the preceding chapters help us to address these questions.

What would it mean to have a victim-centred criminal justice system?

Based on all the data gathered for this project, the following section draws out examples of best practice which would feature in an ideally victim-centred system of justice. At the outset, it is submitted that the victim-centred nature of a criminal trial can be separated into three interrelated forms of centrality illustrated on Figure 7.1.

These three forms of centrality are closely related and interdependent, hence the choice of a triangle. Each component of this model will now be discussed in turn.

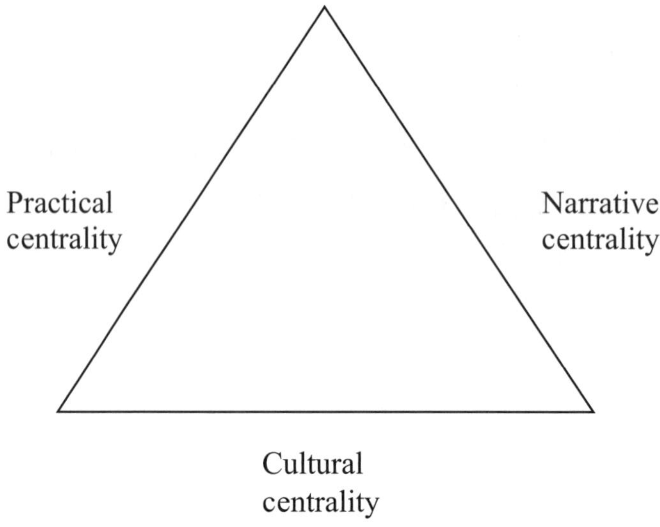

Figure 7.1 Proposed model of victim-centredness

Practical centrality

Many of the most significant problems faced by victims in the criminal trial procedure are grounded in very practical concerns. Practical centrality simply means that the truly victim-centred criminal justice system would be systematically organised with these practical considerations in mind. This means ensuring administrative systems and funding are in place to guarantee that services and facilities are offered consistently and automatically to all victims, and not just in courts with especially pro-active managers or Witness Services.

Evidence from the Witness Surveys (Whitehead 2001; Angle *et al.* 2003) and the wider research (Maguire and Bennett 1982; Shapland *et al.* 1985) indicate that much of what victims require from the criminal justice system amounts to so-called service rights, including increased information and facilities at court (Ashworth 2000). Sanders *et al.* (2001) describe such rights as 'essentially unobjectionable' in principle. Nevertheless, commentators have tended to rely on a standard list of service rights without further deconstruction of the issue (JUSTICE 1998) or its application to the evidential process. As such, the notion of practical centrality used here includes standard service rights such as information (booklets, help desks, signposting) and physical facilities (waiting rooms, seating, a cafeteria) while also emphasising services afforded to victims giving evidence (court design, special measures, non-intrusive noting/recording), and the wider reform of administrative and operational practices to better meet their needs.

Such operational practices include, in particular, those related to the listing and running of criminal trials. Practical centrality means courts have sufficient resources to run trials around victims' availability, rather than fitting the victim in around the schedule of court work and the allocation of staff and judges. The CPS has a key role here too in providing enough prosecutors or agents to meet demand. This suggests an end to the double-listing of trials where victims might attend to give evidence because, at best, this system leads to extended waiting times while, at worst, it results in victims being sent home.

This is not simply a matter of increasing the capacity of courts or the CPS to run trials, but increasing the *flexibility* of court and personnel scheduling so that lists can be changed quickly to meet victims' needs. In other words, while this is a resource question, it is not predominantly an *economic* question of increasing resources, but rather one of adapting organisational structures. It is also a question of effective communication and the sharing of information between agencies, ensuring any problems inherent in a case are flagged up long before the day of the trial. From the CPS perspective, assigning one prosecutor to follow a case from start to finish would be a step forward.

At court, the Effective Trial Management Programme has attempted to address some of the inefficiencies in case management. At present, however, magistrates' court benches in particular can be unwilling to enforce the procedures, so the practical issue becomes one of educating magistrates and district judges to ask relevant and probing questions of prosecutors and defence advocates in the run-up to a trial. In other words, benches must be persuaded (or required) to take a proactive hand in case management.[1] The fact that issues like special measures and bad character applications are still commonly arising on the morning of the trial suggests this is not consistently achieved.

The success of the Effective Trial Management Programme also relies on the appointment of proactive and resourceful case progression officers. We saw in Court C that the case progression officer was fettered by a presumption that solicitors would not start preparing a case until two weeks before the trial. Whether this is based on practicality, culture or tactics on the part of defence advocates and defendants is difficult to discern,[2] but in any case such a presumption would need to be addressed in a truly victim-centred system. Proactiveness is especially important when dealing with the needs and availability of victims and witnesses, which must also be canvassed at review hearings. Gathering such information is a multi-agency effort involving organisations like the witness care unit and/or the CPS victim information bureau. Such bodies must maintain clear avenues of communication and information-sharing between them. The Witness Service also has a key role to play here, albeit this raises questions as to whether its support functions are being subsumed with those of increasing system efficiency.

Practical centrality also means having the facilities and resources in place to keep victims and witnesses informed as cases progress towards trial. This means sending them the trial date promptly, and providing other information concerning the location of the court, public transport links and *realistic* details about the trial procedure. Realistic here means details which prepare victims for less straightforward aspects of coming to court, such as the purpose of giving evidence, the process of cross-examination and the likelihood of delays. Victims should also be offered a courtroom familiarisation visit in advance.

On the day of the trial, courts in a victim-centred system would provide all the usual facilities (standard service rights). These include cafeterias, seating, signposting and – unlike Courts A and B in this study – adequate car parking. It would also mean ensuring the victim knows where to go and understands what is happening at all stages of the process. When a victim first arrives at court he or she would be immediately directed to the Witness Service, preferably by being led there by the security officers, or met by Witness Service volunteers themselves. The Witness Service volunteers would then offer a court familiarisation visit. In the case of more vulnerable or intimidated witnesses, practical centrality would also mean having the capacity at a court to bring witnesses in via a back door if this were necessary to avoid the defendant and/or defence witnesses.

Once at court, the lines of communication between victim and courtroom in this system would be well established and efficient. Ideally, this would involve prosecutors themselves keeping the victim directly informed about developments on the morning of the trial. The Witness Service volunteers or CPS caseworkers would also be well placed to offer regular updates and to collect victims' statements for victims to review before they give evidence. Witness Service volunteers should be willing to approach advocates, legal advisers and clerks directly in order to gather this information and, equally, legal advisers and clerks would be kept up to date so they could relay the information. Lines of communication should not become too convoluted, with information being passed on (as in Court C) from prosecutor to clerk to CPS caseworker to Witness Service volunteer to victim. In cases of long delays or adjourned and otherwise resolved proceedings, some explanation would be offered directly from the bench,[3] who would proactively enquire about waiting witnesses.

If pre-trial review processes operate effectively, waiting times should be significantly reduced. If victims were forced to wait for any significant time, they would be allowed to leave the court building, thus avoiding the impression of being trapped. In such cases, the court would have the facilities in place to either page or text these victims when it was time to return. The staggered calling of witnesses could also be employed to this end, especially in cases where it was known that legal arguments would precede the actual trial. Families of witnesses would inevitably still arrive at court together, but this would be their *choice* and the notion of staggering implies more of the appointments-based culture found in other public services. If the victim was happy to stay at court, then comfortable waiting facilities would be provided.

It is important that a courtroom is practically designed so that when the victim is giving evidence they are neither looking at nor positioned close to the defendant or the public gallery where the defendant's supporters may be seated. The witness box should also be free of any confusing equipment, such as the object that looked like a microphone (but was not) attached to the witness boxes at Court C. Another specific practical issue is the noting that is done in the magistrates' court during evidence, which can lead to the victim being stopped and started by lawyers trying to keep up. In a genuinely victim-centred system, the practical facilities would be available to avoid this, either by recording victim evidence or, as in the Crown Court, noting it through stenography.

When victims are giving evidence through special measures, practical centrality implies the provision of effective equipment that in no way complicates the experience for the victim, or interferes with the judicial process.[4] This means a high standard of video and audio, and a proficient operator. In the case of pre-recorded examination in chief, police officers should be fully trained in the process and the challenges presented by children giving evidence (see Krähenbühl 2008). Ideally, screens should be built into the courtroom to reduce confusion, delay and the debates seen in Court A over where to position them. On the issue of special measures, procedures would be in place from very early on in the criminal justice system to ensure that the victim's need for such facilities be flagged up.

In Chapter 4 it was argued that, in order to integrate a victim's full narrative, the victim-centred criminal justice system must be organised to incorporate the impact of crime on victims. In accordance with existing case law (Shapland 2002) this should be taken into account at the sentencing stage.[5] Practically, this means training police officers to take victim personal statements and ensuring that they can (and do) explain their purpose to victims.[6] Another possibility would be for some other agency to take victim personal statements, leaving the police to concentrate on pursuing the prosecution. Systems would be in place to contact victims sometime after the initial statements were taken to ask whether they wished to change them or make further stage two statements. Possibly, no agency at all would need to 'take' statements from victims, but facilities could be provided for victims to send statements to the court or perhaps upload them online. Lawyers themselves would also need to be educated on the impacts of crime on victims.

Following a criminal trial, mechanisms would be in place both to relay information about the outcome to victims and also to refer them on to any other support organisations (external to the criminal justice process) that might assist them.

As we are presently considering the *practicalities* inherent in a victim-centred system, it is worth emphasising that victim-centred criminal justice should not be inundated with reform to the extent that agencies or advocates cannot keep up with their training and familiarisation with new developments, as appeared to be the case with the introduction of bad character and hearsay provisions under the Criminal Justice Act 2003. Furthermore, while the system outlined here is arguably an efficient ideal, none of this represents truly fundamental reform to the present system. For the most part, the measures advocated here are developments of existing practices, or simply ensure existing mechanisms operate as intended.

Cultural centrality

While practical centrality is integral to the operation of a truly victim-centred system, it perhaps does not take us much beyond established notions of affording victims service rights. Greater challenges lie in promoting real and self-perpetuating changes in the underlying occupational cultures of criminal justice practitioners and staff. The practical changes outlined in the last section will not achieve victim-centred trials without this associated cultural change. For example, providing separate waiting rooms for prosecution witnesses will do little to reduce witness intimidation if, as on several occasions during these observations, Witness Service volunteers lead those witnesses into the court past where the defendant and his witnesses are sitting, or defence advocates bring their clients into court while the victim is having a pre-trial familiarisation visit. Hence, providing the practical facilities and systems is one thing, but practitioners and others must understand their purposes and accept these as legitimate to make them beneficial.

The importance of occupational cultures in shaping a criminal justice system has been highlighted in numerous contexts. Erez (1991, 1999, 2004) criticises the widely held view that only 'normal' levels of impact should affect sentences and blames this for the initial low take-up of victim personal statements. Temkin (1987) and Cretney and Davis (1997) also emphasise the role of occupational cultures as a key prerequisite to victims' discomfort in giving evidence. We have also discussed Shapland *et al.*'s (1985) overarching conclusion that the changes required to achieve victim-centredness were more attitudinal than structural. Occupational cultures of course exist at many levels of a profession. In this case, attitudes need to be addressed at the level of individual courts (local cultures), legal professions (barristers, solicitors, court clerks, etc.) and the wider culture of the legal community (values general to most lawyers instilled by their common training).

Culture in trial preparation and delay

Cultural centrality will underlie practical centrality at all stages of the trial process. For example, the effective systems of case management required by practical centrality must be backed with an enthusiasm among all criminal justice agencies and the courts to work together towards this goal. Case management must not be dismissed as pointless bureaucracy to be engaged with only two weeks before the trial.[7] This also means an end to the blame culture that permeated through the observation sessions and interviews, whereby one part of the criminal justice system blames another for delays and adjournments. Of course, practical and cultural centrality are dependent on each other – for in order to instil this kind of culture into practitioners the system needs to operate in practice in a way that demonstrates the usefulness and relevance of case management systems. In the same way, convincing benches to be proactive in enforcing the Effective

Trial Management process is as much a cultural change as it is a practical issue of training.

In recent years, cultural moves towards reducing delay in criminal proceedings have been spurred on by developments in case law. As discussed by Jackson *et al.* (2003), the case of *Porter* v. *Magill*[8] seems to confirm that defendants have a right under Article 6 (1) of the European Convention on Human Rights to be tried within a reasonable time. In *Porter* v. *Magill* Lord Hope confirmed that this guarantee was independent of a defendant's right to a fair trial. In other words, it was not necessary to demonstrate that unreasonable delay in getting a case to court had prejudiced the chances of a fair hearing. Interpretations by the Strasbourg Court confirm that Article 6 is intended to protect *all* parties from excessive procedural delays, especially in criminal cases.[9] Under this construction, judges would be obliged to take account of not only the defendant's position when deciding on the 'unreasonableness' of delay, but also that of the victim, which again means consulting victims on the impact of such delay. Courts in a victim-centred system would therefore be obliged to ensure delays did not reach the stage where a stay of trial was likely, by moving a case up the list or at least holding a pre-trial review hearing to see if progress could be expedited. Such processes could be initiated at the behest of the victims themselves through their legal representation (if they are to be granted party status).[10] This would also mean an end to tactical delays by defendants (or defence advocates) (Elias 1986; McConville *et al.* 1994).

While defendants can be criticised for not applying their minds to cases beforehand – and the argument made that only the court door will focus their minds – the same applies to some (prosecution and defence) lawyers. This is especially true when delays and problems on the morning of a trial are accepted as an inevitability, such as in cases of domestic violence.[11] This leads to the wider point that in a choice between inconvenience to the system/court/lawyers and inconvenience to the victim, practitioners in a victim-centred system would accept the former. The victim-centred model therefore implies a change of views as to who it is permissible to inconvenience.

Culture and victim contact pre-trial

On the morning of a trial, prosecutors in a victim-centred system would see it as a normal part of their duties to meet victims and keep them informed as to the progress of the case, as opposed to seeing this as unusual 'difficult' work imposed on them by the CPS. Culturally, something as simple as not returning to the safety of the barrister's robing room at every opportunity may be enough to ensure the flow of information to the victim is maintained.[12] Many of the advocates interviewed for this study already accepted the greeting of witnesses as part of their job. Others, however, were still uncomfortable with this role and would ask the defence for permission at the first sign of going beyond culturally prescribed boundaries with victims.

In a system where victims have become culturally central, advocates would also accept the assistance of the Witness Service without dismissing them as busybodies. The suggestion by one barrister that the Crown cannot proceed without the Witness Service suggests such a change in attitudes is possible, although here we must be wary of prosecutors abandoning victims entirely into the hands of volunteers. Reconciliation is necessary between the cultures of lawyers and volunteers, which will involve less emphasis by lawyers on consistency and 'proper procedure' (very much traits of the wider legal culture) and more emphasis on ensuring the victim is comfortable and prepared to give evidence. This might involve more use of staggered witness calling. While several practitioners raised a number of fair points regarding the practical limits of such a system, there was a definite sense that, *culturally*, most advocates are nervous about losing the professional security of having all witnesses present before a trial begins.

Culture and victim participation

Cultural centrality also includes affording victims a degree of participation in any victim-centred system. In Chapter 2 it was suggested that participation in the form of consultation can be grounded in the (existing) principle that benches make decisions based on all available information. As such, the main obstacle to such participation seems to be the resistant culture of lawyers, especially the presumption of a zero sum relationship between victim and defendant rights. Culturally centred victims would therefore be *genuinely* consulted on issues like plea bargaining and bind overs.[13] Following the critique of Ashworth in Chapter 2, this represents a right to consultative participation, such that the views of victims are taken into account by decision-makers. As argued in Chapter 2, the key goal here will be to instil within the minds of practitioners the view that victims' opinions matter, are not necessarily grounded in bias or vengefulness, and will not unduly impact upon the rights of defendants if they are considered along with other factors.

It was also argued in Chapter 2 that a victim-centred system might afford victims some degree of consultative participation in the sentencing process. Again, the same basic argument applies that, culturally, lawyers and the judiciary must become accustomed to taking account of victims' stated views – among other factors – and accept that this does not detract from due process. More specifically, the inclusion of victim impact information as part of a victim's wider narrative would also represent a cultural change for many lawyers and benches. Perhaps more importantly, benches will need to adapt their practices such that it is made clear to victims that this information has been taken into account (if not necessarily followed) during the decision-making process.

Of course, adducing such impact information at trial would also require a change of cultural priorities for police officers, if they continued to take the victim personal statements. Again, the distinction here is between the *practical* facilitation of such changes through distributing information (and offering training and education to lawyers, police and other practitioners) and the *cultural* change required to accept these reforms in real-life working practice. In so doing, lawyers in victim-centred trials would consider it an important aspect of the process to involve victim impact information and to adduce and consider the victims' opinions.

We have seen that victims do not wish to run the criminal justice system (JUSTICE 1998), hence the general lack of decision-making participation in the model presented here.[14] Nevertheless, it is vital for a victim-centred system to take account of victims' views, weigh them fairly alongside other factors, and ensure the victim is able to appreciate that this has been done. The alternative is to raise victims' hopes only to dash them later, leaving them more disappointed with the system.

Culture and the treatment of victims in the courtroom

In the courtroom, practical centrality requires proactive clerks, legal advisers and benches who are willing to enquire about waiting victims. Benches must also ensure information is passed on to the Witness Service and/or CPS caseworkers, as well as offering explanations directly to victims if necessary. As with the pre-trial review hearings, this will require training to ensure judicial, legal or administrative actors understand such roles and carry them out. More specifically, however, it must become integral to the operational cultures of judges and magistrates to take such actions and be proactive. All the actors in the process must share these common values, avoiding a situation where prosecutors deflect magistrates from their intention to bring witnesses into court to provide explanations or thanks.[15] In the Crown Court in particular, this would also involve instilling a sense of urgency about the proceedings on the morning of the trial, which is already present to some degree at the magistrates' court.

During the trial, inviting victims to sit, giving them water and offering them breaks are again culturally based practices, as is the welcoming of supporters into courtrooms – or video-link rooms – if it will assist the victim. The reliance in all courts – especially in the magistrates' court – on handwritten notes may also be more cultural than practical, as lawyers have traditionally relied on written documents to allow for later annotation or quick reference. It would therefore be interesting to pilot the recording of witnesses' evidence electronically. In a victim-centred system, the emphasis would be on facilitating the victim's smooth explanation of the evidence (and the building of accounts, on which see below) rather than the notes made by lawyers. Hence, a cultural shift away from this reliance on paper would be beneficial. In addition, court staff and lawyers need to be aware of issues such as the victim giving evidence near or in the eye line of defendants. It also seems unlikely that a victim-centred system would insist that witnesses face benches of magistrates for the purely cultural reason that it represents 'a courtesy'.[16]

During evidence, advocates are influenced by many cultural precepts which may not be vital to the basic adversarial process itself. Hence, improving the experience for victims means altering these occupational practices rather than the procedure *per se*. As such, in a victim-centred system there would be a broad consensus – expressed by some respondents in this study (especially younger advocates) – that excessive hostility is not required to adduce evidence. Even before evidence begins, there would be fewer cultural reservations about explaining to victims issues like hearsay and the purpose of cross-examination. Generally speaking, lawyers would not be inclined to interrupt victims during the evidence and would avoid labelling them as deceptive, or casting aspersions on their character. In short, the overriding legal culture would be one of ensuring evidence is still an adversarial process, but also a *civilised* process; the opinions of lawyers interviewed for this study confirm that this is not a contradiction in terms.

Regarding special measures, it has been noted that practical centrality requires high-quality audio and video reproduction. Culturally it seems that lawyers in a victim-centred system would accept what is still widely viewed as the problem of not being able to appreciate victims' demeanour though the video-link system. Again, this seems a product of entrenched cultural practices, by which the toolkit of advocates has previously been based around reading the body language of victims standing before them (Chan 1996). Clearly, such a system initially needs lawyers who are prepared to make special measures applications, and are willing to accept evidence adduced in this manner[17] without concern that it will affect the outcome of the case. Victim-centredness also implies that lawyers will not use special measures against victims by subsequently barring them from entering the court to observe the remainder of the trial. It was demonstrated in Chapter 6 that there is generally mixed opinion as to whether special measures – especially video-links – always help witnesses give evidence. How a victim reacts to giving evidence in this way is probably less about the equipment itself and more about the *attitude* of the lawyers asking questions, and whether their individual style is adapted to suit the vulnerability of the victim.

Culture and victimhood

A very important cultural change within a victim-centred system would involve the expansion of practitioners' notions of victimhood beyond the stereotypically vulnerable and blameless victim. Victim-centred implies that the real victims are brought to the heart of the system, not the victims we might hope them to be. This also means developing lawyers' ideas about the impact of crime on victims. Hence, expanding notions of victimhood and vulnerability means, for example, affording special measures to non-ideal victims and to adults. This means treating *all* victims equally, rather than assuming 'professional' victims will come when called while non-ideal (but far more common) victims will steal the court's pager.

Essentially, cultural centrality means instilling a genuine concern for the victim within lawyers and staff at all stages of the criminal justice process.[18] Criminal justice actors must collectively develop an ability to see things from the victim's perspective, such that the facilities and mechanisms discussed under practical centrality will function and the views of the victims are not excluded from the process. Ultimately, this also means establishing such considerations as a key aspect of court culture, and legal culture in general. It was shown in Chapters 5 and 6 that many lawyers are becoming comfortable with *expressing* concern for such victims, but in a truly victim-centred system their occupational practices would allow them to demonstrate such concern in action, and without fear of being ostracised by colleagues.

Narrative centrality

Chapter 4 identified a number of limitations imposed on victims of crime when presenting their narratives in English and Welsh criminal trials. These included interruption, compelling victims to give evidence in an unfamiliar and unnatural manner, and phrasing questions so as to elicit narrow answers. All these examples were evident to varying degrees in the data presented in Chapters 5 and 6. As argued in Chapter 4, a truly victim-centred trial would allow room for the freer construction of victims' narratives. As this is certainly the most far-reaching aspect of the model given in Figure 7.1, some time will be spent here elaborating on its implications.

The role of the audience: the lawyers and the state

The imitations placed on victims' narratives during criminal trials are largely a consequence of the audience(s) of these narratives. Narrative theory has long maintained that audiences are not merely passive consumers, but actively contribute to and shape the accounts they are presented with. As Plummer puts it:

> [T]elling [of stories] cannot be in isolation from hearings, readings, consumings ... There is a flow of action and producers become consumers, whilst consumers become producers. (1995: 25)

When a victim presents an account in a courtroom setting there are many possible consumers: the judge or magistrates; lawyers; jurors; the victim's friends and family in the public gallery; the defendant;[19] the defendant's friends and family; the wider community (usually through the media); and the state in whose name charges are brought. As suggested by Van Duyne (1981), these different audiences will have different interpretations of a victim's story and, from their various perspectives, different features will have greater or lesser significance.

In criminal trials, the capacity of the audience (certainly the legally qualified component of it) to exert influence over the story being told by the victim is particularly apparent from Chapter 6. The courtroom data gathered in this study confirm that, for these lawyers, a 'good story' was one which assisted their arguments[20] and complied with the strict rules of evidence. This legal audience is very different from the audience of sympathetic friends, family members and Victim

Support volunteers that victims may grow accustomed to between their victimisation and the trial. Most victims will have some idea of the needs of this 'family' audience, who are willing to accept (perhaps demand) a much wider range of information and emotional outpouring than is permitted by the criminal justice system. At court, however, many victims face a marked lack of information on the requirements of their new audience, which demonstrated itself in this study through the inclusion of hearsay and other legally contentious material in victims' evidence. If victims do not know their audience, then this inevitably makes it difficult for them to prepare and present their narratives in court.

In the light of the policy issues discussed in Chapter 3, this question of audience has implications well beyond individual courtrooms. Specifically, one can view an audience of legally qualified persons as representatives of the state, and the state itself as the ultimate consumer of the victim's narrative. Of course, only the prosecutor is working directly as an agent of the state during a criminal trial. Nevertheless, all lawyers seek to ensure that the procedural rules handed down by the state are followed. Furthermore, victims become involved in the criminal trial procedure as a result of the state's intervention in citizens' actions[21] with the fundamental goal – according to one branch of legal philosophy (De Smith and Brazier 1998) – of ensuring the state's continued existence. It is therefore important for commentators (and victims) to ascertain what the state hopes to elicit from the victim's account.

Determining what the state actually wants from victims in criminal trials is far from straightforward. In recent years the official purposes of the criminal justice system have been expressed very broadly. The government's cjsonline website lists a multitude of goals for the CJS including: delivering justice; punishing the guilty; rehabilitating the convicted; protecting the public; preventing crime; promoting public confidence; increasing the satisfaction of victims and witnesses; and meeting the wider needs of victims (cjsonline 2005a). This wide assortment of outcomes makes it difficult to determine the state's priorities. One possibility suggested by several commentators is that the goals of the criminal justice system have become increasingly entwined with a punitive populism (Bottoms 1995) engendered by Garland's (2001) 'culture of control'. While, in more recent years, the political parties have established a form of middle ground second order consensus on law and order issues (Downes and Morgan 2002), it seems from the discussion in Chapter 3 that the punitive impetus remains (see Young 2003).

If the system is actually premised on punitive or retributive strategies, then the purpose of asking (or compelling) victims to give evidence in court is to sustain a prosecution and to play the role of the wronged party, providing a justification for punitiveness. This limits the scope of the story a victim is permitted to tell, because all that is required to make it a 'good story' from the state's perspective is that it contains the evidential elements necessary to achieve a conviction, and perhaps to justify a heavy sentence. It also implies that the victim should play down any non-ideal features of their narratives; for instance, if they are not entirely blameless in their victimisation, or are not in favour of a punitive response. This corresponds with Garland's (2001) view that victims become the reference point for success, and a justification for punitive measures, when the public loses faith in the ability of the justice system to control crime.

Chapter 3 also highlighted the recent moves to promote efficiency within the system, in accordance with a new public service ethos (Rock 2004). On this point, it is notable that government targets compel courts to reduce adjournment rates, rather than bring down the number of trials listed to take place on a given day but resolved in some other manner (often with a guilty plea) at the last minute. To the courts, this means that such otherwise resolved trials are preferable to full trials, because they use less time and resources. Otherwise resolved trials ordinarily do not require witnesses to give evidence themselves, but rely on written witness statements to communicate in a succinct manner all 'necessary' information to the court. As such, if the state's primary goal for its criminal justice system is to maximise efficiency, this once again restricts victims' narrative accounts to those recorded in their witness statements, with the added stipulation that victims will not even present these accounts themselves in many cases. Under this interpretation, a good story from the state's perspective is one that is never told.

To summarise, the audience of a victim's story is likely to influence and restrict the scope of the narrative he or she is allowed to present. While this might be viewed in simple terms as individual lawyers in individual courtrooms, at the macro level such attitudes reflect the state's intentions for the criminal justice system. While it is difficult to determine precisely what these intentions might be, the suggestion is that – notwithstanding the promise to put victims at the heart of criminal justice – the state as ultimate consumer of these narratives is likely to restrict a victim's account to that of the evidential witness statement.

Incorporating victims' narratives and voluntary account-making

Bringing victims' narratives to the heart of the criminal justice system has two main aspects: allowing the victim to communicate accounts in a more fluent, less contrived manner than is presently possible under procedural and cultural constraints; and giving the victim the *choice* over whether or not to do so (and how to do so) in the first place.

To address the latter point first, victims in such a system would not be forced to give evidence against their will, because their need to tell *or not to tell* their stories would trump any public interest criteria or even – as is often the case in domestic violence proceedings – the need to protect individuals. Hence, in this limited instance, victims would be afforded decision-making power. For the same reason, the views of victims would be *genuinely* canvassed and considered when deciding on issues like plea bargaining or bind overs because, in such cases, lawyers are effectively negotiating what version of the victim's story to present to the court. Victims would also be permitted to give evidence in whatever way they found easiest to communicate their accounts to the fullest. This might mean affording them special measures (including pre-recorded examination in chief) but it could equally mean *not* compelling them to give evidence in this way if they find it confusing or, for example, they require a more direct relationship with their audience.

Allowing victims to choose whether or not to give evidence is not the same as burdening them with *prosecution* decisions. To do so would place them under undue pressure and signify a denial of the state's responsibility to police and prosecute breaches of the law. Denying victims the authority to block prosecutions initiated by the state is not overly problematic to a victim-centred system, so long as the victim may choose whether or not to give evidence *as part of* such prosecutions. It is then left to the state to promote confidence in the criminal justice system and to provide the facilities and information that make more victims willing to give evidence. If victims still refuse, it is again up to the state to gather sufficient evidence to proceed without the original complainant, rather than putting pressure or applying sanctions to that complainant. Having elected to give evidence – in whatever manner – victims in this system would be permitted to communicate their narrative accounts in a more natural, open manner, less constrained by cultural or procedural restrictions. The expectation in this system would be that victims are rarely interrupted when giving evidence, and certainly should not be troubled by issues like note taking, keeping their voice up, or facing the jury or bench. We have seen that these are largely culturally based practices among advocates rather than fundamental principles of the adversarial system.

Such a system would also focus less exclusively on the original written witness statement and allow more room for the continuing narrative development of a victim's account from the time of victimisation onwards. This would begin right at the start of the process, with less emphasis on getting the statement signed as soon as possible and more on allowing the victim to come to terms with the experience. It would also mean giving victims the option to make subsequent witness statements as a matter of course, just as they are permitted to give stage two victim personal statements. Indeed, it may be simpler to combine the two forms of statement into one victim account statement. The taking of such statements would be conducted in far less evidential terms than is presently the case, and ideally victims would be given the opportunity to physically write them themselves, deriving therapeutic benefits from doing so (Harber and Pennebaker 1992). The system would therefore be organised from the outset to ensure prosecutors (and judges) have access to the full range of victims' accounts as they develop from the point of taking the original witness statement right up to the day of the trial.

Of course, having efficient systems in place to collect wider narratives from victims will mean little if prosecutors are not prepared to consider and present such information to the court and/or allow victims to articulate more of this information in evidence. Hence, narrative centrality is once again co-dependent on cultural centrality. This means addressing the cultural presumption inherent in most legal practitioners[22] that the best evidence is gathered as soon as possible after an event. In keeping with the above discussion on victim participation, benches must be prepared to openly acknowledge their consideration of a victim's account (especially at the sentencing stage) even if aspects of this account are, on balance, rejected during the decision-making process. To the victim, this represents a vindication of their victim status, promoting therapeutic outcomes (Miers 1980).

Due process and limitations on victims' narratives?

It would be wrong to interpret the above proposals as affording victims an unfettered discretion to say, present or have presented anything they wish during a criminal trial. Clearly this would be an affront to due process, even accepting the point made in Chapter 2 that the relationship between victim and defendant rights is not a zero sum game. Nevertheless, as a governing principle, it is submitted that a victim-centred system would be geared around filtering *in* as much of the victims' narrative as possible rather than filtering it *out*. This does not mean that victims' narrative accounts could not be subject to limitations. For example, victims should not be permitted to threaten defendants, defence witnesses or their supporters from the witness box on the grounds that they would find it therapeutically beneficial to do so. Presently such actions might lead to contempt of court proceedings or action under Section 51 of the Criminal Justice and Public Order Act 1994.[23] A victim-centred system would still be justified in imposing such limitations on the basis that unrestricted contempt of court and the harassment of defendants will lead to reduced confidence in the criminal justice system.

During the sentencing exercise, so long as decision-making remains with a judiciary trained to weigh up the evidence provided, there is nothing fundamentally objectionable or unfair in allowing victims to present such information (or opinion) as they feel is important to the court. The notion that a court must take account of all available information when making decisions is already part and parcel of the system. It is simply a matter of making that information available to the existing decision-makers. The more controversial aspect of this narrative model lies in allowing victims to present less restricted accounts during the main evidential process itself, prior to a finding of guilt or innocence. This is unavoidable if the system is to be truly victim-centred because this would be a system that minimises inconvenience to victims while maximising their account-making exercise. Both principles make it objectionable either to force victims to pick and choose information at the evidence stage or to make them effectively give evidence a second time after a finding of guilt.[24]

Initially this may seem like fundamental reform, or certainly prejudicial to defendants. From the observation data presented here, however, it is clear that benches and juries are already being trusted with a far wider range of information than was traditionally allowed, especially through the free narrative phase in the pre-recorded examination in chief of children. The remarkable aspect of this procedure is that it does not follow traditional questioning practices. Official guidelines (Home Office 2001a) maintain that such interviews should include an introductory section where the interviewing officer asks the child about his or her interests, schoolwork and hobbies. More significantly, the officers are required to afford young witnesses a free narrative phase in which they may talk about an incident without being interrupted or asked any fresh questions.

Interestingly, no legal changes were necessary to introduce this effectively new component of evidence for these vulnerable witnesses, but rather the 'rules' are to be found in non-statutory guidelines (Home Office 2001a). As such, it seems there is nothing legally preventing lawyers from adopting this approach with adults, even during traditional live evidence. When special measures are used, the Youth Justice and Criminal Evidence Act 1999 relates only to the use of the equipment, not the specific manner of the questioning. This example illustrates that the existing trial procedure is indeed capable of incorporating a wider class of voluntary evidence than is traditionally permitted, and with it a victim's fuller narrative. Evidence from the observation sessions confirms that pre-recorded examination in chief is far more akin to the genuine account-making exercise described in Chapter 4 than anything afforded to most other witnesses, including those giving evidence via other special measures. Aside from pre-recorded evidence, the discussion in Chapter 6 has demonstrated that hearsay as a concept is practically redundant, and with the new bad character and hearsay provisions under the Criminal Justice Act 2003, more of this wider information is coming before benches and juries than ever before. As such, allowing benches and juries to hear a few emotional outbursts or pieces of 'irrelevant' or impact information in a victim's full narrative does not seem such a big step, especially if accompanied by clear explanations from judges (for juries) and legal advisers (for magistrates) as to how this information may be used. In truth the barriers seem once again cultural.

Indeed, if this is fundamental reform which changes the basic tenets of the evidence process, then it is a fundamental reform already well under way. Hence, in a victim-centred system, just because an outburst from the victim during evidence is considered irrelevant to the decision-making exercise, this would not prevent victims from expressing the information in order to achieve therapeutic outcomes (so long as they do not amount to intimidation or contempt of court) and recognition of their situation. Such recognition of victims' views must in turn be clearly expressed by the court and – certainly in the case of sentencing – by decision-makers when explaining their decisions, even if they ultimately rejected some of that information during the process, the victim having received clear explanation that this is possible, and even to some extent probable.

Fundamentally, the distinction between victims and lawyers may be that one group are storytellers and the others are evidence takers. If the two sides are to be resolved – with the victim as the new focus – it seems unavoidable that lawyers must learn about stories.

Achieving centrality through internally enforceable rights

Given the growth of rights discourse[25] and the long-standing application of the term to defendants in criminal proceedings, it seems inevitable that a victim-centred criminal justice system must afford victims rights to guarantee the three forms of centrality outlined above. Nevertheless, rights enforceable only though complaints mechanisms external to the criminal process seem unsuited to this task, much like the Victim's Charter (Fenwick 1995). Most recently, Casey (2008) has commented that victims still lack clear and accessible methods of redress when the criminal justice system fails to meet their needs despite the provisions made in the Domestic Violence, Crime and Victims Act 2004. As such, only 30 complaints have been taken to the Parliamentary Commissioner for Administration for breaches of the statutory Code of Practice (most of which were dismissed) and no appointment made of a Victims and Witnesses Commissioner. Victims also have the Victims Advisory Panel to represent their interests, although Casey notes that its impact thus far on policy-making has been questionable.

In contrast, the form of rights I am concerned with here would be enforceable *within* the criminal justice (trial) procedure itself through the proactive intervention of benches and lawyers who are specifically designated to represent the interests of victims and ensure they are afforded consultative participation in decision-making. That is to say, victims should be given party status. A key practical advantage of such a system is that (in the majority of cases) victims' grievances could be dealt with immediately during trials by the bench, as opposed to a lengthy complaints procedure initiated after the fact. This raises the crucial point that court staff – and especially legal practitioners – need to see these rights enforced from within the system if they are to gain legitimacy, and to proliferate good practice. Principally this is because lawyers are clearly trained and accustomed to following the judgments of the courts. The observations sessions confirmed that lawyers working regularly in a specific court are keen to keep on the right side of individual magistrates, and certainly judges. As such, coming directly from judges and magistrates, such proactive moves to guarantee victims the three forms of centrality would have a swift effect on the occupational practices of advocates. Such advocates will pay far more attention to the judges they appear before than to a list of standards backed by a remote complaints mechanism for, as Jackson notes:

> One of the problems with putting obligations on criminal justice agencies, however, is that they are unlikely to be taken seriously unless consequences attach to non-compliance. (2003: 319)

In time, such practices will become engrained and form part of local court cultures – whereby everyone from listings officers to judges shares the same victim-assistance values – before moving on to impact upon lawyers' occupational cultures and, ultimately, the wider legal culture passed on to the next generation of practitioners.

In this system, judges and magistrates become willing to guarantee the rights of victims in court, during trials and at pre-trial review (case management) hearings, just as they protect the rights of defendants. In the majority of cases any derogation from victim rights would be picked up by the judge and swiftly remedied on the instructions of the bench. This would mean adapting the occupational cultures of the judiciary to account for matters such as reducing delay and inconvenience for the victim and ensuring account-making principles are upheld during the evidential process. It has been shown that some benches are already taking on such roles (Plotnikoff and Woolfson 2005; Applegate 2006). Through leading by example, judicial actors should thus help achieve the cultural shift in lawyers' occupational practices discussed above. Where benches fail to appreciate or enforce victims' rights, victim advocates would be standing by to raise the issue and request a resolution.

This is the theory. In practice, in keeping with the principle that genuine rights must have consequences attached to their non-compliance, such a system would require mechanisms for remedying cases where victim rights have been breached, despite the expected vigilance of benches and victim advocates. This presents a problem for victim-centredness, because such mechanisms seem likely to exclude victim participation. If such matters become the subject of trials within trials (causing delay and thus conflicting with another principle of victim-centredness) victims may be excluded, just as they are excluded from legal arguments under the present system. The same would be true of a separate system of appeals to adjudicate on victim-centredness. To counteract this, giving victims legal representation (party status) seems especially important in the context of such appeals. Of course, the appeals suggested above would focus only on the alleged breach of victims' rights. Remedies might include compensation to the victim (as can now be *suggested* by the Victims' and Witnesses' Commissioner)[26] or an apology to help reaffirm their victim status. The key here will be to consult victims as to the kinds of remedies they would need.

A fundamental challenge here lies in convincing judicial actors to take a more proactive view towards the needs of victims without infringing upon judicial independence. The option of extending documents like the Victim's Code of Practice to cover judges and magistrates would seem to do just that, and history has taught us that the judiciary find ways to avoid such restrictions (see Ashworth 1998). What can be done, however, is to ensure that the public is aware that judges and magistrates in this new victim-centred system are expected to safeguard the rights of victims during criminal trials. This could be achieved though the publication of a code of judicial ethics. Such a code has previously been suggested in Northern Ireland:

> [T]here might be an advantage in the public having access to material on the standards required of the judiciary, as a confidence booster ... It would also be an opportunity to raise awareness about the nature of judicial responsibilities. (Criminal Justice Review Group 2000: para. 6.138)

Clearly, the goal here was not to intrude upon judicial independence, but to publicise the standards expected of holders of judicial offices. Nevertheless, no such statement of ethics has yet been drawn up in Northern Ireland or the rest of the UK. In England and Wales, the Office for Judicial Complaints was set up in April 2006 to investigate complaints of personal misconduct on the part of judicial office holders, but judicial decisions and judicial case management are expressly excluded from its remit.[27]

Such codes have been successfully employed elsewhere. For example, the International Criminal Court (ICC) has a Code of Judicial Ethics that includes the following requirement:

> Judges shall exercise vigilance in controlling the manner of questioning of witnesses or victims in accordance with the Rules and give special attention to the right of participants to the proceedings to equal protection and benefit of the law. (ICC 2005: Article 8(2))

The rules mentioned here are the ICC's *Rules of Procedure and Evidence* (ICC 2002) which contain many safeguards to what are called the 'rights of victims', including the right to participate in proceedings as a party with legal representation.

Generally speaking it would be hoped that the publication of such a code (coupled with adequate training) would be enough to compel judges to adapt their occupational and cultural practices to perform these kinds of roles. The ICC code itself is 'advisory in nature'. More radically, such a code may need to be backed by a complaints procedure which covered a judge's decisions and case management. The notion of the public complaining against judges has wide implications, not least of which is that they would become a professional group subject to scrutiny, in the same way that barristers can have complaints made against them to the Bar Council. One way to achieve this may be to have a separate body of judges reserved to deal with judicial complaints,[28] along the lines of police complaints before the advent of the Independent Police Complaints Authority.

While a judicial complaints mechanism is controversial, the judicial enforcement of victim rights within the courtroom is itself not so much a fundamental reform as a standardisation of existing practices. Indeed, as the complaints system would be separate from the judicial process, the adversarial model itself remains untouched. So, when a victim is being questioned in an unreasonably forceful manner, or is interrupted in the witness box (contrary to the principles of cultural and narrative centrality), judicial actors in a victim-centred system would – under the ethical code – be expected to intervene. Similarly, in a situation where a trial cannot proceed and victims or other witnesses have attended, it could become the rule rather than the exception for the bench to bring these people into court and ensure they have been given all the relevant information. Even before this stage was reached, judges would quiz advocates as to whether they had taken time to speak to witnesses directly and whether their opinions, availability and so on had been canvassed (possibly through a dedicated victims advocate). The point is that such judicial actions were observed numerous times already during observation sessions carried out for this research. Placing them in a code of ethics simply ensures that such consideration towards victims is extended consistently in all cases.

Judges taking responsibility for victim rights would extend to their openly acknowledging the consideration of victims' accounts – as noted above – and addressing other cultural barriers, such as those that seem to be limiting the use of compensation orders (see Home Office 2004a). This proactive approach to victims would also extend to benches doing their utmost – in accordance with victims' right to minimal inconvenience – to list cases around victims' and other witnesses' availability, as well as defendants'. On this point, the observation sessions revealed that while judges and magistrates are technically in charge of setting dates for court business, in practice the times and dates of hearings are set by administrators (listings officers) and then rubberstamped by the bench. As such, if victims are to be put at the heart of the criminal trial on a practical level, it will be necessary for magistrates and judges to become more insistent when it comes to scheduling cases that involve civilian victims and other witnesses, or else for listing officers to contact victims directly.

Aside from the more controversial notion of complaining about judges, a key benefit of this system is that judges *themselves* become the enforcers of victim rights when other actors detract from victim-centred principles. So, while ultimately the guardian of victim rights may (in the case of judicial complaints, as opposed to appeals and trials within trials) lie outside the justice process (externally enforceable), the vast majority of infractions will be dealt with within it. This may be a case of trusting the judges, but in a system based on judicial independence this seems acceptable provided judges are given appropriate training.[29] Given the indications from Chapters 5 and 6 that judges are already generally sympathetic to the notion of supporting victims, it can be confidently predicted that they would operate in accordance with such an ethical code. It should be remembered that defendants were considered to have rights in England and Wales long before the Human Rights Act 1998 made this a statutory fact. As such, it may well be enough that criminal justice and court actors come to *accept* that victims have rights, which is again a cultural issue, reflected across occupational, court, and legal cultures at all levels.

As for the exact content of such rights, many will be service rights intended to promote practical centrality. These would include the right to respectful treatment, facilities and information but also the right to have effective case management systems, flexible listing strategies and witness calling strategies applied to their cases. Overall, this can be summarised as the right not to be inconvenienced by the system if it can be avoided. Rights intended to achieve practical centrality will be mainly positive rights like the examples given above, or the right to meet the prosecutor before the trial. When one considers narrative centrality, however, the rights involved might well be negative; for example, the right *not* to be interrupted while giving evidence, or not to be asked questions in an unreasonably forceful manner. Phrasing such rights in negative terms is useful, as it removes any implication (and associated pressure) that the victims are *expected* to construct a long and intricate narrative, instead allowing them to say as much or as little as they wish. This would also free judicial actors from the probably impossible task of judging victims' accounts to decide whether they have been restricted or not, leaving them with a much simpler task of ensuring against interruptions and so on, which some benches are doing already.

As argued in Chapter 2 and above, such rights would also include the right to participation, in the form of consultation, on the issue of plea bargains, bind overs and sentencing. The argument has been made that these represent non-fundamental reforms and broadly fall under the category of cultural centrality, as they mainly necessitate the acceptance of such procedures by practitioners rather than a change in decision-making processes *per se*. In fact, this is best seen as an extension of the principle that courts (and other actors within the criminal justice process) should base decisions on all the available information. Hence, the victim's right to participation takes the form of a right to present (or have presented) such information, to have it considered, and to have the fact of its consideration acknowledged. I have also argued that rights would include the right to decide whether to give evidence and how to do so in the interests of narrative centrality. Here it would be the role of judges to ensure that prosecutors adequately canvass the views of victims and take them into account in their decision-making, as well as taking account of such issues themselves during the sentencing exercise and ensuring that victims know such account has been taken. This may be facilitated best through dedicated victim advocates.

Victims themselves are given little decision-making power in this model, save when it comes to deciding whether or not to give evidence and how this will be done. Furthermore, this model is not grounded in the 'rights are common sense' approach frowned upon by Ashworth, but rather on the understanding that changing occupational cultures in criminal justice can only be achieved from the top down, by benches leading through example. In the longer term, the system advocated here becomes victim-centred not because a statute arbitrarily makes it so – or because victims are given unwanted decision-making powers which put them under pressure – but because the attitudes of judges, advocates and legal professionals, along with the practical organisation and running of all aspects of the case, become concerned with and incorporate the needs of victims of crime; including their need to construct narratives in an uninhibited way.

Going beyond trials

The model illustrated in Figure 7.1 can be applied to the victim in many other criminal justice processes beyond the trial itself. For example, research on policing rape and domestic violence has shown that changing police occupational practices (cultural centrality) and the provision of facilities like specialist domestic violence officers or comfortable units in which to give statements (practical centrality) should improve the view such victims take away of the police (Jordan 2004). In Chapter 4 it has been argued that police could reflect more of an appreciation for victims' narrative account-making when taking statements, as opposed to sticking purely to traditional evidential criteria. Similarly, Crown prosecutors could become more culturally attuned to victims' wider accounts when reviewing case files. Hence, while the focus here has been on trials, the wider criminal justice system could also be tested for its degree of victim-centredness by reference to the three forms of centrality.

What factors have driven this 'policy'?

In sum, the essential conclusion drawn from this research question, as discussed fully in Chapter 3, was that the 'policy' had been driven by many interrelated factors, some of which had little to do with victims. As such, the impression of a consistent chain of policy, driven over time by compatible goals, is a retrospective construction and a product of the policy-making process itself. This process requires new policies to be presented as the continuation of established ones. Hence, this is not so much a 'policy' as a web of 'policies'. These findings are consistent with those of Rock (2004), but emphasise macro forces driving these developments, as well as developments in our understanding of victimhood. The findings also indicate that central government seems to be washing its hands of victims by refusing to take financial responsibility for these measures, placing the burden on the resources of local agencies as opposed to committing central resources, such as those of the new Ministry of Justice. It was further concluded that, looking at the features of these policies over time, many have failed significantly to assist victims themselves, which again indicates a reluctance to put victims truly at the heart of the system.

Thus, overall, victims of crime have become prominent in policy-making over recent years because actions that incidentally assist victims and witnesses have frequently been grounded in a quite different set of political concerns, and because – now that victims and witnesses have achieved rhetorical acceptance in the political system – new policies are being packaged as the continuation of work *for* these groups which are in fact intended to achieve *other* aims. It must be said, however, that every central policy-maker spoken to for this research, without exception, seemed genuinely concerned and enthusiastic about victim support and involvement in the criminal justice system. The same is true of local administrators and implementers of such policies.

Having formulated a model of victim-centred criminal justice, it is useful to return briefly to these issues and ask whether the multitude of driving forces behind victim policies has been conducive to victim-centredness as it is understood here. Such a discussion will also serve to illustrate how the model proposed in Figure 7.1 can be used as an analytical tool. So, for example, it has been demonstrated how the general international development in human rights discourse paved the way for victims being afforded the kinds of internally enforceable rights suggested above. More specifically, Chapter 3 indicates that this development of rights language was an important driving force behind victim reform; one that again arose in international circles and led to the eventual announcement of the Victim's Code of Practice.

Chapter 3 also examined how developments in our understating of victimhood – encompassing the discovery of more victims through macro trends – influenced the policies under review. This is clearly conducive to the concept of cultural centrality, which maintains that legal personnel must accept and apply services and facilities to a wider category of non-ideal victims and to victims outside the criminal justice system. At the same time, narrative centrality in particular requires that the stories told by *victims* of crime be given some special place in the trial. Hence, the greater distinctions now being drawn in policy-making circles between victims and witnesses are similarly conducive to this model, as is the greater focus on the suffering caused to victims of crime engendered by wider macro influences. Some aspects of the wider reform agenda have also led to a situation beneficial to this model of victim-centredness. For example, the quest for efficiency in the criminal justice system has the knock-on effect of reducing victims' waiting times and increasing the information afforded to them, which is clearly positive from the view of practical centrality, as is the setting of (efficiency) targets and the development of a joined-up, multi-agency approach to criminal justice.

Hence, despite the fact that many of these reform agendas were not consistently or exclusively focused on victims – and their assistance afforded to victims is often questionable – a significant number of these have contributed to a situation where the kind of victim-centred model discussed above can be realised. Of course, this is not true of all the other politics identified in Chapter 3. For example, the apparent influence of populist punitiveness – albeit tied in with wider macro trends – has led to a situation where some lawyers are distrustful of the government's motives on victims, setting back the cause of cultural centrality. In addition, aspects of the efficiency goal, which lead to the focus on financial savings, means local agencies have less money to implement the training, schemes and facilities required by practical centrality. This also reflects the manner in which these national policies have been implemented locally, in the sense that on most occasions local agencies have been given targets to reach but no extra resources from the centre.

Overall, however, a look back at the political and social influences driving victim policies over time lends some weight to the model of victim-centred criminal justice described above. For the most part, the two seem compatible. This is a retrospective conclusion, but the findings from Chapter 3 confirm that, in policy-making circles, this is often the only form of conclusion available. The point is that while aspects of the above model may seem controversial, the policy context does not preclude it in principle, if so far it has done so in practice.

What has putting victims 'at the heart' of the system meant so far in practice?

This section highlights the main features of the present system – exposed in Chapters 5 and 6 – which either contribute to or depart from the victim-centred ideal described in this chapter. The simplest way to do this is once again to draw on the three forms of centrality, which will also serve to demonstrate the high degree of overlap and interdependence between them.

Practical centrality within the present system

Much of the data gathered for this project support the view that the present criminal justice system is indeed becoming practically centred on victims of crime. The provision of facilities at court was extremely encouraging overall: all courts providing reception desks, signposting, cafeterias, seating and a Witness Service with its own waiting rooms. While the waiting rooms themselves were not ideal – either because they were small and cumbersome or because victims did not feel comfortable confined to even a well-designed room for long periods – it is clear that all three courts had done their best within the limited space and resources. All three courts ensured that the majority of *prosecution* witnesses had contact with the Witness Service.

On the morning of a trial, the flow of communication between the courtroom and the victim was fairly good in most cases. In the magistrates' courts, victims would almost always meet the prosecutor firsthand, although in the Crown Court centre it was less common; and the Witness Service and CPS caseworker took on more of this responsibility. Overall, the flow of information was more restricted at the Crown Court, where clerks were often not entirely up to date with proceedings, and prosecutors would frequently retreat to their own areas of the court. Lacking such facilities at the magistrates' courts, lawyers would often remain in the courtroom, where Witness Service volunteers could reach them. The flow of information was particularly efficient at Court B, where the witness waiting rooms were close to the trial courts.

Under the Effective Trial Management Programme, all three courts had a designated case progression officer and case progression hearings, commonly known as 'pre-trial reviews'. While many lawyers felt this system was improving efficiency, several noted that the procedure was not enforced strictly enough and that the necessary information was often not available at case progression hearings. In practice, many cases still arrived in court with problems on the morning. In such cases, victims would have no choice but to wait, as staggered calling was never used (except during long cases at the Crown Court) and there were no facilities to call victims to court when needed, save in the case of professionals and police officers.[30] Trials were delayed most frequently in the magistrates' court due to listings issues and witness problems, including non-arrival and reluctance. In the Crown Court, proceedings were delayed by legal arguments in over half the cases.

On the issue of listing cases, both magistrates' courts employed a system of double-listing, which was contrary to the notion of practical centrality because it kept prosecutors away from victims and often led to victims being delayed in giving evidence, or even sent home due to lack of court space or time to run both double-listed trials.

Court A did attempt to abandon the system, but had to reinstall it due to lack of facilities. Primarily, then, this was a resource issue in that courts lacked the resources, facilities and personnel to move cases around the building.

The case progression system was failing in many instances to flag up problematic or reluctant witnesses in advance, especially at the magistrates' courts. This was particularly the situation in domestic violence trials, where it was still very common to resolve problems on the morning of the proceedings. That said, the local witness care unit and the CPS Victim Information Bureau were able to refer such victims to outside voluntary agencies for assistance, which sometimes made them more willing to assist the prosecution. If cases had to be adjourned, or were otherwise resolved due to plea bargaining or a bind over, victims did tend to be 'consulted' to some extent at all three courts, albeit the reality was often that the decision had already been taken by lawyers in the courtroom. On the other hand, it was now common for a trial to proceed in the defendant's absence, especially at the Crown Court.

When a case did proceed to trial, many practical facilities and procedures were in place to assist the victim. Victims were usually invited to sit down and were offered breaks. Most had been given a copy of their statement to read over in advance, either by the prosecutors themselves (magistrates' courts) or the Witness Service/CPS caseworkers (Crown Court). Victims were usually referred to by name and thanked after they had given evidence. Supporters – whether Witness Service volunteers or friends and family – were frequently welcomed into the courtroom.[31]

Several practical difficulties were still apparent during the evidence-giving process itself. In the magistrates' court the positioning of witness boxes usually led to a great deal of head-turning as lawyers asked questions and instructed victims to respond towards the bench. At Court A, some witness boxes were positioned immediately next to where the defendant was sitting, and the only alternative was often to move the defendant so that they were positioned behind the defence advocate and directly in the eye line of the victim.

Many victims and other witnesses seemed unprepared for certain aspects of giving evidence, especially cross-examination. This suggests that some of the more practical (or realistic) aspects of the trial process are not conveyed to victims beforehand through leaflets or other resources. On this point, it is interesting to recall the view of one district judge that generally witnesses appeared just as prepared (or unprepared) to give evidence in recent years as at any time in the past.[32] This may, however, be because more vulnerable and intimidated witnesses are coming forward to give evidence, and a smaller percentage of them find the process too daunting.

Special measures facilities for vulnerable and intimidated witnesses generally seemed to operate effectively, while the police MG2 witness evaluation form was in place to flag up such needs at an early stage. There were, however, some issues with setting up the equipment in the morning at the magistrates' courts, and occasional problems with audio feedback at all three courts. Special measures applications were frequently granted on the morning of the proceedings, which again indicates that pre-trial review hearings were not always fruitful.[33] Many lawyers felt it was very easy to succeed in a special measures application, although such measures were still mainly afforded to ideal victims. A common criticism from interviewees was that the video-link rooms were uncomfortable and, on occasion, worse for victims than the courtroom. In the magistrates' court, many administrators and magistrates complained about the cumbersome screens blocking their view of the court.

Following the trial, procedures were in place between the witness care unit and the CPS Victim Information Bureau to provide victims (and witnesses) with information and explanations of a case resolution, and to forward them on to other agencies if they required further help or support. That said, it would be more practical for these two bodies to be joined, and for the police and CPS to share administrative systems so that information could be readily passed between them.

Overall, the system on display here seemed generally well developed in terms of the practical centrality of victims in the process. Nevertheless, there were some key drawbacks. Despite Effective Trial Management initiatives, many victims were still forced to wait for long periods on the morning of the trial and many were sent home without giving evidence. In this research, the view of many lawyers was that it is impossible to completely eliminate such problems. This is fair, but it was also clear that communication between agencies, and the willingness of the court (especially the magistrates' court) to enforce the case management system were sometimes absent.

On the morning of the trial, the flow of information from prosecutor to victim at the Crown Court was still somewhat hampered, and it was clear that fewer victims in Court C had even met the prosecutor in their case directly before giving evidence. The system of passing information (in some cases) from prosecutor to clerk to CPS caseworker to Witness Service volunteer to victim clearly lacks practicality. In addition, several aspects of the evidence-giving process were still not practical from the perspective of victims, especially the need to take handwritten notes at the magistrates' court, and the general frequency of interruptions this caused.

Finally, the issue of funding permeates all aspects of practical centrality. The lack of central funding available for local facilities and initiatives may reflect unwillingness on the part of the government to take responsibility for victims.

Cultural centrality within the present system

While many legal practitioners and other respondents would openly discuss and applaud the merits of assisting victims through the mechanisms described above, many still did not carry out these sentiments in operational practice, or did so in only a limited (sometimes begrudging) fashion. For example, some lawyers accepted the need to talk with the victim before a trial, but generally did not like doing so and considered it difficult or 'messy' work, especially in cases of domestic violence. There were also definite limits on what such advocates were prepared to say to victims, and some were expressly of the view that one should not encourage a victim to think of the prosecutor as 'on their side'. Some would also seek the approval of defence lawyers before saying very much at all to victims and witnesses. Among themselves, almost all advocates referred to victims as 'complainants', many feeling uncomfortable with the term 'victim' being applied before a finding of guilt.

Lawyers and court staff had mixed views about the Witness Service. While many considered them a vital resource, to others they were busybodies who gave inappropriate information and advice to witnesses. Lawyers clearly placed great value on consistency and adherence to strict procedural rules, which was very different from the way Witness Service volunteers approached their role. Hence, while many practitioners and court staff *attempted* to take a victim's-eye view of proceedings, many were still culturally unable to. On this issue, it was interesting to notice some defence lawyers apparently using concern for the victim to gain tactical advantage in their arguments for trial adjournments or alternative resolutions. Especially in domestic violence cases, defence lawyers would often make much of the fact that a victim did not want to give evidence, and should not be made to go through with it.

Many lawyers were not truly conversant with the concept of seeking victims' opinions as to case disposition, even though many *said* they would always canvass the victim's views. In practice, the relevant decision had often already been made in the victim's absence. In the magistrates' courts, most prosecutors would consistently explain matters to the victim after a case had failed to proceed, although in the Crown Court this was commonly left to CPS caseworkers. Also, in the magistrates' court, some prosecutors would deflect magistrates' intentions when they suggested bringing the victim into court for a personal explanation and thanks.

On the point of adjourned and otherwise resolved trials, most lawyers applauded the efforts of the Effective Trial Management Programme, but some believed it was ineffective. More generally, there was a sense of agencies blaming each other for trials failing to proceed rather than working effectively together to avoid this. As already noted, magistrates in particular did not seem especially confident in enforcing Effective Trial Management proceedings and many lawyers believed there was very little one could do to prevent delays and trials failing to proceed on the day, largely because of the fickle, disorganised nature of defendants.

In the courtroom on the morning of a trial, court clerks and legal advisers clearly had victim and witness waiting times in mind, and would remind judges and magistrates of this issue, especially in the case of vulnerable or intimidated witnesses. Generally, however, there was a lack of consistency – among legal advisers in particular – on the extent to which they would raise this point with advocates. Judges and magistrates too seemed to have this issue in mind, and even Crown Court circuit judges were observed remarking on the victim's wait.

During the evidential process, it was clear that advocates, magistrates and judges were still very culturally reliant on demeanour and body language to read witnesses. This often fostered a preference for live rather than video-linked evidence. Other cultural views on special measures were mixed, some believed they could influence conviction rates (either way) and some did not. Some were concerned about slipping evidential standards in pre-recorded examination in chief, but many did not see a problem. Certainly, prosecutors were willing to make special measures applications in increasing numbers. What was clear was that most advocates and court staff believed special measures were only for ideal victims and stereotypically vulnerable witnesses.[34] Also, special measures were sometimes used against victims by defence advocates when such victims subsequently wished to observe the remainder of the proceedings from the public gallery.

The majority of lawyers apparently accepted that one need not be overly hostile to victims in order to adduce evidence. Most lawyers defaulted to a generally formal, but polite, style of questioning even during cross-examination. On the few occasions that questioning became hostile, benches seemed increasingly willing to step in. In the same vein, references to character or misleading the court were rare. Nevertheless, interrupting witnesses was still the norm. In addition, most advocates were still of the view that the proper remit of the victim's evidence was what they had put in their witness statement, and victims would be frequently stopped from giving any further details or attacked by defence lawyers when they did, much to the confusion of victims themselves, who often appeared perplexed by the lawyer's evidential perspective.

Another important point is that lawyers did not appear to vary their questioning style between victims and non-victim witnesses, nor did they make changes for vulnerable and intimidated witnesses giving evidence through special measures, although at interview many *said* they did. Nevertheless, results from Chapter 6 on the length of questioning and the percentage of time different witnesses spoke or contributed to proceedings confirm this finding. Overall, the implication is that it is not victims *per se* who are becoming culturally central in the minds of lawyers, because they are treated in the same way as witnesses in general.

Information on victim impacts was usually not forthcoming during actual trial proceedings. Nevertheless, interview respondents confirmed that the victim personal statement scheme was being offered to more victims by the police, who took the statements in the same manner as regular witness statements. There were, however, numerous complaints that such statements – when they appeared – were brief and offered very limited extra information aside from 'the obvious'. Survey respondents in this project seemed confused as to what a victim personal statement was. Nevertheless, advocates were on the whole willing to adduce such evidence at the sentencing stage, and benches were seeking it out, albeit usually only in cases where they had prejudged from the outset that it would be useful. Such a view would be reached mainly in cases of stereotypical or vulnerable victims, and in domestic violence cases. Beyond the trial process itself, there were also indications that some police officers were confused as to the purposes of the scheme, and were taking victim personal statements in a very traditional, evidential manner.

Overall, the impression derived from interviewing court staff and legal practitioners, and from watching them work, was that most understood and accepted the rationale behind the schemes intended to provide services and support to victims and witnesses. Indeed, most thought these were long-overdue developments. Nevertheless, many had greater difficulty in adapting their practices to comply with this new philosophy. Certain cultural practices were still sacrosanct, such as the need to have all witnesses available from the start of a trial, the reliance on written notes at all three courts, and an apparent inability to engage fully with victims regarding the disposal of cases on the morning of a trial (in other words a denial of consultative participation). At least one district judge equated 'making witnesses comfortable' with being opposed to 'the ends of justice'.[35] In a victim-centred system, however, victim comfort would be prioritised (albeit perhaps not to the extent that the process becomes easy) because this would improve the quality of the evidence (and, importantly, the *narrative*) and this would be considered in the interest of justice.

In addition, many advocates and court personnel appeared to be working with very stereotypical notions of victimhood; hence the view that less innocent (but probably more common) victims should not be afforded special measures. This was expressed through a reluctance to allow adults – especially adult males – the benefits of special measures, because they are not considered vulnerable. This attitude prompts the concern that only a certain category of victims is becoming culturally central in the criminal justice system, a category which excludes far more victims than it embraces (Dignan 2005).[36]

There was a definite sense that at Court B, victims, witnesses and the Witness Service were accepted as part of the court community to a far greater extent than at the other courts. This is an important finding because it suggests the existence of individual court cultures as opposed to the wider legal culture or the more specific occupational cultures of individual professions. It is important to appreciate here that the same lawyers were generally working at all three courts, hence the increased victims spirit at Court B must be attributable to other factors. One possible explanation was the increased interaction at this court between the volunteer Witness Service and the court professionals, as their office/waiting room was situated right next to the two main trial courts. In addition, the Regional Director of the court (also a deputy district judge) seemed especially interested in the plight of victims and witnesses, as did the resident district judge. Hence, this may constitute a practical example of a court which had been moulded from the top down, as recommended earlier in this chapter.

More research will be needed to ascertain exactly how more localised working cultures are proliferated, but the position at Court B indicates that – given the right conditions – it is possible to adapt the engrained cultures within different professions and the wider legal culture to become more sympathetic to victims and witnesses. These findings also imply that volunteers and professionals at courts should interact more to help resolve their conflicted (ultra-consistent versus understanding and practical) working cultures. This seems to imply that Victim Support and its Witness Service should have more say in the running of courts, including representation on the Local Criminal Justice Board.

Narrative centrality within the present system

Narrative centrality was probably the least developed aspect of the model illustrated in Figure 7.1 in the area studied by this research. The reasons for this have for the most part already been covered in other contexts. As such, the narratives presented by victims were restricted by advocates' firm intention to limit a victim's evidence to that which was written in their statement. The interrupting of witnesses while giving evidence, the lawyers' dislike of emotional outbursts, the exclusion of victim impact evidence from the main trial, and lingering concerns over hearsay all served to limit the narrative accounts made by victims during the evidential process. It was also clear from the standardised way that lawyers adduced evidence from *any* witness that the story told by the victim was given no special consideration. In addition, the worrying failure of prosecutors to give some 'officially' vulnerable and intimidated witnesses and victims the choice over whether or not to give evidence through special measures almost certainly restricted some of those witnesses' ability to present full narratives.[37] In any case, T-test analyses of mean percentages of time speaking by witnesses during evidence with and without special measures[38] indicates that (aside from pre-recorded examination in chief) most of these facilities do not in fact increase the verbal contribution of witnesses. Hence, lawyers' cultural precepts about how evidence should be adduced from victims is far more relevant.

Furthermore, in coming to agreements between themselves in the courtroom about case dispositions – without consulting the victim – lawyers again effectively negotiated victims' accounts for them. In the case of witness reluctance, Chapter 5 indicates that victims are effectively already given the choice in many cases as to whether or not they give evidence. Even in domestic violence cases – where officially prosecutors must follow a prescriptive policy of compelling such witnesses handed down by the CPS – the Chief Crown Prosecutor admitted that victims ultimately exercise a choice over whether they give evidence, because prosecutors or courts will rarely take the step of forcing them. A narrative-centred system would simply accept from the outset the reality of the victim's choice and spare them the vigorous or upsetting attempts at persuasion. Instead, the CPS would concentrate attention from the outset on gathering a wider body of evidence from police, neighbours and so on.

Nevertheless, the data indicate this is a system capable of accepting victims' wider narratives. This is most readily demonstrated by the acceptance of a free narrative phase in the evidence of children speaking through pre-recorded examination in chief. During these sessions, magistrates, district judges and juries clearly demonstrated the ability to put 'irrelevant' matters from their minds, and lawyers clearly relied on them to do so. It was also clear that rules like hearsay are becoming less relevant in any event. Hence, with proper training on the part of judges and magistrates, and careful directions given to juries, a broader category of narrative-based evidence from victims could be accepted within this system without abandoning adversarial principles. Indeed, the main difficulty here may lie in training police officers to interview child witnesses effectively, as research has shown that many find this process challenging (Krähenbühl 2008).

A victim-centred system?

In Chapter 1 it was suggested that the greatest developments in the criminal justice system relating to victim-centredness would be in the *practical* infrastructure needed to assist victims. It was further predicted that the *culture* of criminal justice professionals, courts and the wider legal culture would be 'somewhat softened' to the plight of victims and witnesses (p. 12). From the outset, it was suspected that narratives would not feature too heavily in the present system, and that numerous features of this system would restrict the accounts made by victims.

Generally, these hypotheses appear correct, although cultural centrality was if anything more developed than expected. Overall, this research exposed relatively few of the 'crusty', 'old school' lawyers reported in previous studies, dismissive of victim involvement or support and critical of the government's stance. Even defence lawyers largely accepted the measures and considered most to be:

> A step forward in British justice. (a defence solicitor appearing at Court B)

While the occupational applicability of such sentiments was perhaps lagging behind, the will was certainly there for the vast majority of legal practitioners.

Overall, the criminal justice system operating in the three courts under review was not a victim-centred system in the ideal sense postulated in Figure 7.1. In particular, this system still fails to offer the sufficient mechanisms of enforceability and redress that would constitute genuine rights for victims. Nevertheless, this project did reveal a criminal justice system boasting the clear potential to become more victim-centred, without resorting to truly fundamental reform.

Final points

The purpose of this study has been to examine the government's pledge to put victims at the heart of the criminal justice system, to find out where it came from and what it means. If nothing else, this project has demonstrated the complexity of such disarmingly simple questions, and the multifaceted nature of any answers.

What is certain is that victims of crime have become increasingly important in political and policy-making spheres and – given the nature of policy-making – it seems clear that they will remain high on the agenda for criminal justice reformers, administrators and practitioners for the foreseeable future. The knock-on effect of this is that researchers will continue to be called upon to investigate various aspect of victimisation, and the needs of those who are victimised. It is, however, worrying that so many of these reforms seem to have occurred without direct consultation with victims themselves, and certainly without any accompanying ethnographic data on how they have been implemented in practice throughout the country. One area of particular concern for researchers will be the continued development of our understanding of victimhood beyond the realm of ideal victims. In addition, there is a great deal more work to be done on the narrative and narrative account-making needs of crime victims and their applicability to the criminal justice system.

It is my hope that this research will contribute to these upcoming debates, in terms of its findings and its methodology. Ethnography helps us to understand the criminal justice process and the victims within that process without reducing them to statistics. Such positivist methodologies are sometimes in danger of dehumanising a process fundamentally characterised by human interaction. In so doing, we are in danger of committing the very offence so often levied at the criminal justice process: revictimising those who have already suffered greatly.

Notes

1 Criminal Procedure Rules came into force in April 2005 giving benches explicit powers to manage the progression of criminal cases.
2 Although this author suspects the latter two interpretations.
3 On which, see 'cultural centrality' below.
4 For example, the large and cumbersome video-link screens in the Youth Courts at Court A.
5 Discussed in greater detail under 'narrative centrality'.
6 The British Crime Survey indicates that victims are asked by the police about their injury or loss in 52 per cent of incidents (Ringham and Salisbury 2004).
7 See p. 136.
8 [2002] 2 AC 357 (HL).
9 *Stogmuller* v. *Austria* (1979–80) 1 EHRR 155, para. 5.
10 See below.
11 Even though the present results indicate little difference overall between the late running or failure to run of domestic violence trials compared with other trials. See Chapter 5.
12 Although this may be a wider issue than victim avoidance if the nature of the barrister's profession is such that the robing room becomes a key setting for information distribution and career development.
13 The tendency of lawyers in this study to exclude victims from such decisions reflects the findings of McConville *et al.* (1994).
14 See the section on narrative centrality below for some exceptions.
15 See p. 223.
16 See p. 151.
17 Perhaps in the *majority* of cases, if victims so wish, meaning perhaps these would no longer be considered *special* measures.
18 As opposed to tactical concern designed to prevent the victim giving evidence.
19 In relation to victim personal statements, Graham *et al.*'s (2004) report suggests that victims sometimes make VPS statements without realising that defendants might see them. Such defendants may be viewed as an unintended audience.
20 Such versions of the story may have been constructed well in advance of the trial (McConville *et al.* 1991).
21 Having assumed responsibility for their conflicts (Christie 1977).

22 But not all, see page 181
23 Intimidation of witnesses, jurors and others.
24 Thus requiring victims to remain in court till the very end of a trial.
25 See Chapters 2 and 3.
26 If and when one is appointed.
27 The Judicial Discipline Regulations (Prescribed Procedures) 2006 (SI 2006/676), regulation 14(1)(b).
28 Presently, complaints can only be made directly to the Lord Chancellor, a very non-transparent process.
29 This was sorely lacking during the implementation of bad character provisions under the Criminal Justice Act 2003.
30 Culturally, many lawyers were uncomfortable with both ideas.
31 Or at least no objections were made to their presence.
32 See p. 170.
33 The same was true of bad character applications under the Criminal Justice Act 2003.
34 As they are presently stated, upcoming extensions of special measures in the government's draft Law Reform, Victims and Witnesses Bill will do little to dispel this idea, apparently focusing on the relatively small number of victims in cases involving guns and other offensive weapons (Office of the Leader of the House of Commons 2008).
35 See p. 174.
36 The government's recent consultation on the law relating to rape and serious sexual assault suggests that adult witnesses in such cases may become automatically entitled to give evidence through pre-recorded examination in chief (Office for Criminal Justice Reform 2006).
37 Especially when, in the Crown Court, child witnesses were not permitted to have any supporters with them in the video-link room apart from ushers.
38 See Chapter 6.

References

Advisory Group on Video Evidence (1989) *Report of the Advisory Group on Video Evidence*. London: Home Office.

Allen, J., Komy, M., Lovbakke, J. and Roy, H. (2005) *Policing and the criminal justice system – public confidence and perceptions: findings from the 2003/04 British Crime Survey*, Home Office Online Report 31/05. London: Home Office.

Amir, M. (1971) *Patterns in Forcible Rape*. Chicago: University of Chicago Press.

Angle, H., Malam, S. and Carey, C. (2003) *Witness Satisfaction: Findings from the Witness Satisfaction Survey 2002*, Home Office Online Report 19/03, London: Home Office.

Applegate, R. (2006) 'Taking child witnesses out of the Crown Court: a live link initiative', *International Review of Victimology*, 13: 179–200.

Ashworth, A. (1986) 'Punishment and Compensation: Victims, Offenders and the State', *Oxford Journal of Legal Studies*, 6: 86–122.

Ashworth, A. (1993) 'Victim Impact Statements and Sentencing', *Criminal Law Review*, 40: 498–509.

Ashworth, A. (1998) *The Criminal Process: An Evaluative Study* (2nd edn). Oxford: Oxford University Press.

Ashworth, A. (2000) 'Victims' Rights, Defendants' Rights and Criminal Procedure', in A. Crawford and J. Goodey (eds), *Integrating a Victim Perspective Within Criminal Justice: international debates*. Aldershot: Ashgate Dartmouth, 185–204.

Association of Chief Police Officers (2008) *Guidance on Investigating Domestic Abuse*. London: National Police Improvement Agency.

Auld, Lord Justice (2001) *Review of the Criminal Courts of England and Wales*. London: HMSO.

Bache, I. (2003) 'Governing through Governance: Education Policy Control Under New Labour', *Political Studies*, 51: 300–314.

Barberet, R., Fisher, B., Graham, F. and Taylor, H. (2003) *University Student Safety*, Home Office Research Findings 194. London: Home Office.

Bari, F. (2006) *Time Intervals for Criminal Proceedings in the Magistrates' Courts: September 2006*, DCA Statistical Bulletin T4/2006. London: DCA.

BBC (2003) *Jury plans suffer Lords defeat* [online]. Available at: http://news.bbc.co.uk/1/hi/uk_politics/3064551.stm (accessed 03/02/07).

BBC (2006) *Extra £2.5 million for July bomb victims* [online]. Available at: http://news.bbc.co.uk/1/hi/uk/5001734.stm (accessed 03/02/07).

BBC (2008) *Flat fire pair stabbed to death* [online]. Available at: http://news.bbc.co.uk/1/hi/england/london/7486628.stm (accessed 08/07/08).

Birch, D. (2000) 'A Better Deal for Vulnerable Witnesses', *Criminal Law Review*, April: 233–249.

Bottoms, A. (1995) 'The philosophy and politics of punishment and sentencing', in C. Clark and R. Morgan (eds), *The Politics of Sentencing Reform*. Oxford: Clarendon Press, 17–50.

Bottoms, A. (2003) 'Some Sociological Reflections on Restorative Justice', in A. von Hirsh, J. Roberts, A. Bottoms, K. Roach and M. Schiff (eds), *Restorative Justice and Criminal Justice: Competing or Reconcilable Paradigms?* Oxford: Hart Publishing, 79–114.

Boutellier, H. (2000) *Crime and Morality: The Significance of Criminal Justice in Post-Modern Culture.* AA Dordrecht: Kluwer.

Braithwaite, J. (2002) *Restorative Justice and Responsive Regulation.* New York: Oxford University Press.

Braithwaite, J. and Parker, C. (1999) 'Restorative Justice is Republican Justice', in L. Walgrave and G. Bazemore (eds), *Restoring Juvenile Justice: An Exploration of the Restorative Justice Paradigm for Reforming Juvenile Justice.* Monsey: Criminal Justice Press, 103–126.

Brienen, M. and Hoegen, H. (2000) *Victims of Crime in 22 European Criminal Justice Systems: The Implementation of Recommendation (85) 11 of the Council of Europe on the Position of the Victim in the Framework of Criminal Law and Procedure*. Nijmegen: Wolf Legal Productions.

Brownlee, I. (1998) 'New Labour – New Penology? Punitive Rhetoric and the Limits of Managerialism in Criminal Justice Policy', *Journal of Law and Society*, 25: 313–335.

Bull, R. and Corran, E. (2002) 'Interviewing child witnesses: Past and future', *International Journal of Police Science and Management*, 4: 315–322.

Burnham, P. (2001) 'New Labour and the politics of depoliticisation', *British Journal of Politics and International Relations*, 3: 127–149.

Bury, M. (1982) 'Chronic illness as biographical disruption', *Sociology of Health and Illness*, 17: 65–85.

Cabinet Office (1999) *Modernising Government*, Cm 4310. London: The Stationery Office.

Cape, E. (2004) 'Overview : Is reconciliation possible ?', in E. Cape (ed.), *Reconcilable rights? Analysing the tension between victims and defendants*. London: Legal Action Group, 1–18.

Carlen, P. (1976) *Magistrates' Justice*. London: Martin Robertson.

Casey, L. (2008) *Engaging Communities in Fighting Crime*. London: Cabinet Office.

Cavadino, M. and Dignan, J. (2002) *The Penal System: An Introduction* (3rd edn). London: Sage Publications.

Chan, J. (1996) 'Changing Police Culture', *British Journal of Criminology*, 36: 1–26.

Christie, N. (1977) 'Conflicts as Property', *British Journal of Criminology*, 17: 1–15.

Christie, N. (1986) 'The Ideal Victim', in E. Fattah (ed.), *From Crime Policy to Victim Policy*. Basingstoke: Macmillan, 17–30.

cjsonline (2005a) *Aims and Objectives* [online]. Available at: http://www.cjsonline.gov.uk/the_cjs/aims_and_objectives/index.html (accessed 03/02/07).

cjsonline (2005b) *More Specialist Courts to Beat Domestic Violence* [online]. Available at: http://www.cjsonline.gov.uk/the_cjs/whats_new/news-3229.html (accessed 03/02/07).

cjsonline (2006c) *Home Secretary pledges 8,000 new prison places – putting public protection and the law-abiding majority first* [online]. Available at: http://www.cjsonline.gov.uk/the_cjs/whats_new/news-3412.html (accessed 03/02/06).

cjsonline (2006d) *Victims of crime given a voice in government* [online]. Available at: http://www.cjsonline.gov.uk/the_cjs/whats_new/news-3459.html (accessed 03/02/07).

cjsonline (2006e) *Victims Virtual Walkthrough* [online]. Available at: http://www.cjsonline.gov.uk/victim/walkthrough/index.html (accessed 03/02/07).

Coles, R. (1989) *The Call of Stories: Teaching and Moral Imagination*. Boston: Houghton Mifflin.

Crawford, A. (1997) *The Local Governance of Crime: Appeals to Partnerships and Community*. Oxford: Clarendon Press.

Crawford, A. (2001) 'Joined-up but Fragmented: Contradiction, Ambiguity and Ambivalence at the Heart of Labour's "Third Way"', in R. Matthews and J. Pitts (eds), *Crime Prevention, Disorder and Community Safety: A New Agenda?* London: Routledge, 54–80.

Crawford, A. and Enterkin, J. (2001) 'Victim Contact Work in the Probation Service: Paradigm Shift or Pandora's Box?' *British Journal of Criminology*, 41: 707–725.

Crawford, A. and Newburn, T. (2003) *Youth Offending and Restorative Justice: Implementing reform in youth justice*. Cullompton: Willan Publishing.

Cressey, D. (1986) 'Research Implications of Conflicting Conceptions of Victimology', in E. Fattah (ed.), *Towards a Critical Victimology.* London: Macmillan, 43–54.

Cretney, A. and Davis, G. (1997) 'Prosecuting Domestic Assault: Victims Failing Courts or Courts Failing Victims?' *Howard Journal of Criminal Justice*, 36: 146–157.

Criminal Justice Review Group (2000) *Review of the Criminal Justice System in Northern Ireland.* London: The Stationery Office.

Criminal Justice System (2007) *Working together to cut crime and deliver justice: A strategic plan for criminal justice 2008–2011.* London: Home Office.

Crown Prosecution Service (2001) *Provisions of Therapy for Child Witnesses Prior to a Criminal Trial: Practice Guidance.* London: CPS.

Crown Prosecution Service (2004) *The Code for Crown Prosecutors.* London: CPS.

Crown Prosecution Service (2005a) *Children's Charter: Draft for public consultation.* London: CPS.

Crown Prosecution Service (2005b) *The Prosecutors' Pledge* [online]. Available at: http://www.cps.gov.uk/publications/prosecution/prosecutor_pledge.html (accessed 03/02/07).

Dalgleish, T. and Morant, N. (1992) 'Representations of child sexual abuse: a brief psychological commentary', in G. Davies and T. Dalgleish (eds), *Recovered Memories, Seeking the Middle Ground.* Chichester: John Wiley and Sons, 3–22.

Danet, B. (1980). 'Language in the Legal Process', *Law and Society Review*, 14: 514–528.

Davies, G. (1999) 'The impact of television on the presentation and reception of children's testimony', *International Journal of Law and Psychiatry*, 22: 241–256.

Davies, G. and Westcott, H. (1999) *Interviewing Children Under the Memorandum of Good Practice: A Research Review.* London: Home Office.

Davies, P. (2007) 'Criminal (In)Justice for Victim?, in P. Davies, P. Francis and C. Greer (2007), *Victims, Crime and Society.* London: Sage.

Davis, R. and Smith, B. (1994) 'The Effect of Victim Impact Statements on Sentencing Decisions: A test in an Urban Setting', *Justice Quarterly*, 11: 453.

De Smith, S. and Brazier, R. (1998) *Constitutional and Administrative Law.* London: Penguin.

Dignan, J. (1992) 'Repairing the damage: can reparation be made to work in the service of diversion?', *British Journal of Criminology*, 32: 453–472.

Dignan, J. (2002a) 'Restorative justice and the law: the case for an integrated, systemic approach', in L. Walgrave (ed.), *Restorative Justice and the Law.* Cullompton: Willan Publishing, 168–190.

Dignan, J. (2002b) 'Towards a Systematic Model of Restorative Justice', in A. von Hirsh, J. Roberts, A. Bottoms, K. Roach and M. Schiff (eds),

Restorative Justice and Criminal Justice, Oxford: Hart Publishing, 135–156.

Dignan, J. (2005) *Understanding victims and restorative justice,* Maidenhead: Open University Press.

Dignan, J. and Cavadino, M. (1996) 'Towards a framework for conceptualising and evaluating models of criminal justice from a victim's perspective', *International Review of Victimology,* 4: 153–182.

Doak, J. (2003) 'The victim and the criminal process: an analysis of recent trends in regional and international tribunals', *Legal Studies,* 23: 1–32.

Doak, J. (2005) 'Victims' Rights in Criminal Trials: Prospects for Participation', *Journal of Law and Society,* 32: 2294–2316.

Doak, J. (2007) *Victims' Rights, Human Rights and Criminal Justice: Reconceiving the Role of the Third Parties.* Oxford: Hart.

Doak, J. and O'Mahony, D. (2006) 'The vengeful victim? Assessing the attitudes of victims participating in restorative youth conferencing', *British Journal of Criminology,* 13: 1–21.

Dorey, P. (2004) 'Attention to Detail: The Conservative Policy Agenda', *The Political Quarterly,* 373–377.

Downes, D. and Morgan, R. (2002) '"The skeletons in the cupboard": The politics of law and order at the turn of the Millennium', in M. Maguire, R. Morgan and R. Reiner (eds), *The Oxford Handbook of Criminology* (3rd edn). Oxford: Oxford University Press, 286–321.

Edwards, I. (2002) 'The Place of Victims' Preferences in the Sentencing of "their" Offenders', *Criminal Law Review,* September: 689–702.

Edwards, I. (2004) 'An ambiguous participant: The Crime Victim and Criminal Justice Decision-Making', *British Journal of Criminology,* 44: 967–982.

Egeberg, M. (1999) 'The Impact of Bureaucratic Structure on Policy Making', *Public Adminstration,* 77: 155–170.

Elias, R. (1983) *Victims of the system: crime victims and compensation in American politics and criminal justice.* New Brunswick: Transaction.

Elias, R. (1986) *The politics of victimisation: victims, victimology and human rights.* New York: Oxford University Press.

Ellis, C. (2005) 'No Hammock for the Idle: The Conservative Party, "Youth" and the Welfare State in the 1960s', *20th Century British History,* 16: 441–470.

Ellison, L. (1998) 'Cross-examination in Rape Trials', *Criminal Law Review,* September: 605–615.

Ellison, L. (2001) *The Adversarial Process and the Vulnerable Witness.* Oxford: Oxford University Press.

Ellison, L. (2002) 'Cross-examination and the intermediary: bridging the language divide', *Criminal Law Review,* February: 114–127.

Ellison, L. (2003) 'Case Note: The Right of Challenge In Sexual Offence Cases: *Sn* v. *Sweden*', *International Journal of Evidence and Proof,* 7: 1–5.

Erez, E. (1991) 'Victim Participation in Sentencing, Sentence Outcome and Victim's Welfare', in G. Kaiser, H. Kury and H. Albrecht (eds), *Victims and Criminal Justice*. Eigenverlag: Max-Planck Institut, 681–701.

Erez, E. (1994) 'Victim Participation in Sentencing: And the Debate Goes On', *International Review of Victimology*, 3: 17–32.

Erez, E. (1999) 'Who's Afraid of the Big Bad Victim? Victim Impact Statements as Victim Empowerment and Enforcement of Justice', *Criminal Law Review*, July: 545–556.

Erez, E. (2000) 'Integrating a Victim Perspective in Criminal Justice Through Victim Impact Statements', in A. Crawford and J. Goodey (eds), *Integrating a Victim Perspective Within Criminal Justice: international debates*. Aldershot: Ashgate Dartmouth, 165–184.

Erez, E. (2004) 'Integrating Restorative Justice Principles in Adversarial Proceedings Through Victim Impact Statements', in E. Cape (ed.), *Reconcilable Rights? analysing the tension between victims and defendants*. London: Legal Action Group, 81–96.

Erez, E., Roeger, L. and Morgan, F. (1997) 'Victim Harm, Impact Statements and Victim Satisfaction with Justice: An Australian Experience', *International Review of Victimology*, 5: 37–60.

Erez, E. and Rogers, L. (1999) 'Victim Impact Statements and Sentencing Outcomes and Processes: The Perspective of Legal Professions', *British Journal of Criminology*, 39: 216–239.

Fattah, E. (1992) 'Victims and Victimology: The facts and the rhetoric', in E. Fattah (ed.), *Towards a Critical Victimology*. New York: Macmillan, 29–56.

Fenwick, H. (1995) 'Rights of victims in the criminal justice system: rhetoric or reality?', *Criminal Law Review*, November: 843–853.

Ferrero-Waldner, B. (2006) *Combating Trafficking in Human Beings – The EU's Repsonse*. Presented at the 'High-level Conference on Combating Trafficking in Human Beings, Especially Women and Children', Vienna, 17th March 2006.

Garland, D. (2001) *The Culture of Control: Crime and Social Order in Contemporary Society*. Oxford: Oxford University Press.

Giddens, A. (1979) *Central Problems in Social Theory*. London: Macmillan.

Giddens, A. (1994) *Beyond Left and Right: The Future of Radical Politics*. Oxford: Polity.

Giliberti, C. (1991) 'Evaluation of Victim Impact Statement Projects in Canada: A Summary of the Findings', in G. Kaiser, H. Kury and H. Albrecht (eds), *Victims and Criminal Justice*, Eigenverlag: Max-Planck Institut, 703–718.

Glaser, B. and Strauss, A. (1967) *The Discovery of Grounded Theory: Strategies for Qualitative Research*. Chicago: Aldine.

Glidewell, I. (1998) *The Review of the Crown Prosecution Service*. London: The Stationery Office.

Goodey, J. (2005) *Victims and Victimology: Research, Policy and Practice*. Harlow: Pearson.

Gorard, S., Selwyn, N. and Rees, G. (2002) '"Privileging the Visible": a critique of the National Learning Targets', *British Educational Research Journal*, 28: 309–325.

Graham, J., Woodfield, K., Tibble, M. and Kitchen, S. (2004) *Testaments of harm: a qualitative evaluation of the Victim Personal Statement Scheme*. London: National Centre for Social Research.

Greener, I. (2004) 'The three moments of New Labour's health discourse', *Policy and Politics*, 32: 303–316.

Hague, G. (2005) 'Domestic Violence Survivors' Forums in the UK: Experience in Involving Abused Women in Domestic Violence Services and Policy-making', *Journal of Gender Studies*, 14: 191– 203.

Haines, K. (2000) 'Referral Orders and Youth Offender Panels: Restorative Approaches and the New Youth Justice', in B. Goldson (ed.), *The New Youth Justice*. Lyme Regis: Russell House Publishing, 58–80.

Hall, M. (2007) 'The Use and Abuse of Special Measures: Giving Victims the Choice?', *Journal of Scandinavian Studies in Criminology and Crime Prevention*, Vol. 8, Supplement 1: 33–53.

Halliday, J. (2001) *Making Punishments Work: Report of the Review of the Sentencing Framework for England and Wales*. London: HMSO.

Hamlyn, B., Phelps, A. and Sattar, G. (2004a) *Key Findings from the Surveys of Vulnerable and Intimidated Witnesses 2000/01 and 2003*, Home Office Research Findings 240. London: Home Office.

Hamlyn, B., Phelps, A., Turtle, J. and Sattar, G. (2004b) *Are Special Measures Working? Evidence from Surveys of Vulnerable and Intimidated Witnesses*, Home Office Research Study 283. London: Home Office.

Harber, K. and Pennebaker, J. (1992) 'Overcoming Traumatic Memories', in S. Christianson (ed.), *The Handbook of Emotion and Memory: Research and Theory*. London: Lawrence Erlbaum Associates, 359–388.

Harland, A. (1978) 'Compensating the Victim of Crime', *Criminal Law Bulletin*, 14: 203–224.

Hartley, J. and Benington, J. (2006) 'Copy and Paste, or Graft and Transplant? Knowledge Sharing Through Inter-Organizational Networks', *Public Money and Management*, April: 101–108.

Healey, D. (1995) *Victim and Witness Intimidation: New Developments and Emerging Responses*. Washington: US Department of Justice.

Heidensohn, F. (1991) 'Women and Crime in Europe', in F. Heidensohn and M. Farrell (eds), *Crime in Europe*. London: Routledge, 3–13.

Her Majesty's Stationery Office (2003) *Explanatory notes to Domestic Violence, Crime and Victims Bill*. London: HMSO.

Herman, J. (2003) 'The Mental Health of Crime Victims: Impact of Legal Intervention', *Journal of Traumatic Stress*, 16: 159–166.

Hickman, J. (2004) 'Playing games and cheating: fairness in the criminal justice system', in E. Cape (ed.), *Reconcilable rights? analysing the tension between victims and defendants*. London: Legal Action Group, 50–64.

HIllyard, P. (2006) 'Crime obsessions: crime isn't the only harm', *Criminal Justice Matters*, 62: 46.

Holmstrom, L. and Burgess, A. (1978) *The victim of rape: institutional reactions*. Chichester: John Wiley.

Home Office (1990) *Victims' Charter: a statement of the rights of victims*. London: Home Office.

Home Office (1996) *Victims' Charter*. London: Home Office.

Home Office (2001a) *Achieving Best Evidence in Criminal Proceedings: Guidance for Vulnerable or Intimidated Witnesses, including Children*. London: Home Office.

Home Office (2001b) *Criminal Justice: The Way Ahead*, Cm 5074. London: The Stationery Office.

Home Office (2001c) *Making a Victim Personal Statement*. London: Home Office.

Home Office (2001d) *The Review of the Victim's Charter*. London: Home Office.

Home Office (2001e) *The Victim Personal Statement Scheme: Guidance Notes for Practitioners or those Operating the Scheme*. London: Home Office.

Home Office (2002) *Justice for all*, Cm 5563. London: The Stationery Office.

Home Office (2003a) *A new deal for victims and witnesses: national strategy to deliver improved services*. London: Home Office.

Home Office (2003c) *Improving Public Satisfaction with the Criminal Justice System*. London: Home Office.

Home Office (2003d) *Securing the attendance of victims in court: A consultation paper*. London: HMSO.

Home Office (2003e) *Tackling Witness Intimidation – An Outline Strategy*. London: Home Office.

Home Office (2003f) *Victims in Court*. London: Home Office.

Home Office (2003g) *Witness in Court*. London: Home Office.

Home Office (2004a) *Compensation and Support for Victims of Crime: A consultation paper on proposals to amend the Criminal Injuries Compensation Scheme and provide a wide range of support for victims*. London: Home Office.

Home Office (2004b) *Compensation and Support for Victims of Crime: Summary of Reponses to a Home Office Consultation Paper*. London: Home Office.

Home Office (2004c) *Confident Communities in a Secure Britain: The Home Office Strategic Plan 2004–2008*. London: Home Office.

Home Office (2004d) *Criminal Case Management Framework*. London: Home Office.

Home Office (2004e) *Cutting Crime, Delivering Justice: A Strategic Plan for Criminal Justice 2004–08*. London: Home Office.

Home Office (2004f) *Guidance on Part 2 of the Sexual Offences Act 2003*. London: Home Office.

Home Office (2004g) *No Witness, No Justice: The National Victim and Witness Care Programme*. London: Home Office.

Home Office (2004h) *Prosecution Team Manual of Guidance Incorporating the JOPI*. London: Home Office.

Home Office (2005a) *Consultation on Road Traffic Offences Involving Bad Driving*, Home Office Press Release 025/2005. London: Home Office.

Home Office (2005b) *Hearing the Relatives of Murder and Manslaughter Victims: The Government's plans to give the bereaved relatives of murder and manslaughter victims a say in criminal proceedings: Consultation*. London: Home Office.

Home Office (2005c) *Hearing the Relatives of Murder and Manslaughter Victims: The Government's plans to give the bereaved relatives of murder and manslaughter victims a say in criminal proceedings: Summary of responses to the consultation paper*. London: Home Office.

Home Office (2005d) *Rebuilding Lives: supporting victims of crime*. London: The Stationery Office.

Home Office (2005e) *Review of Road Traffic Offences Involving Bad Driving: A Consultation Paper*. London: Home Office.

Home Office (2005f) *The Code of Practice for Victims of Crime*. London: Home Office.

Home Office (2005g) *The Witness Charter: New standards of care for witnesses in the criminal justice system: Consultation*, London: Home Office.

Home Office (2005h) *Victims' Code of Practice Consultation*. London: Home Office.

Home Office (2006a) *Delivering Simple, Speedy, Summary, Justice*. London: Home Office.

Home Office (2006b) *Home Secretary Pledges 8,000 New Prison Places – Putting Public Protection and the Law-abiding Majority First*. Home Office Press Release of 21st July 2006. London: Home Office.

Home Office (2006c) *Rebalancing the criminal justice system in favour of the law abiding majority: Cutting crime, reducing reoffending and protecting the public*. London: Home Office.

Home Office and Scottish Executive (2006) *Tackling Human Trafficking – Consultation on Proposals for a UK Action Plan*. London: HMSO.

Hough, M. (1986) 'Victims of violent crime: findings from the first British crime survey', in E. Fattah (ed.), *From Crime Policy to Victim Policy*. Basingstoke: Macmillan, 117–132.

Hoyano, L. And Keenan, C. (2007) *Child Abuse: Law and Policy Across Boundaries*. Oxford: Oxford University Press.

Hoyle, C., Cape, E., Morgan, R. and Sanders, A. (1999) *Evaluation of the 'One Stop Shop' and Victim Statement Pilot Projects*. London: Home Office.

Inter-agency Working Group on Witnesses (2003) *No Witness – No Justice: Towards a national strategy for witnesses*. London: Home Office.

Interdepartmental Working Group on the Treatment of Vulnerable or Intimidated Witnesses in the Criminal Justice System (1998) *Speaking up for Justice*. London: HMSO.

International Criminal Court (2002) *Rules of Procedure and Evidence*. The Hague: ICC.

International Criminal Court (2005) *Code of Judicial Ethics*. The Hague: ICC.

Irvin, R. and Stansbury, J. (2004) 'Citizen Participation in Decision Making: Is It Worth the Effort?', *Public Administration Review*, 64: 55–65.

Jackson, J. (1990) 'Getting Criminal Justice Out of Balance', in S. Livingstone and J. Morison (eds), *Law, Society and Change*. Aldershot: Dartmouth, 114–133.

Jackson, J. (2003) 'Justice for All: Putting Victims at the Heart of Criminal Justice?', *Journal of Law and Society*, 30: 309–26.

Jackson, J. (2004) 'Putting victims at the heart of criminal justice: the gap between rhetoric and reality', in E. Cape (ed.), *Reconcilable rights? Analysing the tension between victims and defendants*. London: Legal Action Group, 65–80.

Jackson, J., Johnstone, J. and Shapland, J. (2003) 'Delay, Human Rights and the need for Statutory Time Limits in Youth Cases', *Criminal Law Review*, August: 510–524.

Jackson, J., Kilpatrick, R. and Harvey, C. (1991) *Called to Court: A Public Review of Criminal Justice in Northern Ireland*. Belfast: SLS Legal Publications.

Jordan, A., Rüdiger, K. and Zito, A. (2005) 'The Rise of "New Policy" Instruments in Comparative Perspective: Has Governance Eclipsed Government?', *Political Studies*, 53: 477–496.

Jordan, J. (2004) 'Beyond Belief? Police, Rape and Women's Credibility, *Criminal Justice*, 4: 29–59.

Joutsen, M. (1989) 'Foreword', in HEUNI (ed.), *The Role of the Victim of Crime in the European Criminal Justice System*. Helsinki: HEUNI, I.

JUSTICE (1998) *Victims in Criminal Justice, Report of the JUSTICE Committee on the Role of Victims in Criminal Justice*. London: JUSTICE.

Kellas, J. and Manusov, V. (2003) 'What's in a story? The relationship between narrative completeness and adjustment to relationship dissolution', *Journal of Social and Personal Relationships*, 20: 285–307.

Kearon and Godfrey (2007) 'Setting the scene: a question of history', in Walklate, S. (ed.), *Handbook of Victims and Victimology*. Willan: Cullompton, 17–36.

Kenney, J. (2003) 'Gender Roles and Grief Cycles: Observations of Models of Grief and Coping in Homicide Survivors', *International Review of Victimology*, 10: 19–49.

Kenney, J. (2004) 'Human Agency Revisited: The Paradoxical Experiences of Victims of Crime', *International Review of Victimology*, 11: 225–257.

Kirchhoff, G. (1994) 'Victimology – History and basic concepts', in G. Kirchhoff, E. Kosovski and H. Schneider (eds), *International debates of victimology*. Mönchen-Gladbach: WSV Publishing.

Kitchen, S. and Elliott, R. (2001) *Key Findings from the Vulnerable Witness Survey*, Home Office Research Findings 147. London: Home Office.

Kleinman, A. (1988) *The Illness Narratives: Suffering, Healing and The Human Condition*. New York: Basic Books.

Konrad, H. (2006) 'Combating Human Trafficking', *Refugee Survey Quarterly*, 25: 51–55.

Krähenbühl, S. (2008) 'Interviewing young children: protocol, practice and perceptions in police interviews', *Childhoods Today*, 2 (1) [online]. Available at: http://www.childhoodstoday.org/index.php (accessed 4/7/08).

Lawrence, R. (2006) 'Research dissemination: activity bringing the research and policy worlds together', *Evidence and Policy*, 2: 373–384.

Lees, S. (2002) *Carnal Knowledge: Rape on trial*. London: Women's Press.

Leggett, W. (2000) 'New Labour's Third Way: From "New Times" to "No Choice"?' Paper presented at a 'workshop on models of European Social Democracy', Sussex European Institute, 26th May 2000.

Lindblom, C. and Woodhouse, E. (1993) *The Policy-Making Process* (3rd edn). New Jersey: Prentice Hall.

Loader, I. and Sparks, R. (2002) 'Contemporary Landscapes of Crime, Order and Control: Governance, Risk and Globalization', in M. Maguire, R. Morgan and R. Reiner (eds), *The Oxford Handbook of Criminology* (3rd edn). Oxford: Oxford University Press, 83–111.

Lord Chancellor's Department (2001) *Practice Direction – Victim Personal Statements*. London: Lord Chancellor's Department (now the Department for Constitutional Affairs).

Luchjenbroers, J. (1996) '"In your own words...": Questions and answers in a Supreme Court trial', *Journal of Pragmatics*, 27: 477–503.

Macleavy, J. (2006) 'The Language of Politics and the Politics of Language: Unpacking "Social Exclusion" in New Labour Policy', *Space and Polity*, 1: 87–98.

Macpherson (1999) *The Stephen Lawrence Inquiry: Report of an inquiry by Sir William Macpherson of Cluny*. London: HMSO.

Magistrates' Court Committee (2004) *Annual Report 2002–2003*.[1]

Maguire, M. (1991) 'The Needs and Rights of Victims of Crime', in M. Tonry (ed.), *Crime and Justice: A Review of Research*, 14: Chicago: Chicago University Press, 363–433.

[1]The specific name of this MCC and the publication details of this report have been omitted to preserve the confidentiality of the area under review.

Maguire, M. (2002) 'Crime statistics: the "data explosion" and its implications', in M. Maguire, R. Morgan and R. Reiner (eds), *The Oxford Handbook of Criminology* (3rd edn). Oxford: Oxford University Press, 322–375.

Maguire, M. with Bennett, T. (1982) *Burglary in a Dwelling: the Offence, the Offender and the Victim*. London: Heinemann.

Maguire M. and Shapland, J. (1997) 'Provision for Victims in an International Context', in R. Davis, A. Lurigio and W. Skogan (eds), *Victims of Crime* (2nd edn). Thousand Oaks: Sage Publications, 211–230.

Maines, D. (1993) 'Narrative's Moment and Sociology's Phenomena: Toward a Narrative Sociology', *Sociological Quarterly*, 34: 17–38.

Maloney, W., Grant, J. and McLaughlin, A. (1994) 'Interest groups and public policy: the insider/outsider model revisited', *Journal of Public Policy* 14 (1): 17–38.

Matheson, C. (2000) 'Policy Formulation in Australian Government: Vertical and Horizontal Axis', *Australian Journal of Public Administration*, 59: 44–55.

Mattinson, J. and Mirrlees-Black, C. (2000) *Attitudes to Crime and Criminal Justice: Findings from the 1998 British Crime Survey*, Home Office Research Study 200. London: Home Office.

Mawby, R. and Walklate, S. (1994) *Critical victimology*. Thousand Oaks: Sage Publications.

Mayer, I., Edelenbos, J. and Monnikhof, R. (2005) 'Interactive policy development: undermining or sustaining democracy?', *Public Administration*, 83: 179–199.

McConville, M., Hodgson, J., Bridges, L. and Pavlovic, A. (1994) *Standing Accused: The Organisation and Practice of Criminal Defence Lawyers in Britain*. Oxford: Clarendon Press.

McConville, M., Sanders, A. and Leng, R. (1991) *The Case for the Prosecution*. London: Routledge.

McGrath, C. (2000) 'Policy making in political memoirs – The case of the poll tax', *Journal of Public Affairs*, 2: 71–84.

Mendelsohn, B. (1956) 'A New Branch of Bio-psychological Science: la victimology', *Revue Internationale de Criminologie et de Police Technique*, 2.

Miers, D. (1980) 'Victim compensation as a labelling process'. *Victimology*, 5: 3–16.

Miers, D. (1991) *Compensation for Criminal Injuries*. London: Butterworths.

Milbourne, S., Macrae, S. and Maguire, M. (2003) 'Collaborative solutions or new policy problems: exploring multi-agency partnerships in education and health work', *Journal of Education Policy*, 18: 19–35.

Ministry of Justice (2008) *Our strategy* [online]. Available at: http://www.justice.gov.uk/about/our-strategy.htm (accessed 07/07/08).

Morgan, R. and Sanders, A. (1999) *The Use of Victim Statements*. London: Home Office.

Moxon, D., Martin, J. and Hedderman, C. (1992) *Developments in the use of compensation orders in magistrates' courts since October 1988*, Home Office Research Study 126. London: Home Office.

Nakamura, R. and Smallwood, F. (1980) *The Politics of Implementation*. New York: St Martin's Press.

Nelken, D. (2002) 'White-Collar Crime', in M. Maguire, R. Morgan and R. Reiner (eds), *The Oxford Handbook of Criminology* (3rd edn). Oxford: Oxford University Press, 844–877.

Newburn, T. (1988) *The Use and Enforcement of Compensation Orders in Magistrates' Courts*, Home Office Research Study 102. London: Home Office.

Newburn, T. (2003) *Crime and Criminal Justice Policy* (2nd edn). London: Longman.

Office for Criminal Justice Reform (2005) *Increasing victims' and witnesses' satisfaction with the criminal justice system: delivering a high quality service*. London: Home Office.

Office for Criminal Justice Reform (2006) *Convicting Rapists and Protecting Victims – Justice for Victims of Rape: A Consultation Paper*. London: Home Office.

Office of the Leader of the House of Commons (2008) *Draft Legislation Programme 2008/09* [online]. Available at: http://www.commonsleader.gov.uk/output/Page2440.asp (accessed 27/06/08)

Orbuch, T. (1997) 'People's Accounts Count: The Sociology of Accounts', *Annual Review of Sociology*, 23: 455–478.

Orbuch, T., Harvey, J., Davis, S. and Merbach, N. (1994) 'Account-Making and Confiding as Acts of Meaning in Response to Sexual Assault', *Journal of Family Violence*, 9: 249–263.

Pearce, G. and Mawson, J. (2003) 'Delivering developed approaches to local governance', *Policy and Politics*, 31: 51–67.

Pennebaker, J. and Beall, S. (1986) 'Confronting a traumatic event: Toward an understanding of inhibition and disease', *Journal of Abnormal Psychology*, 95: 274–281.

Pennebaker, J., Colder, M. and Sharp, L. (1990) 'Accelerating the coping process', *Journal of Personality and Social Psychology*, 58: 528–537.

Pennebaker, J., Kiecolt-Glaser, J. and Glaser, R. (1988) 'Disclosure of traumas and immune function: Health implications for psychotherapy', *Journal of Consulting and Clinical Psychology*, 56: 239–245.

Plotnikoff, J. and Woolfson, R. (2005) *In their own words: the experiences of 50 young witnesses in criminal proceedings. London: NSPCC.*

Plummer, K. (1995) *Telling Sexual Stories: power, change and social worlds.* Routledge: London.

Pointing, J. and Maguire, M. (1988) 'Introduction: the rediscovery of the crime victim', in M. Maguire and J. Pointing (eds), *Victims of Crime: A New Deal?* Milton Keynes: Open University Press, 1–13.

Priestley, M. (2002) 'Whose voices? Representing the claims of older disabled people under New Labour', *Policy and Politics*, 30: 361–372.

Rein, M. and Rabinovitz, F. (1978) 'Implementation: A Theoretical Perspective', cited in Nakamura, R. and Smallwood, F. (1980) *The Politics of Implementation*. New York: St Martin's Press.

Reiner, R. (2000) *The Politics of the Police* (3rd edn). Oxford: Oxford University Press.

Richardson, J. (2000) 'Government, Interest Groups and Policy Change', *Political Studies*, 48: 1006–1025.

Riessman, C. (1992) 'Making sense of marital violence: one woman's narrative', in C. Rosenwald and R. Ochberg (eds), *Storied lives: the cultural politics of self-understanding*. New Haven: Yale University Press, 231–249.

Ringham, L. and Salisbury, H. (2004) *Support for Victims of Crime: findings from the 2002/2003 British Crime Survey*. Home Office Online Report 31/04, London: Home Office.

Roberts, J. and Erez, E. (2004) 'Communication in Sentencing: Exploring the Expressive and the Impact Model of Victim Impact Statements', *International Review of Victimology*, 10: 223–244.

Rock, P. (1986) *A view from the Shadows: the Ministry of the Solicitor General of Canada and the making of the justice for victims of crime initiative*. Oxford: Clarendon Press.

Rock, P. (1990) *Helping Victims of Crime: The Home Office and the Rise of Victim Support in England and Wales*. Oxford: Oxford University Press.

Rock, P. (1993) *The Social World of an English Crown Court: witnesses and professionals in the Crown Court Centre at Wood Green*. Oxford: Clarendon Press.

Rock, P. (1998) *After Homicide: Practical and Political responses to Bereavement*. Oxford: Clarendon Press.

Rock, P. (2002) 'On Becoming a Victim', in C. Hoyle and R. Young (eds), *New Visions of Crime Victims*. Oxford: Hart Publishing.

Rock, P. (2004) *Constructing Victims' Rights: The Home Office, New Labour and Victims*. Oxford: Clarendon Press.

Rock, P. (2007) 'Theoretical perspectives on victimisation', in S. Walklate (ed.), *Handbook of Victims and Victimology*. Cullompton: Willan, 37–61.

Rottman, D. (2000) 'Does Effective Therapeutic Jurisprudence Require Special Courts (and Do Specialized Courts Imply Specialist Judges)?', *Court Review*, 37: 22.

Rottman, D. and Casey, P. (1999) 'Therapeutic Jurisprudence and the Emergence of Problem-Solving courts', *National Institute of Justice Journal*, July: 12–19.

Ryan, M. (1999) 'Penal Policy Making Towards the Millennium: Elites and Populists; New Labour and the New Criminology', *International Journal of Sociology and Law*, 27: 1–22.

Salisbury, H. (2004) *Public attitudes to the criminal justice system: the impact of providing information to British Crime Survey respondents*, Home Office Online Report 64/04. London: Home Office.

Sanders, A. (2002) 'Victim Participation in an Exclusionary Criminal Justice System', in C. Hoyle and R. Young (eds), *New Visions of Crime Victims*. Portland: Hart Publishing, 197–222.

Sanders, A. (2004) 'Involving victims in sentencing: a conflict with defendants' rights?', in E. Cape (ed.), *Reconcilable rights? Analysing the tension between victims and defendants*. London: Legal Action Group, 97–110.

Sanders, A., Hoyle, C., Morgan, R. and Cape, E. (2001) 'Victim Impact Statements: Don't work, Can't work', *Criminal Law Review*, June: 437–458.

Sanders, A. and Young, R. (2000) *Criminal Justice*. London: Butterworths.

Sanderson, I. (2003) 'Is it "what works" that matters? Evaluation and evidence-based policy-making', *Research Papers in Education*, 18: 331–345.

Schneider, H. (1991) 'Restitution Instead of Punishment – Reorientation of Crime Prevention and Criminal Justice in the Context of Development', in G. Kaiser, H. Kury and H. Albrecht (eds), *Victims and Criminal Justice*. Eigenverlag: Max-Planck Institut, 363–380.

Selwyn, N. and Fitz, J. (2001) 'The national grid for learning: a case study of new labour education policy-making', *Journal of Education Policy*, 2: 127–147.

Sewell, K. and Williams, A. (2002) 'Broken Narratives: Trauma, Metaconstructive Gaps, and the Audience of Psychotherapy', *Journal of Constructivist Psychology*, 15: 205–218.

Shapland, J. (2000) 'Victims and Criminal Justice: Creating Responsible Criminal Justice Agencies', in A. Crawford and J. Goodey (eds), *Integrating a Victim Perspective Within Criminal Justice: international debates*. Aldershot: Ashgate Dartmouth, 147–164.

Shapland, J. (2002) 'Sentencing: an art or a Science?' Paper presented at the 'SLS/Criminal Bar Association of Northern Ireland Conference', Belfast, 19 October 2002.

Shapland, J., Atkinson, A., Colledge, E., Dignan, J., Howes, M., Johnstone, J., Pennant, R., Robinson, G. and Sorsby, A. (2004) *Implementing restorative justice schemes (Crime Reduction Programme) A report on the first year*, Home Office Online Report 32/04. London: Home Office.

Shapland, J., Atkinson, A., Atkinson, H., Chapman, B., Colledge, E., Dignan, J., Howes, M., Johnstone, J., Robinson, G. and Sorsby, A. (2006) *Restorative justice in practice – findings from the second phase of the evaluation of three schemes*, Home Office Research Findings 274. London: Home Office.

Shapland, J. and Hall, M. (2007) 'What do we know about the effect of crime on victims?', *International Review of Victimology*, 14: 175–217.

Shapland, J., Willmore, J. and Duff, P. (1985) *Victims in the Criminal Justice System*. Aldershot: Gower.

Shaxson, L. (2005) 'Is your evidence robust enough? Questions for policy makers and practitioners', *Evidence and Policy*, 1: 101–111.

Sieber, J. (1998) 'Planning Ethically Responsible Research', in L. Bickman and D. Rog (eds), *Handbook of Applied Social Research Methods*. Thousand Oaks: Sage Publications, 127–156.

Smith, M. (2004) 'Toward a theory of EU foreign policy-making: multi-level governance, domestic politics, and national adaptation to Europe's common foreign and security policy', *Journal of European Public Policy*, 11: 740–758.

Spalek, B. (2006) *Crime victims: theory, policy and practice*. New York: Palgrave Macmillan.

Spencer, J. and Flin, R. (1993) *The Evidence of Children: The Law and the Psychology* (2nd edn). London: Blackstone.

Stolle, D. (2000) 'Introduction', in D. Stolle, D. Wexler and B. Winick (eds), *Practicing Therapeutic Jurisprudence: Law as a Helping Profession*. Durham: Carolina Academics Press, xv–xvii.

Tapley, J. (2002) *From Good Citizen to Deserving Client. Relationships between Victims and the State using Citizenship as the Conceptualizing Tool*. Southampton: University of Southampton.

Tarling, R., Dowds, L. and Budd, T. (2000) *Victim and Witness Intimidation: Key Findings from the British Crime Survey*, Home Office Research Findings 124. London: Home Office.

Temkin (1987) *Rape and the Legal Process*. London: Sweet and Maxwell.

Temkin (1999) 'Reporting Rape in London: A Qualitative Study', *Howard Journal of Criminal Justice*, 38: 17–41.

Tisdall, E. and Davis, M. (2004) 'Making a Difference? Bringing Children's and Young People's Views into Policy-Making', *Children and Society*, 18: 131–142.

Tyler, T. (1990) *Why People Obey the Law*. New Haven: Yale University Press.

Valler, D. and Betteley, D. (2001) 'The Politics of "Integrated" Local Policy in England', *Urban Studies*, 38: 2393–2413.

van Dijk, J. (1983) 'Victimologie in theorie en praktijk; een kritische reflectie op de bestaande en nog te ceëren voorzieningen voor slachtoffers Van Delicten', *Justitiële verkenningen*, 6: 5–35.

van Dijk, J. (1997) *Introducing Victimology*. Paper presented at the '9th Symposium of the World Society of Victimology', Free University of Amsterdam, 25–29 August 1997.

van Duyne, C. (1981) *A Psychological Approach to Differences in Sentencing*. The Hague: Ministry of Justice.

Victim Support (1995) *The Rights of Victims of Crime: A Policy Paper*. London: Victim Support.

Victim Support (2001) *Manifesto 2001*. London: Victim Support.

Victim Support (2002a) *Criminal Neglect: No justice beyond criminal justice*. London: Victim Support.

Victim Support (2002b) *New rights for victims of crime in Europe: Council Framework Decision on the standing of victims in criminal proceedings*. London: Victim Support.

Victim Support (2003) *Annual Report and Accounts*. London: Victim Support.
Victim Support (2004) *Annual Review 2004: The Story Unfolds*. London: Victim Support.
Victim Support (2005) *One crime, five voices: annual review 2005*. London: Victim Support.
Victim Support (2006) *Annual reports and accounts 2006*. London: Victim Support.
Victim Support (2007) *Annual reports and accounts 2007*. London: Victim Support.
von Hentig, H. (1948) *The Criminal and his Victim*. New Haven: Yale University Press.

Walker, A., Kershaw, C. and Nicholas, S. (2006) *Crime in England and Wales 2005/06*, Home Office Statistical Bulleting 12/06. London: Home Office.
Walklate, S. (2007) *Imagining the victim of crime*. Maidenhead: Open University Press.
Welbourne, P. (2002) 'Videotaped Evidence of Children: Application and Implications of the Memorandum of Good Practice', *British Journal of Social Work*, 32: 553–571.
Wertham, F. (1949) *The Show of Violence*. New York: Doubleday.
Wexler, D. and Winick, B. (1996) 'Introduction', in D. Wexler and B. Winick (eds), *Law in a Therapeutic Key*. Durham: Carolina Academic Press, xvii–xx.
White, M. and Epston, D. (1990) *Narrative Means to Therapeutic Ends*. London: W.W. Norton and Company.
Whitehead, E. (2001) *Witness Satisfaction: findings from the Witness Satisfaction Survey 2000*, Home Office Research Study 230. London: Home Office.
Williams, B. (2005) *Victims of Crime and Community Justice*. London: Jessica Kingsley.
Williams, G. (1984) 'The genesis of chronic illness: narrative reconstruction, *Sociology of Health and Illness*, 6: 175–200.
Williams, N. (1999) 'Modernising Government: Policy-making within Whitehall', *Political Quarterly*, 452–459.
Wolfgang, M. (1958) *Patterns in Criminal Homicide*. New York: New York University Press.

Young, A. (1996) *Imagining Crime*. London: Sage Publications.
Young, J. (2003) '"Winning the fight against crime?" New Labour, populism and lost opportunities', in J. Young, and R. Matthews (eds), *The New Politics of Crime and Punishment*. Cullompton: Willan Publishing, 23–47.
Young, M. (1997) 'Victim Rights and Services: A Modern Saga', in R. Davis, A. Lurigio and W. Skogan (eds), *Victims of Crime* (2nd edn). Thousand Oaks: Sage Publications, 194–210.
Young, R. (2000) 'Integrating a Multi-Victim Perspective into Criminal Justice Through Restorative Justice Conferences', in A. Crawford and J. Goodey

(eds), *Integrating a Victim Perspective Within Criminal Justice: international debates*. Aldershot: Ashgate Dartmouth, 227–252.

Young, R. and Goold, B. (1999) 'Restorative Police Cautioning in Aylesbury – From Degrading to Reintegrative Shaming Ceremonies?', *Criminal Law Review*, February: 126–38.

Zauberman, R. (2002) 'Victims as Consumers of the Criminal Justice System?' in A. Crawford and J. Goodey (eds), *Integrating a Victim Perspective within Criminal Justice: international debates*. Aldershot: Ashgate Dartmouth, 37–54.

Zedner, L. (2002) 'Victims', in M. Maguire, R. Morgan and R. Reiner (eds), *The Oxford Handbook of Criminology* (3rd edn). Oxford: Oxford University Press, 419–456.

Index

Added to a page number 't' denotes a table.

academia, victims in 3–9
accommodation approach, cross-examination 34
account-making
  benefits of 97–100
  definition 96
  distinguished from court-based evidence 105, 109–13
  distinguished from narrative 96
  psychological and social implications 96
  in victim-centred criminal justice 206–7
adjourned trials 128t
  cost-cutting 70
  domestic violence 147t
  inevitability of 138–9
  informing victims of decisions 186–7
  late starting 129t
  present national target rate 126
  reasons for 136t, 137t
administrative problems
  late starting trials 131t
  trials adjourned or resolved in another way 136t
adversarial system 9, 18, 33, 34, 36, 39, 42, 101
advocacy 31
advocates
  acceptance of Witness Service 199
  informing victims of outcomes 186–7
  reference to VPSs 182–3
  reliance on demeanour to read witnesses 223
  victim contact 122
  views
    on special measures 223
    on witnesses in the public gallery 186
  see also defence advocates; solicitor advocates; victims' advocates
agreements/deals
  late starting trials 131t, 134t
  trials adjourned or resolved in another way 136t, 137t
appeals, breach of victim rights 211
Attorney General Reference No. 2 of 1995 (R v. S) 25
audiences, victims' narratives 203–5
Auld Report (2001) 29–30, 50, 71

Bache, I. 46
bad character, evidence of 81

Baegen v. Netherlands 24
barristers
  contact with victims 122
  control of witness information 110
  questioning style 163
beacon areas (LCJB) 59
A better deal for victims and witnesses 47
blame culture, criminal justice 197
British Crime Surveys 30, 75, 83, 91, 124
burglary victims, study on 27–8

calling witnesses 142, 150–3, 164, 195
case law, victim rights 24
case management 70, 136, 197, 221
case progression officers 136–8, 193
case progression system 220
Casey report (2008) 83
child witnesses
  at magistrates' courts 151–2
  pre-recorded examination in chief 35–6, 175–6
  pre-trial familiarisation 31
  special protection 37–8
  unwillingness to use special measures 171–2
Children's Charter 27, 85
Christie, Nils 4
civilian non-victims
  interruptions when giving evidence 160t
  lack of supporters 153
civilian victims
  average length of questioning 154t
  interruptions when giving evidence 160t, 161
  percentage of time speaking
    during different components of evidence 155t
    during examination in chief 159t
    with special measures 156t, 157t
civilian witnesses
  supporters 152–3
  treated as offenders 142
civilians
  average length of questioning 154t
  interruptions when giving evidence 160t
  percentage of time speaking
    during cross-examination 158t
    during different components of evidence 155t
    during examination in chief 159t
    with special measures 156t, 157t
civilised process, giving evidence as 201
civility, towards victims 34
Code for Crown Prosecutors 26
Code of Judicial Ethics (ICC) 212–13
communication
  between agencies 78–9
  between prosecutors and victims 221–2
  between Witness Service and courtroom staff 119–20
  victims and court staff 194–5, 219
communicative function, victim impact statements 108
community, concept of 74–5
community justice 103
Community Justice Centres 74
conditional discharge 81
confidence target, policy-making 75
confrontational approach, to clients 101–2
consolidation process, policy-making 49
consultative participation 17, 19, 20, 23–4, 29, 199–200
consumers, victims as 5, 8, 66
Convention on the Rights of the Child (UN) 37, 85
cost-cutting and trial adjournments 70
court facilities 123–4
  overall satisfaction with 127t
  in present CJ system 220
  users' rating of 126t
  victim-centred 194
  see also Witness Service

court scheduling 193, 214
court staff
communication
between victims and 194–5, 219
between Witness Service and 119–20
enforcement of victim rights 210–11
views about Witness Service 222
see also individual members
court-based compensation orders 69–70
court-based evidence, distinguished from account-making 109–13
courtrooms
culture and treatment of victims in 200–2
design 195
courts
impact of VPSs on 182
research methodology 12–13
waiting at *see* waiting times
see also Crown Courts; magistrates' courts; Youth Courts
Courts Act (2003) 81
Crawford, A. 46
crime, impact of, in trials 178–85
Criminal Case Management Framework 70, 136
Criminal Evidence (Witness Anonymity) Act (2008) 24
Criminal Evidence (Witness Anonymity) Bill 48, 72–3
Criminal Injuries Compensation Authority 26
Criminal Injuries Compensation Scheme 52, 62, 65, 66, 68, 69
Criminal Justice: The Way Ahead 54–5, 65, 66, 71
criminal justice
inclusive model 18
joined-up approach 78
public perceptions 75–6
review (2001) 81
therapeutic jurisprudence 103
victim-centred *see* victim-centred criminal justice
Criminal Justice Act (1991) 48
Criminal Justice Act (2003) 81, 92, 196
criminal justice policies
implementation 57–8
victim prominence 8
Criminal Justice and Public Order Act (1994) 208
criminal justice system
balance of protection 83
concerns about low public confidence 72
cultural centrality within 222–6
efficiency 70–3
goals and policy-making 73–6
lack of redress in failure of 210
narrative centrality within 226–7
occupational cultures and shaping of 197
official purposes 204
participation *see* victim participation
practical centrality within 218–22
satisfaction with *see* victim satisfaction; witness satisfaction
speeding up of 82
Strategic Plan 59
Criminal Justice System Agencies and Partners 66
cross-examination
accommodation approach 34
derogations from 164
intimidatory 33
percentage of time speaking during 158t
pre-recorded 34
views about decline in 162
witness interruptions 161
witness reactions 165t
though special measures 167t
Crown Court judges, taking account of impact information 184
Crown Courts
impact of VPSs on 182
trial proceedings *see* trials
video-links 152

Crown Prosecution Service (CPS) 40
  Children's Charter 27, 85
  domestic violence
    policy to bring cases to justice 143–4
    reaction to poor conviction rates 112–13
  informing victims of outcomes 186
  provision of prosecutors 193
  tensions between police and 79–80
  witness reluctance 220
cultural centrality
  victim-centred CJ system 196–202, 215
  within the present CJ system 222–6
culture of control 204
Cutting Crime, Delivering Justice 86

decision-makers, victims as 17, 40–1, 215
decision-making
  involvement of children in 37
  rejection of victim participation 18–19, 20
Declaration of Basic Principles of Justice for Victims of Crime and Abuse of Power (UN) 23
defence advocates, views on special measures 173
defence lawyers
  concern for vulnerable witnesses 188
  criticisms of video-links 175
  questioning about impact of a crime 178
defence solicitors
  confrontational attitude to clients 101–2
  use of VPSs in mitigation 185
  views
    on special measures 172
    on victims' advocates 185
defence witnesses, interruptions when giving evidence 160t
defendant problems, late starting trials 131t
defendant rights, and victim rights, as a zero sum game 17–18, 21–2
defendants
  average length of questioning 154t
  balance of protection weighted towards 83
  interruptions when giving evidence 160t
  time speaking during different components of evidence 155t
delays, reducing, in criminal proceedings 198
Delivering Simple, Speedy, Summary Justice 82
derogations, cross-examination 164
district judges
  receipt of impact information in trials 178–9
  views
    on pre-recorded evidence 176–7
    on special measures 174
domestic violence
  CPS reaction to poor conviction rates 112–13
  international agenda 84
  police culture and difficulty of prosecuting 112
  trials 143–6, 147t, 148t
Domestic Violence, Crime and Victims Act (2004) 25, 34, 52, 82, 84, 210
Domestic Violence, Crime and Victims Bill (2003) 7, 63
domestic violence victims
  forced narratives 112–13
  intimidation 33
  treated as parties with reduced capacity 144
  vulnerability while giving evidence 32
Doorsen v. Netherlands 24
double jeopardy, abolishment of 81
double-listing system 130–2, 219–20
due process
  limitations on victims' narratives 207–9

versus crime control dichotomy 18

Effective Trial Management Programme 70, 136–8, 193, 197–8, 223
efficiency, policy-making 70–3
Elias, Robert 6, 45
emotional reactions, to giving evidence 164–70
equipment/logistics, late starting trials 131t
'essentially unobjectionable' rights 192
ethnography 228
European Convention on Human Rights (ECHR) 24, 84, 198
European Union Council Framework Decision (2001) 23, 25, 66, 67, 68, 84
evidence
of bad character 81
collection, domestic violence cases 143–4
electronic recording 201
see also giving evidence
evidential issues, late starting trials 131t
examination in chief
percentage of time speaking during 159t
pre-recorded 35–6, 48, 159t, 175–7
witness interruptions 161
witness reactions 165t
through special measures 167t
expression, account-making and giving evidence 110–11
expressive participation 17
'externally enforceable rights' 22

facilities, *see also* court facilities
fairness, to victims 22
feelings, during and after giving evidence 168t, 169t
financial concerns, victim policies 69–70
forced narratives 112–13
freedom perspective 18, 19
full trial proceedings 128t
domestic violence 147t
starting late 129t
fundamental reform 9, 39–42, 208
funding, and victim policy 60–2, 91

gender, likelihood of intimidation 33
'general victimology' 4
giving evidence 153–64
allowing victims choice of 206
as a civilised process 201
distinguished from narrative account-making 109–13
interruptions while 31–2, 160–1
occupational cultures and victim discomfort 197
orality principle 112
practical difficulties 220
reactions to 164–70
via special measures *see* special measures
victim preparedness 220–1
see also waiting times, before giving evidence
Glidewell Report (1998) 71
governance 46
governments, influence on policy networks 68

Halliday Report (2001) 54
handwritten notes, shift away from 201
harm 18
hearsay 81, 111
Home Office 37, 45–6, 62, 85
homicide survivors
coping strategy 99
as indirect victims 89
victims' advocates for 27, 64
hostile questioning 224
hours of waiting *see* waiting times
human rights 84
Human Rights Act (1998) 24, 214
Human Rights Act (2000) 84, 85
human rights culture 85
human trafficking 84–5

ideal victims 4–5, 64, 183, 223
ideologies, victimogogic 6
impact information
  inclusion in victims' narratives 200
  in trials 178–85
indirect victims 5, 64, 67, 89
information
  complaints about non-recording by police 164
  given at court 123–4
    different interpretations 101–2
    lack of objectivity 101
    overall satisfaction with 127t
    users' rating of different sources 125t
  providing to victims 19
  victim participation 17
  see also communication; impact information
information gathering
  policy-making 49, 52–4
  practical centrality 194–5
information sharing 59, 194
inquisitorial system 18, 34, 40
interactive policy-making 52–4
internally enforceable rights 24–7
  achieving centrality through 210–15
  victims' lack of 90
International Criminal Court (ICC) 212–13
international influences, victim policy 83–5
interruptions, while giving evidence 31–2, 160–1
intimidated witnesses *see* vulnerable and intimidated witnesses

judges
  as enforcers of victim rights 214
  guarantee of victim rights 211
  re-interpretation of stories 102
  reliance on demeanour to read witnesses 223
  see also Crown Court judges; district judges
judicial complaints mechanism 213
judicial proceedings, intimidation of witnesses 31–2
judiciary
  enforcement, victims' rights 213
  problems, late starting trials 131t
  safeguarding of victim rights during trials 212
  taking account of victims' stated views 200
  taking a proactive view towards victims' needs 212
juries
  impact of special measures on findings 173–4
  interpretation of evidence 102
  range of information entrusted to 208
  receipt of impact information during trials 178–9
Justice for all (2002) 1, 23, 47, 74, 81
JUSTICE committee (1998) 18–19, 20, 22, 23, 28–9, 31, 32

late modernity
  concept of community 74–5
  populist punitiveness 80
'law-abiding majority' 74–5
lawyer problems, late starting trials 131t
lawyers
  concerns about video-links 174
  confusion, CPS policy on domestic violence cases 144
  departing from established practices 188–9
  expressing concern for victims 188, 202
  perceptions of VPSs 181
  seeking victim's views 222–3
  taking account of victims' stated views 200
  use of misleading strategy 163
  and victims' narratives 203–5
  views
    about Witness Service 222
    of ETMP 223
    on special measures 170, 177

on use of VPSs 185
and volunteers, reconciliation of cultures 199
see also defence lawyers; prosecution lawyers; questioning lawyers
learning difficulties, witnesses with 35
legal advisers, provision of information to Witness Service 119
legal arguments, late starting trials 131t, 134–5t
legal audience 203–4
life events, coping though account-making 99
life stories 96
listening, to victims 18
listings issues, late starting trials 131t, 133t
Local Criminal Justice Boards 55–60, 62, 71, 91
local funding, victim policies 60–2, 91

McCourt v. UK 25
magistrates
guarantee of victim rights 211
impact of special measures on findings 173–4
interpretation of evidence 102
receipt of impact information in trials 178–9, 183–4
reliance on demeanour to read witnesses 223
safeguarding of victim rights during trials 212
Magistrates' Court Committee 184
magistrates' courts 12
enquiries about witness waiting times 142–3
giving evidence 153
judicial proceedings 31–2
portable screens 152
trial proceedings *see* trials
video-links 151–2
managerialism 76–7
media coverage, and government policies 76
MG2 form 37, 38
MG11 form 37, 180
Ministry of Justice 92, 216
misleading strategy, use of 163
mitigation, use of VPSs in 185
multi-agency approach 45, 78–80
multi-level governance 84

narrative(s)
distinguished from account-making 96
impact of multiple, in trials 100–1
narrative centrality
victim-centred CJ system 203–9, 214–15
within the present CJ system 226–7
narrative-based model, victim-centredness 95–115
stories in criminal trials 100–2
storytelling and narrative 95–100
see also victims' narratives
national minimum standards, implementation of policies 57
national targets, meeting 77
New Labour 1, 2, 80
A new deal for victims and witnesses 45–6, 47, 56, 63, 74, 81, 84
No Justice Beyond Criminal Justice 66
No Witness, No Justice 37, 47, 58, 61, 70, 91, 184
non-fundamental reforms 40–1, 42, 215
non-molestation orders, new sentences for breaching 82
non-running trial proceedings 132–6
non-victim reform 68–9
normative argument, incorporating victims' narratives in trials 103

occupational cultures
shaping of criminal justice systems 197
victim discomfort 32
Office for Criminal Justice Reform (OCJR) 56–7
One-Stop Shops 18

orality principle, giving evidence 112
'other politics' 11
outcomes, informing victims of 186–7

Parents of Murdered Children (POMC) 68
Parole Boards 26
participation *see* victim participation
participatory rights 25
Peace and Security Package 55
penal victimology 4
penal welfarism 8
personnel flexibility 193
Pigot report 34
Plummer, Ken 96
police
  at courts
    average length of questioning 154t
    time speaking during different components of evidence 155t
  complaints about non-recording of information 164
  culture, and prosecution of domestic violence 112
  guidelines
    assessment of vulnerability 37–8
    for pre-recorded examinations 35–6
  non-forwarding of information 79
  and prosecution, case construction 101
  skills, pre-recorded evidence 177
  'taking' witness statements 104–5
  tensions between CPS and 79–80
  victim satisfaction 28
  victim-blaming 32
  witness satisfaction 30
police reform, user satisfaction information 54
policing, citizen-focused 57
Policing Performance Assessment Framework (PPAF) 54
policy communities 46, 53
policy networks 46
policy-making
  adaptability to suit situations 51–2
  consolidation process 49
  implementation stage 50
  interactive 52–4
  nature of 48–52
  packaged as a continuation of work 47
  as a sequential process 48–9
  victims, importance in 228
  see also victim policy
political pressures, victim policy 44
politics, victims in 1, 3–9
Poppy projects 85
populist punitiveness 80, 204
Porter v. Magill 198
positivist research 228–9
Powers of Criminal Courts (Sentencing) Act (2000) 69
practical centrality
  victim-centred CJ system 192–6, 214
  within the present CJ system 218–22
Practice Direction, VPS scheme 109
pre-court familiarisation 30–1
pre-recorded cross-examination 34
pre-recorded examination in chief 35–6, 48, 175–7
pre-trial familiarisation 118
pre-trial reviews 195, 200, 219
pre-trial victim contact, culture and 198–9
'precipitation' debates 3
'principle of circularity', policy-making 49
proactiveness 194, 200, 213
probation service 26, 79
procedural rights 17, 18, 30
proportionality 20
prosecution
  decisions, victim participation 19, 27
  denying victims the authority to block 206
  and police, case construction 101
  see also Crown Prosecution Service

prosecution lawyers, criticisms of video-links 175
Prosecution Team Manual of Guidance 104–5
prosecution witnesses
giving evidence via video-link 174
interruptions when giving evidence 160t
prosecutors
contact with victims 121–3, 221–2
CPS provision of 193
in domestic violence cases 145
eliciting impact information from victims 178
special measure applications 223
Prosecutors' Pledge 65
public gallery, witnesses in 186
public interest criterion, domestic violence cases 144
public morality 7–8
Public Service Agreement (PSA) targets 45, 72, 75
public support, for reform, buying 54–5
punitive policies 8
punitive reforms 92
punitiveness 20, 21, 80–3, 88, 204

questioning
about impact of a crime 178
average length of 154t
hostile 224
questioning lawyers
adapting style to account for victim needs 161–3, 224
control of court evidence 110

R v. Davis (Iain) 24, 48, 73
R v. Perks 25
R v. Secretary of State for the Home Department and another, ex parte *Bulger* 25
radical victimology 5
rape victims 32, 33, 100
real victims 5
Rebalancing the criminal justice system in favour of the law-abiding majority: Cutting crime, reducing reoffending and protecting the public 74
referral orders 80
reform(s)
buying public support for 54–5
and 'community' 74–5
consolidation process 49
in favour of victims 74
see also fundamental reform; non-fundamental reform; non-victim reform
relationship dissolutions, coping though account-making 99
resolved trial proceedings 128t
domestic violence 147t
inevitability of 138–9
informing victims of decisions 186–7
late starting 129t
reasons for 136t, 137t
restorative justice 18, 21, 40, 74, 103
restraining orders 82
retraction statements 112
rights *see* human rights; victim rights
rights language 25, 84, 85–7
Roberts, Linda 32
Rock, P. 7
Rules of Procedure and Evidence (ICC) 212

satisfaction *see* victim satisfaction; witness satisfaction
scapegoating 187
schema theory 98
screens/screening, of witnesses 152, 174–5
secondary victimisation 5
sentencing
victim personal statements 182–3, 184–5
victim rights in 19–21
service rights 17, 18, 30
'essentially unobjectionable' 192
practical centrality 192–3, 214
severity of sentencing 21
sexual abuse, account-making in relation to 99–100

sexual offences, special protection, child witnesses 37–8
Sexual Offences Act (2003) 63, 81, 87
sexual victimisation 63, 87
short-term residence permit issues 85
Sn v. Sweden 24
social processes
  conceptions of victimisation 5
  victim policies as products of 7–9
solicitor advocates
  concerns about screening off witnesses 174–5
  view on VPSs 181–2
solicitors *see* defence solicitors
Speaking Up for Justice (1998) 32, 33, 48
special measures, giving evidence via 33–4, 88
  being forced upon victims 37
  child witnesses 38
  cultural centrality 201–2
  development of 48
  percentage of time speaking
    during cross-examination 158t
    during different components of evidence 156t, 157t
    during examination in chief 159t
  practical centrality 195–6
  views on 170–7, 223
  vulnerable and intimidated witnesses
    facilities for 221
    identification 37–8
  witness reactions 167t
  witness surveys 36–7
  see also pre-recorded examination in chief; screens/screening; video-links
special protection, child witnesses 37–8
staggered calling 142, 195
stakeholders, in policy-making 53
standardized case theories, enforcement of 101–2
state compensation programmes 68, 69
state control, and victim policy 6, 80–3
stories, in criminal trials 100–2
storytelling 95–100
Strategic Plan 59
suffering, defining victims by 63–4
support, offered by Witness Service 118
Support After Murder and Manslaughter (SAMM) 67, 68
support groups 66–8
supporters 152–3
  see also Witness Service, volunteers

T and V v. UK 25
Tackling Witness Intimidation – An Outline Strategy 78
target culture, policy-making 76–8
therapeutic benefits
  account-making 97–100
  incorporating victims' narratives within trials 103
therapeutic jurisprudence 103
trauma, benefits of account-making 97–8
treatment of victims, culture and 200–2
trial procedures, realistic details for victims 194
trial process, cultural centrality 197–8
'trial without jury' 81
trials
  calling witnesses 142, 150–3, 164, 195
  domestic violence 143–6, 147t, 148t
  double-listing system 130–2, 219–20
  effective management *see* Effective Trial Management Programme
  evidence at *see* evidence
  impact information in 178–85
  late-starting 130–2
    lateness averages 130t, 148t
    numbers 129t
    reasons for 131t, 133–5t
    in which witnesses were on time and waiting 140t, 141t

non-running 132–6
reducing delay in 198
research methodology 13
running of 126–30
stories in 100–2
victim-centred 10
see also victims' narratives
victims and witnesses after 186–8
see also adjourned trials; full trial proceedings; resolved trial proceedings

United Nations
Convention on the Rights of the Child 37, 85
Declaration of Basic Principles of Justice for Victims of Crime and Abuse of Power 23
drawing of attention to victims 3–4
United States, victims movement/groups 3, 4

victim care 71
victim categories 87
victim comfort 174
victim contact 187
court scheduling 214
culture and pre-trial 198–9
in probation service 79
prosecutors 121–3
Victim of Crime 72
victim discomfort 32, 197
victim groups 4, 66–8
victim impact statements 19–21, 108
Victim Information Bureau 80, 220, 221
victim participation
culture and 199–200
four possible forms 17
see also consultative participation
victim personal statements 20, 65, 106–9
acknowledgement of limitations 87–8
advocates' reference to 182–3
common criticism of 181
complaints about 224
as fundamentally flawed 20
lack of targets and low take-up rates 77
limitations of use in sentencing 184–5
mentioned in court 179
numbers being taken 179
participatory goals 55
stage one 107
stage two 107, 180
training of agencies and police officers 196
victims' knowledge about 180
victim policy
centred on vulnerable and intimidated witnesses 5
driving forces behind 5–7, 11, 216–18
interpreting 45
as a policy chain 47–92
political pressures and influences 44, 47–88
buying public support for reform 54–5
criminal justice and non-victim reform 68–9
distinguishing victims and witnesses 64–6
financial concerns 69–70
goals for criminal justice 73–6
growing understandings of victimhood 63–4
increasing efficiency 70–3
international influences 83–5
local context 55–60
local funding 60–2, 91
local responsibility 62
macro influences 87–8
multi-agency approach 78–80
punitiveness and state control 80–3
rights language 85–7
support groups and charities 66–8
target culture 76–8

as products of broader social processes 7–9
retrospectively developed 7
victims and witnesses, shaping 45–7
see also policy-making
victim rights
assessing 17–19
automatic granting of special measures 172–3
consequences attached to non-compliance 211
debates about 16–17
and defendant rights, as a zero sum game 21–2
enforceability 22
externally enforceable 22
finding
early developments 23–4
later developments 24–7
internally enforceable 24–7, 90, 210–15
remedies for breach of 211–12
in sentencing 19–21
see also Convention on the Rights of the Child
victim satisfaction, with police 28
Victim Support 20, 34, 45, 47, 62, 66–7, 68, 84
Victim and Witness Intimidation: Findings from the British Crime Survey 64
victim-blaming 32
victim-centred criminal justice
best practice 191–216
practical centrality 192–6
cultural centrality 196–202
narrative centrality 203–9
achieving centrality through internally enforceable rights 210–15
factors driving 216–18
fundamental reform 39–42
narrative-based model 95–115
research questions
what are the factors driving this policy 11
what has it meant so far in practice? 11–12
what would it mean to have? 9–10
research methodology 12–14
'victimalization of morality' 8, 9
victimhood
concept of 4–5
culture and 202
understanding of
researchers and development of 228
victim policy 63–4
victimisation
affect on personal assumptions 98
society's narrow conception of 5
surveys 30–1
see also secondary victimisation; sexual victimisation
victimogogic ideologies 6
victimology 1–2, 3–4, 5
victims
after trials 186–8
being informed of outcomes 186–7
staying in court to watch trials 186
as capable of attacking defendants' characters 81
communication
between court staff and 194–5, 219
between prosecutors and 221–2
as consumers of criminal justice 5, 8, 66
culture and treatment of 200–2
as decision-makers 17, 40–1, 215
describing impact of crime 178
distinguishing from witnesses 64–6
facilities, services and support for
early studies 27–8
later studies 28–30
as 'fragmented actor' 4
giving party status to 210, 211
government relinquishing of

responsibility for 2
participation *see* victim participation
and policy *see* victim policy
preparedness for giving evidence 220–1
researching 1–2
as a shared priority 62, 80
as topical issue 1
treated as offenders 142
see also civilian victims; domestic violence victims; homicide survivors; ideal victims; indirect victims; rape victims; real victims
Victims' Advisory Panel 26, 52–3, 86, 210
victims' advocates
for homicide survivors 27, 64
reservations about 185
Victim's Charters 22, 23, 26, 49, 50, 90
Victim's Code of Practice 10, 25–7, 51, 57, 66, 84, 90, 139, 212
Victims in the Criminal Justice System (1995) 28
victims minister 50, 80, 91
victims movement
as action-orientated 89–90
United States 3, 4
victims' narratives, in trials
due process and limitations on 207–9
giving evidence 109–13
inclusion of impact information in 200
incorporating 102–4, 206–7
limitations on capacity to tell 113–14
timeline of 113–14
victim personal statements *see* victim personal statements
witness statements 104–6
Victims and Witnesses Commissioner 26
video-link rooms
problems associated with 172
supporters allowed in 153
video-links 151–2
concerns and criticisms 174–5
NSPCC research 37
volunteers *see* Witness Service, volunteers
vulnerable and intimidated witnesses 31–9
defence lawyer's concern for 188
identifying, police guidelines 37–8
identifying needs 31–3
special measures *see* special measures
surveys 30, 36–7, 52
victim policy focused on 5

waiting rooms 117, 172
waiting times, before giving evidence 124–43, 221
conflict between reducing and not wasting court's time 77–8
numbers of hours 31
reinterpretation and development of victims' narratives 113–14
victim-centred CJ systems 195
witness anonymity 24, 48
witness boxes 150, 195, 220
witness care 122, 123
witness care units 61, 79–80, 184, 186, 188, 220
witness comfort 225
Witness in Court 37, 124
witness dissatisfaction 36, 103
witness orders 71, 72, 81–2
witness problems
late starting trials 131t, 132, 133t
trials adjourned or resolved in another way 137t
witness reluctance 131t, 132, 220
witness satisfaction 30, 36–7, 167
Witness Satisfaction Surveys 30–1, 49, 51, 52
(2002) 33, 36, 103, 124, 167
Witness Service 47, 48, 88, 116–21
advocates' acceptance of 199

communication between court staff and 119–20
information gathering/sharing 194
number of witnesses having contact with 30
provision of information to 119
support offered by 118
views about 222
volunteers 117, 197
brought into court 153
getting information on running/non-running of trials 119
information gathering 194–5
keeping victims and witnesses apart 118
and lawyers, reconciliation of cultures 199
pre-trial familiarisation 118
witness statements 104–6
see also MG2 form; MG11 form; victim personal statements
witness surveys 36–9, 49
Witness and Victim Experience Survey (WAVES) 49, 180
witness warrants 113, 146
witnesses
after trials 186–8
being thanked 186
staying in court to watch trials 186
calling 142, 150–3, 164, 195
as capable of attacking defendants' characters 81
demeanour, reliance on to read 223
deserving of special measures 173
disparity of treatment between courts 116–21
distinguishing from victims 64–6
giving evidence *see* giving evidence
Home Office guidance for 37
shaping policy 45–7
see also child witnesses; defence witnesses; prosecution witnesses; vulnerable and intimidated witnesses
Witnesses Charter 27, 65
Workings of Criminal Courts (Auld 2001) 29
writing experiments 98, 111

Youth Courts 150, 171
Youth and Justice Criminal Evidence Act (1999) 33–4, 37, 38, 39, 48, 52, 56, 80, 209
Youth Offending Panels 80

zero sum game
between defendants' and victims' rights 17–18, 21–2
between victim and offender needs 88